# FOOD AND COOKING IN VICTORIAN ENGLAND

**Recent Title in**
**Victorian Life and Times**

Family Ties in Victorian England
*Claudia Nelson*

# FOOD AND COOKING IN VICTORIAN ENGLAND

## A History

*Andrea Broomfield*

VICTORIAN LIFE AND TIMES
Sally Mitchell, Series Editor

**Westport, Connecticut
London**

**Library of Congress Cataloging-in-Publication Data**

Broomfield, Andrea.
Food and cooking in Victorian England : a history / Andrea Broomfield.
p. cm. — (Victorian life and times, ISSN 1932–944X)
Includes bibliographical references and index.
ISBN 978–0–275–98708–4 (alk. paper)
1. Cookery, English—History. 2. Cookery, British—History. 3. Great Britain—History—Victoria, 1837–1901. I. Title.
TX717.B754 2007
641.5–dc22 2007000069

British Library Cataloguing in Publication Data is available.



Library of Congress Catalog Card Number: 2007000069
ISBN–13: 978–0–275–98708–4
ISBN–10: 0–275–98708–6
ISSN: 1932–944X

First published in 2007

Praeger Publishers, 88 Post Road West, Westport, CT 06881
An imprint of Greenwood Publishing Group, Inc.
www.praeger.com

Printed in the United States of America

The paper used in this book complies with the Permanent Paper Standard issued by the National Information Standards Organization (Z39.48–1984).

10 9 8 7 6 5 4 3 2 1

The publisher has done its best to make sure the instructions and/or recipes in this book are correct. However, users should apply judgment and experience when preparing recipes, especially parents and teachers working with young people. The publisher accepts no responsibility for the outcome of any recipe included in this volume.

# CONTENTS

*Series Foreword* vii

*Preface and Acknowledgments* xi

*Chronology: Important Dates in English Victorian Culinary History* xv

1. The Industrial Roots of Victorian Cooking 1
2. Much Depends on Toast: Making and Serving Breakfast in the Victorian Middle-Class Home 23
3. Luncheon or Dinner? The Victorian Midday Meal 41
4. "An Invention of Comparatively Recent Date": Afternoon Tea 58
5. "The Chief Meal of the Day": The Victorian Working-Class Tea 78
6. The Effects of Industrial and Technological Innovation on Dinner *à la Française,* 1830–1870 100
7. The Multiple Meanings and Purposes of Dinner *à la Russe,* 1880–1900 122
8. The Holidays, Celebrations, and Other Festivities 148

*Appendix: Victorian Recipes* 165

*Notes* 173

*Glossary of Cooking Terms* 183

*Bibliography* 187
*Index* 193

# SERIES FOREWORD

Although the nineteenth century has now almost faded from living memory—most people who heard first-hand stories from grandparents who grew up before 1900 have adult grandchildren by now—impressions of the Victorian world continue to influence both popular culture and public debates. These impressions may well be vivid yet contradictory. Many people, for example, believe that Victorian society was safe, family-centered, and stable because women could not work outside the home, although every census taken during the period records hundreds of thousands of female laborers in fields, factories, shops, and schools as well as more than a million domestic servants—often girls of fourteen or fifteen—whose long and unregulated workdays created the comfortable leisured world we see in Merchant and Ivory films. Yet it is also true that there were women who had no household duties and desperately wished for some purpose in life but found that social expectations and family pressure absolutely prohibited their presence in the workplace.

The goal of books in the Victorian Life and Times series is to explain and enrich the simple pictures that show only a partial truth. Although the Victorian period in Great Britain is often portrayed as peaceful, comfortable, and traditional, it was actually a time of truly breathtaking change. In 1837, when eighteen-year-old Victoria became Queen, relatively few of England's people had ever traveled more than 10 miles from the place where they were born. Little more than half the population could read and write, children as young as five worked in factories and mines, and political power was entirely in the hands of a small minority of men who held property. By the time Queen Victoria died in 1901, railways provided fast and cheap transportation for both goods and people, telegraph messages sped to the far corners of the British Empire in minutes, education was compulsory, a man's religion (or lack of it) no longer barred him from sitting in Parliament, and women were not only wives and domestic servants but also physicians, dentists, elected school-board members, telephone operators, and university lecturers. Virtually every aspect of life had been transformed either by technology or by the massive political and legal reforms that reshaped Parliament, elections, universities, the army, education, sanitation, public health, marriage, working conditions, trade unions, and civil and criminal law.

The continuing popularity of Victoriana among decorators and collectors, the strong market for historical novels and for mysteries set in the age of Jack the Ripper and Sherlock Holmes, the new interest in books by George Eliot and Charles Dickens and Wilkie Collins whenever one is presented on television, and the desire of amateur genealogists to discover the lives, as well as the names, of nineteenth-century British ancestors all reveal the need for accurate information about the period's social history and material culture. In the years since my book *Daily Life in Victorian England* was published in 1996 I have been contacted by many people who want more detailed information about some area covered in that overview. Each book in the Victorian Life and Times series will focus on a single topic, describe changes during the period, and consider the differences between country and city, between industrial life and rural life, and above all, the differences made by class, social position, religion, tradition, gender, and economics. Each book is an original work, illustrated with drawings and pictures taken from Victorian sources, enriched by quotations from Victorian publications, based on current research, and written by a qualified scholar. All of the authors have doctoral degrees and many years' experience in teaching; they have been chosen not only for their academic qualifications but also for their ability to write clearly and to explain complex ideas to people without extensive background in the subject. Thus the books are authoritative and dependable but written in straightforward language; explanations are supplied whenever specialized terminology is used, and a bibliography lists resources for further information.

The Internet has made it possible for people who cannot visit archives and reference libraries to conduct serious family and historical research. Careful hobbyists and scholars have scanned large numbers of primary sources—nineteenth-century cookbooks, advice manuals, maps, city directories, magazines, sermons, church records, illustrated newspapers, guidebooks, political cartoons, photographs, paintings, published investigations of slum conditions and poor people's budgets, political essays, inventories of scientists' correspondence, and many other materials formerly accessible only to academic historians. Yet the World Wide Web also contains misleading documents and false information, even on educational sites created by students and enthusiasts who don't have the experience to put material in useful contexts. So far as possible, therefore, the bibliographies for books in the Victorian Life and Times series will also offer guidance on using publicly available electronic resources.

In *Food and Cooking in Victorian England: A History,* Andrea Broomfield not only answers typical questions such as "what is served at a 'high tea'?" and "did Victorians really eat eight-course dinners with three or four different kinds of meat?" but also considers the food available to ordinary people in the laboring and middle classes who could not afford elaborate dishes and did not have the servants to prepare them. More importantly, she provides a detailed explanation of the changes brought about by nineteenth-century revolutions in industry, agriculture, transportation, and technology—changes that transformed eating habits, mealtimes, the availability and cost of various foods, the means of cooking and preserving them, and people's understanding of diet and nutrition. It is perhaps not an exaggeration to say that foods and cooking were altered more than any other aspect of ordinary daily life during the period between 1830 and 1900.

In addition to consulting successive editions of well-known books such as Isabella Beeton's *Book of Household Management* (first published in 1861), the author has looked at hand-written recipe collections handed down in families. Some of these manuscripts now held by library archives cover more than a century; others provide evidence about regional differences, local specialties, and holiday traditions. While preparing the book, Andrea Broomfield has cooked on coal ranges, handled heavy iron toasting forks, and tried out recipes. Her explanations about ingredients and technology should therefore help bold explorers who acquire a reprinted edition of "Mrs. Beeton" or another nineteenth-century cookbook to make their own experiments. The rest of us will learn to interpret the financial and social clues exposed by the meals in Victorian novels and to appreciate the complex history of food and cooking.

Sally Mitchell, Series Editor

# PREFACE AND ACKNOWLEDGMENTS

"Food is perhaps the most distinctive expression of an ethnic group, a culture, or, in modern times, a nation." This salient statement by Albert Sonnenfeld from *Food: A Culinary History from Antiquity to the Present* (1999) helps explain culinary history's exploding popularity among academics and the public at large. Food: what people ate, how they procured it, how they cooked it, and how they served it, offers us insight into a country's wider historical and cultural context in an absorbing, refreshing fashion. While I attempt to offer readers a history of food production, cooking, and diet in England from roughly 1830 to 1900, I also explore what Victorian cuisine tells us about the Victorians themselves, including their class structures, intergenerational and gender relationships, national and regional identities, customs and values, and their economy. I rely on a wealth of material to help bring to life the meals that Victorians ate and how they prepared them, including manuscript and published cookbooks, etiquette guides, periodicals, travel literature, diaries, journals, novels, and Parliamentary reports.

At the same time that I move chronologically through the decades of the nineteenth century, exploring changes in English food and cooking that result from industrialization, I also move through the major meals of the day, offering as I go a brief historical overview and also an examination of it during the Victorian era specifically. Nonetheless, my approach is introductory; my book is designed to inform those interested in English culinary history and also to serve as a reference for Victorian scholars. At key junctures in my research, I have been sobered by the complexity of many topics related to Victorian food and cooking, and rather than relegate them to a superficial (and thus counterproductive) overview, I have chosen to leave them out, as better monographs exist where readers can find in-depth information. This history does not, for example, cover in detail Great Britain's colonies and colonial influences on English cooking. Those interested in India's influence on English cuisine might consult *Curry: A Tale of Cooks and Conquerors* (Oxford 2006) by Lizzie Collingham. Nor does this history explore how Welsh, Scottish, and Irish culinary histories intersect with England's. Colin Spencer, in *British Food: An Extraordinary Thousand Years of History* (Columbia 2002), does cover all three, however. Other topics that warrant a more thorough investigation than what my introductory history can offer include the rise of vegetarianism and its sociopolitical ramifications, institutional food, alcoholism, and nutritional science.

Through all stages of research and writing this book, I have relied most heavily on Roger Adams, Special Collections Curator at Kansas State University and Associate Professor and Rare Books Librarian. Roger's knowledge of and enthusiasm for culinary history has proved invaluable, and his willingness to read portions of this manuscript, ask probing questions, and unfailingly extend his assistance means that this book is significantly better than what it would have been without his involvement. Likewise, I wish to thank the staff at the Special Collections Library at Kansas State University for all their help in facilitating my many visits to the campus. While initially unaware of it, I came to realize in the course of my research that many other United States universities are important repositories of English cookbooks, including rare manuscripts. I thank David Schoonover, Kathleen Neeley, Steven Fisher, Katherine Reagan, Debra Featherstone, and Andrea Kempf for their valuable assistance and expertise in managing such fine archival collections and research libraries. Acting at times as my personal librarian and always as a valued mentor, I also wish to thank Martha Vicinus. For answering no end of technical questions and for helping me to finalize this book and bring it to production, I also thank Suzanne Staszak-Silva, Senior Editor, of Praeger Publishers, and Saloni Jain, Project Manager at Techbooks.

In the earliest stages of this project, I relied on the knowledge of living historians, including my colleague Sally Bennet, and Seleena Lanza, Director of the Lombard Historical Museum, Lombard, Illinois. I also would like to thank the staff at the Living History Farms in Urbandale, Iowa, for their expertise and willingness to show me all the intricacies of hearth and closed-range cooking.

The Johnson County Community College Writing Circle read and critiqued many chapters of this book. I thank Maureen Fitzpatrick, Keith Geekie, and Ellen Mohr for their generosity and shrewd insight when I presented work to the group. Via the VICTORIA listserv, I have received advice and help from many of the group's participants, including Michael Flowers, Catherine Golden, Jill Grey, Lee Jackson, Teresa Mangum, Keith Ramsey, Charles Robinson, Tracey Rosenberg, and most importantly, Janet Tanke. Colleagues in the Research Society for Victorian Periodicals (RSVP) have not only listened to my papers on food and cooking at RSVP conferences, but have also been willing to share their knowledge and advice. Thanks to Margaret Beetham, Eileen Curran, Maria Frawley, Tara Moore, and Jennifer Phegley. I likewise acknowledge the help I have received from colleagues in the United Kingdom: Sharon Britten, Pam Carter, Tom Jaine, Laura Mason, John B. Hanson, and most especially, Mike Dawes, whose willingness to give me detailed background information regarding his family history, particularly about Agnes Beaufoy, has been essential to the quality of this book. Elene McKenna has also proven to be a most helpful source, particularly when it comes to the traditions associated with English Christmastime foods.

Friends have offered me emotional and at times logistical support. Thank you to Jay Antle, Don Duey, Andrea and Brian Nelson, Cynthia and Robb Urschel. Likewise, thanks goes to Wilbur and Millie Miller for hunting down hard-to-find food items and sharing many helpful memories of their parents and grandparents, particularly how they farmed, preserved food, and carried to the United States their own culinary practices and traditions. Most importantly, I thank my parents, Charlie and Marsha Broomfield, who in some cases literally did my research for me and always offered me whatever support and encouragement I sought.

As with all my scholarly endeavors, Sally Mitchell has been invaluable, giving me not only her time, keen editorial comments, and expert knowledge, but also fifteen-plus years of friendship. Finally, this book is dedicated to my husband, Vince, and my children, Clara and Gavin, who for the last three years have cheerfully been willing to eat new kinds of foods, have read the manuscript, made insightful comments, put up with my obsessions and occasional absent-mindedness, and even listened to me read aloud Victorian-era novels that concerned not so much absorbing plots and characters, but rather, interesting scenes involving food and drink.

# CHRONOLOGY: IMPORTANT DATES IN ENGLISH VICTORIAN CULINARY HISTORY

1802 A closed iron range is patented by George Bodley.

1810 Englishman Peter Durand takes out a patent for the use of tin canisters as a means of preserving food.

1815 The Corn Laws, or high taxes on imported grain, go into effect.

1816 Major uprising of agricultural workers in the south of England. The next uprisings occur in 1822 and again in 1830.

1820 Chemist Frederick Accum publishes *Treatise on Adulteration of Food and Culinary Poisons.*

1830 Over 90 percent of food consumed in Britain is still being grown in the British Isles.

1832 Over 5,000 Londoners die in the first of four major nineteenth-century outbreaks of cholera due to the infected water supply.

1833 East India Company loses its monopoly over the China tea trade.

1834 Substantial drop in tea duty goes into effect, quickly making tea the preferred beverage of choice in England.

1835 The number of pigs taken to Manchester from Liverpool for slaughter is roughly divided between rail and canal.

1839 Tin-coated steel cans are now more widely in use.

1841 Gas stoves are installed at the London Reform Club.

1845 The Irish potato crop fails; beginning of the Irish potato famine.

Coffee consumption rises to 2 pounds per person a year. At the beginning of the century, consumption was a mere 1 ounce per person a year.

1846 Corn Laws are repealed.

North-West Public Soup Kitchen, established at 295 Euston Road, London, serves 140 gallons of soup to over 500 people per day.

1849 Approximately 14,000 people in London are killed by a cholera outbreak.

1850 *The Lancet* appoints an Analytical and Sanitary Commission to "inquire into and report on the quality of the solids and fluids consumed by all classes of the public."

1851 Approximately a quarter of British males are employed in agriculture, according to the 1851 census.

1854 More than 10,000 fatalities are due to another cholera outbreak in London.

1855 An Englishman named Grimwade takes out a patent for drying milk in a powder form. This becomes the basis for infant and invalid foods. Glass baby bottles with rubber nipples also become available.

Cheap canned meat is now imported to the United Kingdom from North America and Australia.

1857 Amount of tea consumed reaches an average of nearly 2 ½ pounds per person a year, or one to two cups of tea each day.

1858 The can opener is invented, replacing the hammer and chisel.

1861 Isabella Beeton's *Book of Household Management* is published in volume form.

1866 A mere 470,000 water connections exist in London (including standpipes for communal use in poor areas), and private water companies rarely supply customers with water more than an hour a day, three days a week, and never on Sunday.

1869 The opening of the Suez Canal clears way for increased imports from India and other Asian countries.

The French food technologist, Hippolyte Mège-Mouriès, takes out a patent in England for his butter substitute, oleomargarine.

1870 The first cheese factory is established.

1872 Adulteration of Food, Drink, and Drugs Act is passed and enforcement begins.

1875 Fruits and vegetables from Europe are now easily imported. Bananas imported via steamship from the Canary Islands and the West Indies become a popular fruit for wealthy Britons.

1876 Frenchman Charles Tellier builds a ship equipped with a refrigeration system.

1880 *SS Strathleven* arrives in London with its refrigerated hold packed with mutton and beef. Imports from the United States, Argentina, and New Zealand make fresh meat cheaper for consumers.

1881 Roughly 17 percent of British males are employed in agriculture.

1887 Margarine Act makes it illegal for traders to adulterate butter with margarine.

1894 Shredded Wheat is invented in Denver, Colorado, by Henry D. Perky.

1900 Number of British males employed in agriculture falls to 12 percent.

1902 Metropolitan Water Board is created in London, thus ensuring a uniform standard of water supply throughout the city.

# The Industrial Roots of Victorian Cooking

> **Almond Cheesecakes.** Take half a pound of allmonds blanchd and beaten fine with orange flower water, 3 quarters of a pound of Sugar beaten and sifted, 3 quarters of a pound of Butter melted and almost cold again, 8 eggs half the whites very well beaten, mix all together with some Sack & put it in your crust which should be in pans and made very good & light let not yr oven be very hot a little time bakes them you may ad sweetmeats if you pleas—
>
> —Jane Reade and Mrs. Symonds Ensham, *Mss. Cookbook*, ca. 1728–1822

On June 29, 1728, a woman utterly obscure to us today decided to start a family recipe book, or what scholars call a manuscript cookery book. She acquired a small, vellum-covered journal and on the inside front flap wrote her name, "Jane Reade." Under it in a bigger script she wrote, as if proudly, "Her Book." Although we have no history of this Englishwoman, we can nonetheless tell something about her and her circumstances. For a woman to have access to a vellum-covered journal and to be able to write indicates that she was almost surely a gentlewoman. In the early 1700s, roughly three-fourths of women were illiterate and an even higher percentage could not have afforded paper or journals, even if they had some rudimentary knowledge of writing. For a girl to have been educated to the degree that Jane Reade was (based not only on her handwriting, but also on her detailed directions and notations concerning her recipes), her family would have had the money and leisure to educate her themselves (perhaps her mother or father took on this responsibility), or they would have had the money to hire a governess for their daughter or perhaps send her to school.

Jane Reade's first recipe entry, "To make a Bread puding" was followed by "Ginger Bread." She then wrote out recipes for "a white frigasee of Chicken" and "forst balls or Sausages."[1] From just these first four entries, we learn more about Jane Reade's circumstances. The family ate well, although not lavishly or extravagantly. They could afford eggs, milk, pork, and poultry, as well as sugar, expensive spices, and even more expensive citrus fruits such as oranges and lemons. Such luxuries were limited to those who had enough money to go beyond buying the basic staples of bread, fat bacon, cheese, and oatmeal. Readers today might browse through Jane Reade's collection and come away from it with ideas of their own about what to cook for dinner; many of the recipes, in other words, are appetizing and full of variety, as well as somewhat easy to prepare, even in a small kitchen with basic cooking equipment.

Although Jane Reade is the main author of "Her Book," five others also recorded their recipes, and on the book's end flap, a "Mrs. Symonds Ensham" recorded her name and the date, August 16, 1822. Over the course of a century, Jane Reade and perhaps her daughters, granddaughters, and daughters-in-law inadvertently left us a picture of preindustrial English life. Along with the family's favorite recipes are those that detailed how to preserve all types of food, from eels to unripe walnuts; how to do without important ingredients such as eggs should the hens not be laying or the grocer run short; and how to make a variety of medicines, including "a Syrup of Garlic to cure a Asmah, or Shortness of Breath." An eighteenth-century woman's recipe book, in other words, was a storehouse of knowledge that she used on her family's behalf. In it, she recorded new recipes that a family member might have brought from traveling elsewhere (Bath buns for example), or recipes that were passed around among neighbors because they produced exceptional results or offered an interesting variation on a standard recipe (such as potted fish). When a child became ill with a cough that would not go away or a rash that would not respond to an ointment on hand, the mistress of the house might seek an alternative from an acquaintance and write down how she mixed its components, as Jane Reade did for cough pills.

Up through the late 1700s, English people of all classes made their own medicines and much of their own food. Furthermore, they procured food, preserved it, and cooked it in largely the same way that they had been doing for centuries. After all, these ways worked and alternative ways were few. A Renaissance household depended, as much as a Georgian household, on daylight hours, the season, basic food preservation techniques, and geographical region for what and how they ate. Fancy medicines were scarce, but wild roses bloomed in profusion in the roadways, as did yarrow, peppermint, and tansy, plants that had known medicinal properties. Light and fuel were costly, but the summer daylight hours were long enough to see to the important work of planting and harvesting, as well as cooking and eating. In winter, when less work could be accomplished outdoors and it was cold, most people retired early to save fuel and keep warm under down-filled quilts. Hot weather could spoil butter, but salt—plentiful and cheap—could help preserve it through several weeks if necessary. Meat likewise spoiled quickly in summer heat, but most animals were still too lean or still growing in the summer and thus not ready for slaughter. November 11, Martinmas, was the appropriate time to butcher the animals and cure meat for winter. Animals had grazed on harvest stubble to the point that they were fat and ready to be eaten. No one, regardless of money and status, could work very successfully outside these variables, and as a result, people's diet and cooking were largely the same, although the rich could afford more food and more variety than could the poor.

Around the time that Mrs. Symonds Ensham's family acquired Jane Reade's cookbook in the early 1800s, the wife of a prosperous vinegar distiller from Upton Grey, Hampshire, also began recording her family recipes in a small bound book. Agnes Beaufoy, most likely assisted by her daughter Louisa and other family members when she became elderly, wrote out recipes from 1819 up through the 1860s. Her recipe book is distinctive and important to culinary historians because it acts as a bridge between the preindustrial cooking and food of Jane Reade's day and the industrial, or what we might call Victorian, cooking and food that remained popular in England up through the end of the nineteenth century. For by the time that Agnes Beaufoy's family stopped recording recipes in the late 1860s, stunning and far-reaching changes in food and cooking had begun to occur, many in the middle of Queen Victoria's reign. Such variables as one's location and the season now had less impact on food and cooking, and prosperous people in particular confronted options—and sometimes frustrating dilemmas—that had been unknown to previous generations: whether to buy food readymade or to make it themselves, whether to install a coal-fired range or continue to use the hearth, whether to buy a powdered soup packet and add water or make soup from meat bones and vegetables. When people had little notion of alternative ways to procure food and cook it, they also had less dissatisfaction and frustration. Tradition and custom had been important to families and communities, and the methods that a woman's mother and grandmother used to smoke meat, churn cream into butter, and pickle garden produce for winter-time eating did not cause that young woman to feel vaguely deprived because she did not have more sophisticated machines or tools to help her. However, industrialization revolutionized cooking, and as a result, we might regard the Victorian era as more modern than otherwise. Like the Victorians, we have options when it comes to what and how to eat, and also like the Victorians, we understand that our economic status has a bearing on those options. Learning to live with constant innovation and its ensuing choices helped define Victorian cooking, and this history will detail that process in full.

To begin, I rely in this introductory chapter on several recipes, including three for a perennially popular food, cheesecake. Each one signifies a shift away from ancient flavors and preindustrial customs toward an industrial mindset when it comes to food and cooking. The Reade-Ensham cookbook reflects several centuries' worth of culinary traditions in England—not only the eighteenth century; the Beaufoy cookbook reflects England at the beginning of industrialization and in the throes of it. Taken together, the two offer us an overview of the most important themes in this culinary history.

## ENGLISH COOKING IN PREINDUSTRIAL ENGLAND

Jane Reade began recording recipes at a time when most English people lived in small towns, villages, and hamlets. In 1750, only two British cities had more than fifty thousand inhabitants, London and Edinburgh. Even those who lived in good-sized towns often maintained large kitchen gardens or a garden allotment close to their home, and most kept swine and poultry. The majority of men worked in agriculture, i.e., farming, fishing, herding livestock, and dairying, so the economy was largely agrarian. Significant numbers of people also worked in cottage or home-based industries where they spun thread, wove cloth, and made lace, among other goods. Laborers of all types relied not only on their gardens but also on common land that was available for everyone's use. Access to such land allowed laborers to fatten a pig during the summer, graze a milk cow, gather brushwood to start their fires, and sometimes even raise enough grain to make the family's weekly bread. Roadsides, wasteland, and open meadows harbored an abundance of edible foods there for the taking: mushrooms, nuts, berries, greens, and hundreds of varieties of herbs for medicines and flavor. Likewise, the coasts allowed its nearby inhabitants to take in many forms of edible seaweed, along with mussels, whelks, oysters, and the fish that swam close to the shoreline.

If they could not raise, collect, or make the food themselves, people obtained it at weekly markets and from dry goods grocers in their nearest market town. Grocers sold many imported, expensive goods including tea, coffee, chocolate, rice, macaroni, and sugar. Once a week, farmers and dealers brought in their produce and other goods and services to sell and trade. But aside from relying on the market town, people had to be self-sufficient and resourceful to be well fed. Those who lived in London or a larger city with a navigable river or access to a seaport were able to obtain a wider variety of food from around the nation and England's colonies than were most others.

People's access to common land and their work rhythms allowed time for gardening, preserving food, and tending to livestock. As a result, most ate a varied diet that included some protein. Aside from chickens and geese, laborers relied heavily on one or two pigs per year to supply meat. A 200-pound pig produced roughly 122 pounds of bacon, ham, pork, sausage, and offal—enough to help feed a family of five or six during the winter. Pigs did not cost much to maintain because they ate food scraps and foraged on common land for most of their short lives. Families also ate an abundance of garden vegetables, including lettuces and cabbages, parsnips, swedes (rutabagas), carrots, onions, beets, turnips, cucumbers, radishes, peas, and, as the eighteenth century progressed, potatoes. They ate these foods as soon as they were ripe, and they also stored excess root vegetables and apples for winter eating. Cabbages and their relative, kale, grew well in colder weather, and families relied heavily on both when little else was available fresh. Highly perishable food was preserved by drying, smoking, pickling, stewing in sugar, or simply salting. Milk, butter, buttermilk, and whey were also available, either from the family's cow or from a close-by farmer's. Depending on a person's region, the staple grains of wheat, oat, and barley were turned into flummery and frumenty (see Glossary for these and other obscure cooking terms), bread loaves, porridge, or griddlecakes. People also ate a lot of pulses, including the pease porridge of nursery-rhyme fame, and any number of thick stews composed of beans, vegetables, and meat if it was available.

One of the most important differences between a preindustrial and industrial cuisine, at least in terms of England, had to do with one's access to land. At the time that Jane Reade and Mrs. Symonds Ensham were recording their recipes, most people did not own any land, even if they still had rights to use some of it for their own sustenance. To understand how industrialization would radically affect people's livelihoods and thus their food production and consumption, it is first necessary to understand how the land itself was parceled out and how it was controlled in the 1700s. Later in this chapter, we will turn to how that control of the land changed.

Those who worked as farm laborers, in cottage industries, mining, fishing, and other physically demanding jobs were known as the working class—the largest class in England in the 1700s, constituting 75 percent of the population. The remaining 25 percent constituted an expanding middle class of professionals and merchants whose income was not tied directly to land, and a tiny number of the upper class who owned land and gained their income from renting it to farmers. From a North American perspective, where pioneers had viewed land as "free" to those most able to successfully farm or ranch, it can be difficult to conceptualize what it would have been like to live in a country where almost all land was owned and controlled by a tiny number of families, and where the nation's affairs were largely in the hands of landowners, many of whom sat in Parliament and also controlled the highest levels of the court system and the Church of England.

England's upper class included the nobility, or those who for generations had inherited thousands of acres of land along with a title (such as "Duke" or "Baron"). It also included the landed gentry who owned equally large tracts of land in some cases, but who did not have hereditary titles. They resembled the nobility in other respects as well, including their social standing, income derived from the land, and political power, particularly at the county level. Before the Industrial Revolution, a small number of people composed the middle class, those who practiced a profession such as law or medicine, who served as military officers, or as clergy in the Church of England. As the eighteenth century progressed, industrialists and merchants swelled the numbers and power of the middle class, and significantly, their income was not tied to land. Somewhere in between the middle class and the laboring class in terms of prestige and power were yeoman farmers, or men who owned a modest number of acres (usually around one hundred) and who often farmed the land alongside their hired men and women, rather than delegating such work solely to others.

No matter if a person owned a great deal of land, a few acres, or none, what he preferred to eat was probably similar to what others preferred to eat. I say "preferred" because poor people did not have the same diet as the rich, but they would have found the same kinds of foods desirable if money were not scarce. Common people, in other words, did not crave a pottage of beans while rich people craved peacock's brains. Most Englishmen and -women, irrespective of their class and breeding, would have enjoyed a spit-roasted joint of beef or mutton accompanied with a brown gravy, and a boiled plum pudding made rich with spices and dried fruits. They would have gladly washed down such a meal with mugs of ale.

These rather plain foods—what many today think of if asked to describe an English meal—came to symbolize England itself, and they did so because taste was at least partially predicated on the technology available to cook food, as well as on foods that were available in this northern European climate. While people's class dictated the size of their kitchens and how many bowls, pots, and pans they owned, the brick ovens in which people baked were largely the same, and the majority of household cooking was carried out in front of an open fire, be it on a country estate or in a cottage. Some wealthy people might have gone to extreme lengths to find and consume what they considered delicacies (including peacock's brains) or to serve their guests vegetables that were out of season and thus outrageously expensive (garden peas in January, for example), but most did not care to go to such efforts.

The English were renowned for their enthusiasm and appetite when it came to food, with foreign visitors often commenting on this fact in travel memoirs and letters home. Dinner tables were loaded with as many dishes as the family could afford, and among the better off, entertaining guests over four-hour-long dinners was commonplace. Food in general was celebrated, and the bounty of each season showcased, even in February and March when winter supplies were running out, and the monotony of what was left threatened the creativity of resourceful and prosperous wives. Men and women took great pride in their husbandry, or their ability to raise livestock and improve breeds, grow as many fruits and vegetables as possible, and craft cheeses, wines, and ales.

Although a genteel woman was presumed to be more delicate in appetite than a man (and would have probably been willing to act as such if there were company), she nonetheless played a fundamental role in her kitchen, knowing how food should taste and how to prepare it, no matter whether she had a staff of servants or merely her older daughters to assist her. Up through much of the eighteenth century, a woman's education in the domestic arts went unheralded outside her home because it was what was expected of her; however, within the family, her abilities were respected, and they granted her status. Such was the case for all but the poorest English women, who simply suffered too much to care about their "status" or their "respect." But in many cottages, mothers taught their girls to grind grain to make bread and to prepare an oven for baking. They also taught their girls how to collect and preserve wild foods and how to cook an entire meal, complete with bacon, dried peas, greens, and a boiled pudding, in one large pot suspended over the fire. The girls watched their mothers identify and pick herbs that the family used for flavorings and also for a wide range of medicines, salves, and teas. Even in the wealthiest families as far back as Elizabethan times, a gentlewoman with servants nonetheless found that her status and worth in the family was intricately tied to how well she mastered "housewifely activities," among them cookery, confectionery (particularly cake baking), wine making, and distilling spirits into medicines.[2]

Jane Reade was likely to have been an efficient housewife and kitchen manager if her cookbook is any indication. Based on her and her family's recipes, we know that the Reades were prosperous enough to eat a variety and quantity of meat that poorer people would not have been able to afford, that they maintained a kitchen garden and perhaps an orchard, kept bees, and had a poultry yard with dovecote. Given her recipes' ingredients and costs, we might also assume that Jane Reade had at least one or two servants. While she garnished the roast beef with intricate turnip flowers and bright green cress, her servants scoured pots, plucked and larded pigeons, and pounded the hard loaf sugar in a large wooden mortar so that Jane Reade could then use it to crystallize spring violets and angelica for cakes.

Money and social class meant that the Reade family ate well, but neither money nor class exempted them from the daily concerns that most people had when preparing for winter and its inevitable food shortages. Indeed, the running theme of Jane Reade's cookbook is food preservation: how to make full use of whatever foods, wild or cultivated, were in season and briefly abundant. In this respect, her cookbook is representative of others from the eighteenth century kept by prosperous but not fabulously wealthy people. Interspersed with recipes on how to prepare a rolled joint of beef, bread and fry mutton cutlets, and how to make forcemeat are ones such as:

To Souse Maycrull [to pickle fresh Mackerel]
To pot fish
To pot Pigeons
To Pott Eells
A Custard without Eggs
To make a Tansey
Nettle Hash
To dry Aples [apples]
To make Ketchap of Wallnuts
To Pickle Wallnuts
To pickle Pods of Radishes
ConServe of hipps
To make mead in October

These recipes offer us insight regarding how people made use of an extraordinary variety of foods that are now obscure or not treated as food sources, and they also illustrate how people prepared meals before industrialized food processing and widely available imported foods became the norm. Jane Reade's recipes for "ConServe of hipps" and "To make a Tansey" are particularly revealing in this regard.

Rose hips, the fleshy fruit of wild rose, provided an excellent source of vitamin C. While vitamins and minerals were not widely understood until the twentieth century, people knew that certain foods prevented debilitating and fatal diseases such as scurvy and rickets. Recipes for a conserve (fruit preserve) of rose hips date as far back as the Middle Ages, and the word originally came from the Middle English word "hepe." To make the conserve, people gathered hips in November. They juiced them, combined them with a simple sugar syrup, and then boiled the mixture. The resulting conserve, according to Jane Reade's instructions, was to be taken in "the size of a walnut" every morning to keep a person strong and healthy.

A tansy, or tansy cake, also served a medicinal purpose, but its origins are rooted in England's early Roman Catholic heritage. Tansy was a bitter herb whose young stalks were juiced and then mixed, according to Jane Reade's recipe, with a "pint or less of ye juice of green wheat, spinage, or any thing else that is green & is not strong tasted." The juice was then mixed with a pint of cream, twelve eggs, nutmeg, sugar, and salt. A "quantity of white bread to make it thick enuf for a bread pudding" was mixed in. The batter was placed in a buttered dish and put before "a soft fire or a oven" until it was "hard enuf to turn out on the dish." People had been eating tansy cakes since the Middle Ages to purify their bodies, especially after Lent ended and when it was thought wise to counteract the effects of a long fast. By the 1700s, many also ate a tansy cake at Easter in remembrance of the Jewish Passover.[3] Religious reasoning aside, tansy was considered a vital green food for people who had spent the winter eating too much salted meat and pickled vegetables; it was a welcome harbinger of spring's bounty.

Several other English flavors were likewise the result of marrying a practical need with a long-held religious or regional custom, and for the most part, the resulting flavors remained entrenched throughout the eighteenth and into the nineteenth century. For example, Roman Catholic precepts were bound up in the English love for almonds, just as they were for tansy cakes; Jane Reade's recipe for almond cheesecake owes its flavor and heritage to ones that come from centuries earlier. English people in the Middle Ages were subject to the Catholic Church's numerous fast days, when meat (except for fish), eggs, and dairy products were prohibited. To replace milk, cream, and cheese, people used almonds. Almond "milk" replaced cow or goat milk in frumenty; almond "cream" took the place of dairy cream in fish stews and soups. Almond cream could also be thickened to make the equivalent of "junket," when fresh cheese is drained of whey to leave behind the soft curds. Mixed with sugar and flavored with orange-flower or rose water and sack, the resulting mixture—what many eighteenth-century people called "cheesecake"—could then be used to fill tarts or pies.[4] By the 1700s, most English Protestants had abandoned or greatly reduced fasting obligations and other traditions that were tied to Roman Catholicism, but they did not necessarily lose their penchant for flavors that had derived from medieval Catholic traditions.

Some of Jane Reade's recipes were also part of a continuum that stretched as far back as the Norman invasion in 1066. Many, as with her almond cheesecake, were flavored with orange-flower water, orange rind, or orange juice. Bitter oranges, the main ingredient of the orange marmalade that many people today still see as distinctly English, were cultivated in Sicily and southern Italy, areas that were at one time under Norman control. Like the Normans, the English embraced this flavor, along with that of lemons, citron, and pomegranate. Wealthy people relied on these fruits to create the hallmark sweet-sour and bitter-sweet flavors that eventually defined English cookery.[5] Jane Reade and her successors in the Victorian era could not have imagined a bread pudding without cinnamon, a plum cake without nutmeg, a fricassee of chicken without mace (the papery covering of the nutmeg itself), a gingerbread without cloves and of course ginger. The most important spice was pepper. In the 800s, the English cleric Bede distributed this precious spice to his brethren while he was on his deathbed. German merchants paid their customs duties to King Aethelred II (978–1016) in pepper rather than in money. Many Asian spices such as pepper were so important by 1000 that they found their way into school textbook translation exercises written around 1005 by Aelfric, Abbot of Eynsham, in Oxfordshire.[6]

The use of these spices, as well as rose and orange-flower water, points to the earliest cosmopolitan roots of English cookery, particularly influences from Persia, France, Italy, and Sicily. After the Norman Conquest, England increased its importation of spices, along with almonds, citrus fruits, and vegetables. These foods were then used alongside England's native ones. Some distinct flavors, particularly saffron and garlic, did fall out of popularity in England before the eighteenth century, but mace, nutmeg, cinnamon, almond, and citrus were commonplace flavorings and/or ingredients in eighteenth-century English cuisine.

Sugar deserves our attention as well, given that it, along with pepper, was one of the most important commodities in England. Imported from Morocco, Cyprus, and Alexandria via Venice and Genoa up through the 1400s, its cost was too exorbitant for anyone but the most wealthy to purchase, and even then it was more often treated as a spice or medicine—not a key ingredient. Sold in small loaves (a practice that lasted throughout the nineteenth century), sugar was valued at 1 to 2 shillings per pound in the thirteenth and fourteenth centuries, but the price could climb as high as 8 shillings and 4 pence. To put the price in perspective, consider that a dozen eggs cost a mere penny. The most ancient English sweetener was honey, the ingredient not only of cakes and breads, but also of the fermented drink called mead. Once sugar was cultivated in the British Caribbean colonies, especially Barbados and Jamaica, it was easier to obtain, and its price began to fall significantly, making it more affordable to the middle classes.[7] The number of recipes in Jane Reade's cookbook that call for cane sugar testified to England's imperial expansion.

Imported goods were thus more available by the late seventeenth and early eighteenth centuries, but the poor quality of roads combined with the slow speed of overland and water transportation meant that such goods remained expensive, and their availability was inconsistent. The quality of the product was likewise not guaranteed. The vast majority of the population thus relied most on what was at hand, be it at local markets, on their own holdings, or from what grew in open areas. Once again, cheesecake is illustrative. Several pages after Jane Reade's almond cheesecake recipe, another one appears based on dairy cheese:

> **Cheese Cakes**
> *2 penny worth of milk and Rennet then strain it thro a thin Cloath when all the Whey is out add to that curd a little spice and sugar to your taste one spoonful of Brandy—6 oz of Butter and a Tea Cup full of Cream mix it together with a quarter lb Currants.*

Significantly, Jane Reade's earlier recipes do not call for ingredients by cost. This one, a dairy cheesecake or a curd tart, with its "2 penny worth of milk," would suggest that the family no longer kept milk cows (if it had done so previously) and was at that point purchasing milk, probably from a neighboring farmer. Making cheese was a typical domestic chore for many country people up to the early 1800s because fresh milk was cheap and plentiful, as was rennet, a strip of lining from the calf's fourth stomach which causes milk to coagulate and make curds. Likewise, many families brewed their own beer because they had room to store the equipment, it was easy to obtain high-quality malt for a good price, and many people could use their own grain for beer as well as for bread. Equally important, creating such foods as cheese, beer, and bread fit into the daily life patterns of not only families, but also entire village and farm communities.

Out of necessity, people also ensured that no edible item was wasted. Just as excess or cheap milk would become cheese and thus find its way into any number of sweet and savory dishes, an abundance of wild mushrooms would be dried and later turned into powder to thicken winter stews and gravies and any number of wild berries would be gathered, chopped, and turned into preserves. Dishes such as pickled radish pods (from a variety of radish grown for its edible seed pods and not its roots), pickled walnuts, and nettle hash are for most of us obsolete because we have no need to view them as food sources. The same became increasingly true of the Victorians because of the Industrial Revolution, as this history will detail.

## ENGLISH COOKING IN THE EARLY TO MID-VICTORIAN ERA

First, some disclaimers and qualifications: Because the Industrial Revolution was a lengthy and complex process, affecting different classes and regions of people at different times and in different manners, it did not suddenly end one way of cooking and eating and ignite another. Likewise, English food and cooking did not change just because Victoria became Queen in 1837, or just because she died in 1901. The catalysts to change that are important to our discussion include the exploitation of steam power; a recognized need for agricultural reform so that the nation could feed an exploding population; and the creation of stronger, cheaper metals. Victoria's sovereignty works as an appropriate time frame to discuss industrialization's effect on food because innovations put in place in the eighteenth century culminated during her sixty-four-year reign. Nonetheless, many Victorians held onto old recipes and continued to enjoy many of the flavors and foods of their ancestors. Published cookbooks do not necessarily reflect such a continuity, but family recipe files do. When a particular dish did fall from favor, it was often because the technology on which it had depended was rendered obsolete, or because people's daily work rhythms had altered to such a degree that it was difficult to find time to prepare that dish. In other instances, a dish retained its name, but ingredients changed because people found that substitutes were cheaper, easier to find, or better tasting than what one's mother or grandmother had traditionally used.

Exemplifying both the continuity and change endemic to cooking in the early industrial era was Agnes Beaufoy's cookery book. Some of her recipes could just as easily be found in Jane Reade's, a century earlier. "To make Black Hogs Puddings" suggests, for example, that the Beaufoys probably raised pigs and used up all parts of the slaughtered animals. Her recipe "To preserve Plumbs, Apricots, &c &c without Sugar" takes into account not only the need to prepare a winter food stock from summer's abundance, but also the resourcefulness when a key ingredient such as sugar was unavailable or too expensive. "Recipe for Ginger Beer," like Black Hogs Puddings, indicates that the Beaufoys were largely self-sufficient when it came to supplying everything from meat to drink. Several other recipes, however, situate this cookbook at the end of the agrarian era and at the beginning of an industrial one; read against the backdrop of technological and economic innovations, they tell us a great deal about the difficulties and the advantages that accompanied that transition.

In 1800, roughly 80 percent of the British population still lived in rural areas and small towns, and men were still employed largely in agriculture; however, by 1900, 80 percent of the population lived in cities, and agriculture employed a mere 12 percent of men.[8] As a result of this mass migration from countryside to city, people slowly lost their self-sufficiency when it came to procuring their food, and they became reliant on others to do it for them. In 1887, the year of Victoria's Golden Jubilee (her fiftieth anniversary as Queen), people could buy baked beans in cans, they purchased margarine more often than butter (it was cheaper), and they bought cheap imported meat more often than expensive British meat. By 1897, the year of Victoria's Diamond Jubilee, people often ate lunch or tea in restaurants or in a teashop chain rather than at home. Middle-class people could purchase bananas, and working-class people could sometimes splurge and buy oranges for a special treat. City children were routinely given pennies by their parents to buy a "penny lick" of ice cream from the numerous Italian vendors who had recently immigrated to England and Scotland. However, to have reached such stability, convenience, and overall lower prices when it came to food, the nation first had to go through decades of tremendous hardship and challenge. Two of Agnes Beaufoy's recipes directly testify to that hardship. One was attributed to a Mrs. Barton (see illustration). The other, which appears later in her cookbook, was copied from Chef Alexis Soyer's famous soup-kitchen recipe that he devised in 1847 when commissioned to go to Dublin and set up kitchens during the "Great Hunger" or what became known as the Irish Potato Famine.

### Early Industrialization's Effect on Laborers

**"Mrs Barton's Rec't: for Soup, sold to the Poor"**
*10 Pounds Beef—3 lbs Scotch Barley—1 Gallon Turnips—12 Carrots—8 Onions—Salt & Pepper at discretion.—The meat to be cut small–& a sufficient quantity of Water to leave 40 Quarts of Soup, when finished. The price when sold is $1\frac{1}{2}$ d per Quart.*

Most of Agnes Beaufoy's recipes reflect her prosperity and privileged social status. The Beaufoy fortune had been made in vinegar distilling starting in the 1740s, and like other successful merchants, the Beaufoys belonged to a growing, increasingly powerful middle class that evolved because of England's industrialization and colonial expansion. By the time that Agnes married John in 1796, he had taken over the distillery, and the family lived on a large estate, Upton Grey, in Hampshire. The distillery was located in London, as was the family's second residence at Grosvenor Place. Later, when the business was managed by a nephew, John, Agnes, and their daughter Louisa resided primarily at Upton Grey. John acted for a time as High Sheriff for Hampshire, and Agnes oversaw a substantial household, complete with a large garden. People of this class were largely unaffected by industrialization, except to profit financially from it. Nonetheless, the Beaufoys and other prosperous families were eyewitnesses to the misery that industrialization began to cause many in their midst, and the family made attempts to alleviate some of the worst suffering caused directly by hunger.

Such hunger was in part the result of human initiative and eagerness to find better ways of handling procedures that had been both slow and costly, and herein lies one of the more complex conundrums of industrialization. The Victorian age, often dubbed the "Age of Reform" after the spirit of the first Reform Bill of 1832, resulted in industrial, political, and religious leaders

1830 Mrs Barton's Rec.t for Soup, sold to the Poor

10 Pounds Beef – 3 lbs Scotch Barley – 1 Gallon Turnips – 12 Carrots – 8. Onions – Salt & Pepper at discretion. – The meat to be cut small – & a sufficient quantity of Water to leave 40 Quarts of Soup when finished. The price when sold is 1½ p.r Quart. —

Westphalia Hams – Mrs Barton –

Rub each Ham all over with 4 Ounces of Sal: Petre – the next day put ½ a lb of Bay salt – ½ lb Common Salt – ½ lb of coarse Sugar into a Quart of Stale Beer – Boil this & pour it hot over the Ham – Let it be in this Pickle a fortnight rubbing it well & turning it twice a day – Smoke it for 3 days over a fire of Saw dust after which let it be smoked in a Chimney (where Wood only is burned) for a Month or Six weeks Put a Wisp of Hay in a Pot of cold Water when the Ham is to be simmered 3 Hours

Agnes Beufoy. Recipes, including "Mrs Barton's Rec't for Soup, sold to the Poor, 1830" and "Westfalia Hams." Illustration courtesy of the Morse Department of Special Collections, Hale Library, Kansas State University.

recognizing endemic problems and attempting to solve them. In executing their reforms, the most vulnerable—and sometimes ironically, the ones who would finally most benefit—suffered during the transitions that occurred. Of course, greed, selfishness, and prejudice also were rife during this transition, and in the earliest years of industrialization, such traits were oftentimes more apparent to the majority of people than any good-willed desire to make the nation more powerful and self-sufficient.

Consider mechanization in the textiles industry. In the mid-1700s, several inventors and entrepreneurs were attempting to develop faster, cheaper methods for spinning thread and weaving cloth. However, such labor-intensive tasks had for centuries provided jobs for a vast cottage industry, particularly in the Midlands. Improving on an early spinning machine, James Hargreaves invented a spinning jenny that allowed a person to operate a line of spindles with just one wheel, thus cutting human labor to one-eighth and accelerating the speed at which thread or yarn could be produced. This breakthrough was then followed by other innovations, including Richard Arkwright's 1769 spinning or "water" frame that used water power to move the spindles. This was followed in 1779 by Samuel Crompten's spinning mule that could be operated by steam power. Refined versions of Crompton's machine, in other words, took advantage of the separate-condenser steam engines that James Watt and his business partner, Matthew Boulton, were manufacturing in their foundry outside Birmingham.

The handloom weavers were likewise threatened when in the 1830s Edmund Cartwright created a power loom that was quickly refined by other innovators. By the time that Victoria became Queen, cotton bales arriving from the United States via Liverpool's ports were sent to Manchester to be spun into thread and then woven into fabric by powerful machines, many of which were also utilizing James Watt's steam engines.[9] Even though the consequence for most people was positive—thread and fabric became much cheaper—the thousands who spun at home lost their livelihoods. This steam technology was concurrently applied to England's other core industries, particularly metal works, mining, and coal; by the 1820s, steam technology was also being applied to train locomotives and to ships.

By the early 1800s, therefore, many cottage laborers had little choice but to move to cities and seek work in the factories that had in essence taken their livelihoods and their homes. A town of 85,000 during the first half of the nineteenth century, Manchester, the center of the textile industry, was suddenly bursting with roughly 400,000 inhabitants by 1851. Elsewhere, city populations were also exploding; the workforce of Birmingham, for example, went from 73,000 in 1801 to around 200,000 by 1844, the result of manufacturing.[10] Some factory workers fared better than others, with male operatives earning around 32 shillings a week and able to afford enough food and adequate housing for their families, especially if their wives and older children also worked outside the home, which they often did. Among the urban working classes in general, few women and children over the age of eight could afford *not* to work for a wage, even though it might be as little as one-third what a man made. Unskilled factory workers, no matter their sex or age, fared the worst. Men were lucky to make a pound (20 shillings) a week in the textile mills, and in some industries, such as in the newly industrialized pottery works, the pay could bottom out at 14 shillings a week, which was barely a subsistence wage.

While the Midlands and the North experienced upheaval from the growing textile industry, the South and Southeast struggled with the effects of agricultural reform, the final years of the Napoleonic Wars, and the protectionist Corn Laws that went into effect in 1815 ("corn" being the generic word for all grain). To increase hardship for thousands, grain harvests in the 1790s and into the 1800s were repeatedly disastrous. The counties worst effected by bad harvests and laborer unrest included Hampshire, where the Beaufoys resided. Rents for farmland during the early nineteenth century were high, and in order to make a profit themselves, many farmers cut costs by altering traditional farming practices, such as hiring laborers on a yearly basis and giving them a steady wage and room and board for their families, no matter the time of year and the amount of work. Such labor–employee relationships fell out more quickly in the South than in the North, and by the Victorian era, yearly employment for agricultural laborers in that area was a dying custom.

Hired often on a monthly and at times even a weekly basis, many agricultural laborers no longer had any employment security. As with the worst-off urban laborers, some were attempting to feed themselves and families on as little as 14 shillings a week. A labor surplus did not help matters. While in the North factories and the agricultural sector competed for laborers, in the South, where fewer factories existed and where work on farms was decreasing, plenty of people worked willingly for "starvation wages."

Hardship compounded hardship. Farming, like the textiles industry, was itself becoming mechanized, beginning with Jethro Tull's seed drill. Although he had perfected its mechanisms by the 1730s (having initially invented the machine in 1701), it was not until the early 1800s that the technology became more widely instituted. The seed drill began to replace sowing seeds by hand. It required far less labor and was marvelously efficient at planting seeds, covering them with soil, ripping out weeds that always threatened to take over the seeds, and thus ensuring excellent germination. Another innovation that caused difficulty for laborers was Andrew Meikle's steam-driven thresher which was in limited use as early as the 1780s. Frustration and fear reached a pitch, and significant riots broke out in the worst-effected counties in 1816, 1822, and 1830. The Beaufoys would have heard much about these, and they may have been in some way affected by the November 18, 1830, Swing Riots, which started in West Sussex, spread into Hampshire, and then Wiltshire. Within a week, more than three hundred laborers had been arrested and were awaiting trial for burning ricks and breaking farmers' threshing machines.[11]

In its obligation to feed an everexpanding population without relying on other countries to supply the bulk of its grain, English scientists and agricultural experts began developing crop rotation methods and creating more effective fertilizers (especially ones based on guano, or bat and bird dung) that produced significantly better grain yields. With more efficient ways to plant seeds, apply crop rotation technology, and harvest grain, landowners also understood the benefit of enclosing common land and thus increasing the size of their fields. By 1850, little land was left for average people to use. With no access to brushwood, to forests for fattening pigs, and to fields for growing some grain, many were without recourse, and thus, migration to cities in desperation to look for better work meant that all around England, people were leaving behind their rural lifestyles and also leaving behind what sociologists call their foodways—the food traditions or customs that define groups of people.

Cities were too crowded and work too regimented to allow people the necessary time and space to maintain those rural foodways or culinary customs. When parents and children had worked together at home, they tended to their own gardens and cooking. Lancashire's best-known dish, Lancashire Hotpot, reflected this lifestyle. Family members spun thread while a stew of mutton neck meat (scrag) and potatoes simmered on the hearth in a brown-glazed pot. Because the meat was gristly and tough, lengthy stewing time was essential to create this dish, but the family was close by to monitor its cooking while they worked. Significantly, the family could afford some meat (albeit cheap), and they could afford fuel to keep a fire going long enough to cook such stews.

In 1800s urban England, men and women workers of all skill sets and ages were subject to long, strictly regulated hours that made it impossible for them to cook food that required time and attention, including the Lancashire hotpot, pease pudding, pottages, and frummeties that had been their dietary staples. Cottage workers had of course also been subject to equally long hours and oftentimes grueling work, but as Frederick Engels noted in his famous polemic, *Condition of the Working Class in England* (1845), they at least had been able to "save a little money and to rent smallholdings on which they could work in their spare time."[12] In other words, they had set their own schedules and found time to tend the garden or allotment and cook food that came from it.

Instead of baking and brewing, raising vegetables, curing hams and bacon, making cheese, and keeping an apiary, thousands of people had to turn to bakers, butchers, costermongers (street sellers), and grocers to supply them with food. Their living quarters, usually squalid "back to back" houses where families of ten or more were crammed into two small rooms, did not have adequate kitchens or cooking equipment. Furthermore, space was too limited to accommodate the equipment that had been fundamental to a family's earlier self-reliance, including butter churns, barrels for holding salted meat, and kettles for brewing beer. As a result, most depended on food stalls to buy already-prepared food, and for the Sunday dinner, the wife made up a pudding or pie and carried it to the baker to cook for her.

As a result of low wages, depending on others for food, and often living with inadequate cooking facilities, urban laborers' diets in the early nineteenth century were notoriously inadequate both in terms of the amount of food they consumed, as well as in nutrition. Many survived on poor-quality bakery bread, weak tea, and an overabundance of cold, boiled potatoes—the cheapest food available, and sometimes the only choice when a person's wages were low. Meat, if a laborer could afford it, was now more for flavoring potatoes and their cooking water; it was hardly a sufficient protein source. During the 1830s and 1840s, some laborers earned as little as 5 shillings a week. If one made 5 shillings in 1841, that wage bought no more than seven 4-pound loaves of bread—only enough to half fill the stomachs of a family of two adults and three children, leaving nothing left over for rent, clothes, or other food. But if a family consumed mainly potatoes, purchased at 2 shillings for 20 pounds, they could stretch their money further. For example, eating mainly potatoes allowed the family some weak tea, some bread, and Father's meat pie or sausage from a coffee stall at midday. The family might also be able to then afford a Sunday dinner of broth, stew with a bit of meat, and a plain boiled pudding with treacle.[13] However, this scenario was idealistic, and even in weeks where the family had that much food, no one wanted to survive on potatoes for six days just to be able to afford a bit of cheap meat for Sunday dinner.

Thus, in the early years of Victoria's reign, many people suffered from industrialization more than they benefited. While widespread starvation was largely avoided, the swelling numbers of those who sickened and died from complications of malnutrition were sobering enough to ignite public outcry and ultimately to put in place policies designed to improve working conditions, lower food prices, and protect children. The countless recipes to feed the poor, including the two in the Agnes Beaufoy's cookbook, testify to that outcry. By the middle years of Victoria's reign more working-class people were able to find stable and better-paying jobs, many took advantage of a more fluid class system that allowed some upward mobility and, important for our purposes, they were as likely as the middle classes to begin taking advantage of the processed foods industry that had been born and was now beginning to thrive.

## Processed Foods: Cooking in the Mid-Victorian Era

**"To Make Lemon Cheesecakes"**
*Grate the Peel of two Lemons–& squeeze the juice of One—Beat 1/2 lb of Butter into 4 or 5 Spoonefuls of Cream.—Twelve Eggs (leaving out 4 whites) beat very well—1/2 Lb of fine Sugar—stir it altogether & set it over the fire—keep stirring it 'till it begins to thicken. Put a thin paste at the bottom of your tins, & fill your tins a little more than half full with the above mixture when it is cold—Bake for half an Hour in a quick Oven. (Agnes Beaufoy)*

By the mid-nineteenth century, lemon "cheesecakes" similar to this one recorded by Agnes Beaufoy had begun to overtake the dairy or curd cheesecake in popularity. Part of the reason was probably because of the difficulty that urban people had in making cheese, and the ready availability of lemon curd, one of the first traditional home-produced specialties to become available in cans or jars. Not only did many city people have difficulty obtaining rennet and large quantities of fresh milk to make cheese, they had also lost over a couple of generations the knowledge to make it themselves. Until cheese began to be factory-produced in the 1870s, one had to make fresh cheese for cheesecake, or buy cheese from a dairy farmer (increasingly difficult, given that farms receded further and further away from cities). Reasons for lemon cheesecake's rise in popularity was as linked to industrialization as was the dairy cheesecake's decline. Those with servants, such as the Beaufoys, could make many of their sweets "from scratch," but less equipped urban housewives found the newly available array of bottled or canned preserves, lemon curd, and fruit cheeses (what North Americans often call fruit butters) an attractive alternative to the labor-intensive homemade varieties. The Duerr Family of Manchester made a fortune bottling and selling fruits, as did Blackwell & Crosse, Fortnum & Mason, and Wilkin & Sons.

Canning and industrial preservation techniques had been discovered in the early 1800s by the French chemist Nicolas Appert, and Englishman Peter Durand refined the technology, taking out a patent on his tin food canisters in 1810. Donkin & Hall, an English firm, bought Peter Durand's tin can patent and began to supply the Royal Navy with canned meat by the 1820s; by 1839, tin-coated steel containers were being used all over the world, and their popularity was clinched when in 1858 the can opener replaced the hammer and chisel as a convenient means to open them.

By the 1850s, around the time that recipes for curd cheesecake fell out of popularity and ones for lemon cheesecake rose, middle-class housewives increasingly bought their preserves, pickles, and sauces from dry-goods grocers rather than making them at home. By the end of the nineteenth century, some cookbooks and guidebooks such as the four-volume *Cassell's Book of the Household* (1889–1891) went so far as to chide women for bad economy if they insisted on producing such goods in their own kitchen—even if the final product from one's garden was superior to what one purchased at the store:

> Very often mistresses of households do not grasp the fact, that *time is money*. For instance, suppose we insist upon having our bread made at home as well as our cakes, and also that we buy our fruit and vegetables for the purpose of making jam and pickles. Unless this work is performed by members of the household who would otherwise be idle, so far from a saving, there is a loss.[14]

Regardless of the virtue that became tied to whether one purchased food ready-made or cooked it oneself, the fact is that by the mid-nineteenth century, Victorians took advantage of innovations that came specifically from the food industry. As the standard of living rose slightly and the economy stabilized in the 1850s, more were equipped to do so. A kitchen maid's or housewife's burdens could be slightly eased if she had on hand some purchased sauces to help her prepare the numerous dishes that composed a Victorian-era meal. As the century progressed, pantries in many homes began to resemble pantries of today because of the availability of processed foods.

By the 1870s, for example, a Victorian working-class pantry might include such things as cans of corned beef from Argentina, sweetened condensed milk, purchased jam, and "oleomargarine," a butter substitute that then became known as margarine or butterine. Middle-class people were even better equipped financially to take advantage of processed goods, and their pantry might include any number of the following: an assortment of canned fruits including apricots and peaches, canned vegetables such as peas and asparagus, quick-acting compressed yeast, baking powder, self-raising flour, biscuits (what North Americans call cookies), instant soup packets, and Bird's custard powder. Such items made it possible for a woman with little time and of only moderate financial means to create seemingly elaborate desserts that mimicked those created by professional chefs.[15]

Starting with a significant drop in tea duties in the 1830s and then again in the 1850s, the government systematically began to lower or abolish taxes on other food staples. When the sugar tax was reduced in the 1850s and abolished in 1874, the jam and preserves industry immediately benefited, and so did people who bought such goods from grocers. Most importantly, Prime Minister William Peel abolished the Corn Laws in 1846, for reasons that this history will explore in detail. As a result, the free-market economic strategies championed by industrialists won out over protectionist measures.

Free-market economic policies were partly responsible for lower food prices, but so too was British transportation's increasing speed and efficiency. The faster food could be transported without fear of spoilage, and the more consistent supplies were, the greater the market for goods, and ultimately, the less expensive many of them became. Beginning in the mid-1700s, newly paved roads allowed six firms to operate coaches from Manchester to London. Gas lighting facilitated faster travel in urban areas and suburbs. It had been exhibited in London by 1802, illuminated London's Pall Mall by 1813, supplied lighting for major city buildings such as the *Times* printing office and the Drury Lane Theater by 1825, and most of the capital by the end of the 1820s.[16]

Soon thereafter, the railway began to replace stage coaches and the canal barges. As early as 1830, train service began between Liverpool and Manchester, and by 1850, 6,000 miles of railway had been built.[17] In part because of the railway, London grew from a city of one million to roughly two million by 1850. Its terminals and connections to the rest of the country likewise made constant food deliveries into the city possible.

Equally important to falling food prices and consistent supplies were steam-powered trawlers and ships. By the second half of the nineteenth century, England routinely imported canned beef from South America, bacon and pickled pork from the United States, fresh mutton from Australia and, most importantly, massive amounts of cheap wheat from North America as well as Europe. Not only did the cheap price of imported wheat make it easier for working-class people to afford bread, but it also diminished the possibility of famine—a fear that had defined all previous generations of Britons. Even if the Continent suffered from disastrous wheat harvests, it was abundant elsewhere. Steamships could also import cheaper fresh meat, while British rail could make perishables such as fresh fish and milk more available to all but the poorest. Such an advance was the result of a French engineer's pioneering work with refrigeration. Between 1868 and 1876, Charles Tellier began building ships equipped with refrigeration systems, and by 1890, refrigerated rail cars and ships were commonplace. Fresh fish, particularly cod, was then available at more affordable prices throughout the British Isles. The shipping industry nullified the monopolies that sea ports such as Dorking had enjoyed when fishmongers had been obligated to travel there via horse and wagon to buy their wares, cart them back to their towns and cities, and pass the expense on to their customers.[18]

Such transportation and speed would have been impossible without improved iron and ultimately, steel. Experiments with iron ore began in the early 1700s when Abraham Darby discovered that "baked coal," or coke, could be heated hot enough to burn more impurities out of iron and thus produce a stronger, less brittle metal. In the late 1700s, even stronger iron was produced by puddling, a process by which smelted iron was reheated while workers with long rods stirred it quickly enough to incorporate air. Doing so reduced impurities in the iron. Such innovations resulted in iron bridges (the first spanned the Severn River in Shropshire in 1779) that were essential to transporting goods by rail. To carry even heavier cargo, the nation needed an efficient and quick way to produce steel. A breakthrough came in the 1850s when Englishman Henry Bessemer discovered how to blast huge amounts of air into molten iron. Henry Bessemer's iron-to-steel converter thus made it possible for industries to manufacture as much steel as necessary to build the nation's transportation infrastructure, produce large steamships, and build London's underground railroad—not to mention numerous buildings. The result of stronger metal indirectly impacted the cost of food, as it could be shipped from anywhere in the world for cheaper prices.

The kitchen itself was also revolutionized by innovations involving metal. Cast-iron ranges complete with a flat top for boiling, frying, and stewing, as well as a boiler and one or two enclosed ovens began to replace hearthside cooking by the 1830s and 1840s. Innovations with metal also changed cooking utensils. In Jane Reade's lifetime, spoons, pots, baking tins, and frying pans would have most been made of iron, wood, or pottery. Those of iron rusted easily and often cracked after prolonged usage. The process whereby steel was coated with tin in order to keep the steel from corroding was time-consuming and expensive and yet absolutely essential if iron was to become more useful not only in large industries, but also in home technologies. John Hanbury modernized the tin-plating process by using rolling machines that replaced the earlier method of beating tin sheets with hammers.[19] This new technology revolutionized the manufacturing of basic cooking implements and also made them affordable by most classes by the 1830s. Pie and bread pans, baking hoops necessary for large cakes, pastry-cutters, and jelly molds had become commonplace in many English homes by the 1850s, and by the 1890s they were even more affordable.

* * * *

The meals to which Jane Reade sat down in the early 1700s were based on traditional tastes and ways of cooking. They celebrated the season's abundance and made otherwise unpalatable foods like nettles appetizing. Cooking methods themselves had remained largely unchanged from what they had been centuries earlier. However, by the time that the last entries were recorded in Agnes Beaufoy's cookbook in the 1860s, cooking was based less on the season or even the region. The food supply itself was reliable, and food prices often cheaper than they had been earlier in the century. Significantly, families also became more aware of what food conveyed about them and their socioeconomic status. What one ate was not necessarily what one most craved.

And so an animated debate that began in the mid-Victorian era is still with us today, perhaps more so than ever before. It might be summarized in two questions: What was the cost, and what was the benefit of industrialization to the English diet? What was the Victorian legacy in regards to English cuisine, and should that legacy be celebrated or criticized? Victorian cookbook authors, domestic authorities, and certainly many new food companies from Cadbury's to Lipton's championed the benefits that industrialization brought the nation. *Cassell's Book of the Household* perhaps summed up that view best in 1890 when extolling the cheap availability of preserved and canned meats, vegetables, fruits and imported, frozen meat: "By means of this wonderful modern invention the food supply of the whole world has been increased, as the superfluities of one country can supply the deficiencies for another." *Cassell's* editors then added that those who benefited most from the canning and exporting of food were the poor, fortunately for whom "we have free trade in the necessaries of life in the shape of wheat and meat—for in the present day we can now number meat among the necessaries. Some fifty years ago, or more, the poorer classes rarely tasted meat at all; now the exception is the other way."[20]

Partly as a result of such technology and free trade laws, the cost of living fell by 30 percent by the 1880s. Basic commodities such as tea and sugar became affordable. The workweek became shorter. Gas began to replace the coal ranges, and cooking became easier as a result. Food was also more safe to eat after the 1875 Sale of Food and Drugs Act gave force to previous, inefficient laws that were designed to stop manufacturers and merchants from adulterating food and drink. People could more easily trust the products they purchased. Equally important, the majority of people had, perhaps for the first time, access to cleaner water, improved sanitation, indoor plumbing, cheaper fuel, and better housing.

However, plenty of critics bemoaned the state of the nation's cuisine in the 1880s and 1890s. The results of industrialization in regards to food, be it canned, bottled, boxed, or dried, were not so much to be celebrated as evidence of

Victorian progress, but rather, to be condemned as evidence that food scientists and manufacturers were aggressively supporting a new type of economy and social organization that destroyed established social structures, including family relationships, the farmer's or landowner's sense of obligation to his laborers, and the farmer's relationship with the masses he fed. Industrialization instituted new economic structures, where work and leisure, as well as private and public life, became separate entities. It resulted in people losing their connection to the land; and most troubling, industrialization made it unnecessary for people to be self-sufficient in regards to how they procured food and how they prepared it.

One of the purposes of this history is to help readers understand the dimensions of this debate and its continued importance to the subject of English culinary studies. Another purpose is to examine carefully the transformation of the English diet that happened as a result of new technologies and shifting social patterns, and finally, to detail how people in many parts of the British Isles held fast to regional customs and practices in spite of industrialization. The Victorian era is much closer to us than we might have thought, and the challenges that Victorians themselves faced are ones that have stubbornly endured until today in part because of the formation of the European Union and the globalization of the food economy, both of which have encouraged even more food standardization and industrialization. From the Victorians we might discover not only our shared identity, but also strategies to maintain our foodways and traditions, while at the same time taking advantage of innovations and easier cooking procedures that arose in the Victorian era.

# Much Depends on Toast: Making and Serving Breakfast in the Victorian Middle-Class Home

> **Toast.** Procure a nice square loaf of bread that has been baked one or two days previously (for new bread cannot be cut, and would eat very heavy), then with a sharp knife cut off the bottom crust very evenly, and then as many slices as you require, about a quarter of an inch in thickness (I generally use a carving-knife for cutting bread for toast, being longer in the blade, it is more handy, and less liable to waste the bread); contrive to have rather a clear fire; place a slice of bread upon a toasting-fork, about an inch from one of the sides, hold it a minute before the fire, then turn it, hold it before the fire another minute, by which time the bread will be thoroughly hot, then begin to move it gradually to and fro until the whole surface has assumed a yellowish-brown color, when again turn it, toasting the other side in the same manner; then lay it upon a hot plate, have some fresh or salt butter (which must not be too hard, as pressing it upon the toast would make it heavy), spread a piece, rather less than an ounce, over, and cut into four or six pieces; should you require six such slices for a numerous family, about a quarter of a pound of butter would suffice for the whole; but cut each slice into pieces as soon as buttered, and pile them lightly upon the plate or dish you intend to serve it.
> —Alexis Soyer, *The Modern Housewife or, Ménagère*, 1849

Of the many Victorian legacies still with us, the Full English Breakfast is one of the best known and most appreciated by English citizens and visitors alike. While those in the eighteenth-century preferred a light continental-style breakfast, Victorians preferred that now-recognized trinity of eggs, bacon, and sausage, accompanied with an assortment of breads and various cold dishes.

Along with detailing the origins of the Victorian breakfast, its food, and serving rituals, this chapter will also explore some of the roles that servant and mistress played in a typical middle-class home. More so than other household members, these two were to be praised when all ran smoothly—and blamed when things did not.

## BREAKFAST IN A BRIEF HISTORICAL CONTEXT

In medieval times and into the Renaissance, most people ate two main meals a day. Dinner, served from around ten o'clock to noon, was as large a meal as the family could afford. Supper, served in the afternoon or evening, was generally smaller than dinner. Breakfast did not yet exist as a formal meal, nor did lunch. Nonetheless, most people worked too hard to survive comfortably on dinner and supper alone. A farmer who had been out plowing in his field before sun-up would be hungry enough by eight o'clock to pause and eat something, even if his actual dinner was another two hours away. Likewise, a maidservant whose day began by the light of a single taper in the master's kitchen would have eaten something if at all possible, even if it were no more than a crust of stale bread. One of the first learned men to acknowledge that a lot of physical activity resulted in understandable hunger was the sixteenth-century physician Andrew Boorde. In his *Compendyous Regyment, or a Dyetary of Helth* (1542), Boorde allowed that indeed "a labourer maye eate thre tymes a day" because his work was hard, and he needed extra fuel to do his job effectively. But a "rest man" or a person of leisure, Boorde cautioned, should find that "two meales a daye is suffycyent"—and if one eats more often than twice, he "lyueth a beastly lyfe."[1]

By the seventeenth century, the dinner hour had moved from around noon to early afternoon, and thus, many people, regardless of whether they were sedentary or not, began to eat routinely a meal they called "breakfast." Records indicate that Oliver Cromwell, head of the Commonwealth of England, breakfasted with his wife on broth and marrow pudding (soft sausages made of bone marrow and ground almond).[2] Other wealthy people might eat bacon with boiled or poached eggs. The majority ate less expensive foods for breakfast, such as porridge, salted herrings, fresh curd cheese, and bread.

Although Boorde had rightly observed that eating sometimes had little to do with hunger and a lot to do with indicating one's social and economic status via the stomach, most people regarded breakfast as a perfunctory, casual meal. They did not invest it with much symbolic significance. Even the most wealthy treated the meal as casual, almost happenstance. As the Frenchman François de la Rochefoucauld observed in 1784, "in the houses of the rich you have coffee, chocolate, and so on. The morning newspapers are on the table and those who want to do so, read them during breakfast, so that the conversation is not of a lively nature." What he most appreciated was that one need not dress for this meal. "In the morning you come down in riding-boots and a shabby coat, you sit where you like, you behave exactly as if you were by yourself, no one takes any notice of you, and it is all extremely comfortable."[3] Wealthy Georgians often limited their breakfast to soft rolls, breads, jams, and orange marmalade, a relatively new treat in England. Toast—an English invention, according to culinary historian Colin Spencer—also became a popular food, probably out of necessity. Houses were often so cold that the rock-hard butter would not spread. German pastor Carl Philip Moritz wrote in *Journeys of a German in England in 1872* about how much he enjoyed this novel food: "The slices of bread and butter given to you with tea are as thin as poppy-leaves, but there is a way of roasting slices of buttered bread before the fire which is incomparable. One slice after another is taken and held to the fire with a fork until the butter is melted. . . . This is called 'toast'."[4]

We can imagine Moritz sitting in front of a blazing fire enjoying this ritual, and indeed, characters seated around the fire with the toasting fork in one hand and a stack of hot buttered toast in the other are common enough in Victorian-era fiction as well. The time of day that these cozy scenes usually take place in novels, however, is seldom morning, the meal seldom breakfast. By the 1830s and 1840s, prosperous Victorians had altered the Georgian-era breakfast in significant ways and "cozy" was not a word that could characterize that meal. Working-class people had little choice but to see breakfast as a purely perfunctory affair, but the middle classes began to weigh the meal and its foods with meanings that took it far from both its pragmatic and its casual roots.

## THE VICTORIAN WORKING-CLASS BREAKFAST

Working-class Victorians ate as much food for breakfast as they could afford, but with perhaps the exception of Sunday morning, they seldom had leisure to sit and enjoy their food. Urban laborers often ate as they walked to work. Investigative journalist Henry Mayhew recorded in his classic study, *London Labour and the London Poor* (1851) that more than three hundred vendors lined London's main thoroughfares, selling the working poor mugs of coffee, tea, or drinking chocolate for a penny. Morning before sunrise was one of the vendors' busiest times. Industrialization had resulted in an urban laborer's day becoming a regimented affair, defined by the blowing of a factory or mine whistle or the clanging of a dock bell. Most worked extremely long hours, up to sixteen, six days a week (Sunday was one day granted for rest). Given the low wages that many people were making, steady work—no matter how many hours—was a blessing, even if it meant that a person was up before daybreak and not to bed until nine or ten o'clock at night. Such a regimen dramatically affected a laborer's diet. Similar to fast-food restaurants today, urban food stalls offered cheap meals of amazing variety that catered to tired, hurried people who could not see to much cooking themselves. Along with a hot mug of coffee, a customer could purchase a readymade breakfast: a slice of bread and butter or a slice of current cake for half a penny, a boiled egg for 1 penny, and a ham sandwich for 2 pence.[5] Soft, large rolls, known as baps in Scotland, were popular with laborers because they were cheap and designed to hold a ham, fried egg, or sausage filling. After swallowing a mug of coffee and returning the mug to the vendor, the laborer continued on to work while eating breakfast.

Most rural laborers still had a bit more leisure in the mornings unless it was spring planting or fall harvest. They usually sat at the table with their families for breakfast. Northerners continued to eat porridge, as oats grew so well in that damper, colder clime. The housewife boiled water in a pan and sprinkled in the oats, stirring as she did so. When the mixture was thick, she ladled it into bowls. Family members first took a spoonful of oatmeal, dunked it into a bowl of milk or cream, and then swallowed it. It was not customary in that era to mix the milk with the oatmeal in the same bowl as people do today. Southern laborers continued to eat bread for breakfast. All over England, tea was replacing small (low alcohol) beer as the preferred breakfast choice. If times were bad, as they often were in the early Victorian era, many ate little but potatoes for all three meals, and in the morning, these were eaten cold as leftovers from last night's boiled mess of them. A "donkey tea" sometimes replaced the real thing if the family had little money. One submerged burnt bread crusts in boiling water and steeped them for several minutes. The drink was hot, and it at least resembled tea in color. By the 1850s and 1860s the economy stabilized, and prices for staples such as bread, sugar, and tea had fallen; however, most urban and rural laborers continued to begin their days with bread and porridge, although now the bread was smeared with store-bought jam or margarine ("marg") and the oat porridge mixed with treacle. When one could afford meat, it appeared on the table for as many breakfasts as possible. This remained the case throughout the entire Victorian era for all people but vegetarians, of which there were few.

## THE VICTORIAN MIDDLE-CLASS BREAKFAST: FOOD AND VALUES

While working-class people were usually preoccupied with finding enough food to eat and a spare moment in which to eat it, middle-class people elevated breakfast to one of the most important meals of the day and began to give it a great deal of symbolic significance. They saw all their meals, including when, how, and what they ate, as a way to differentiate themselves from those below and above them, and perhaps inadvertently, as a way to create class solidarity or identity.[6] Indeed, food and values became intricately linked for many middle-class people. In the course of any given morning, the mistress of the house in particular was to showcase orderliness, punctuality, diligence, and efficiency along with presenting the food. Surprisingly, given its rather humble nature, the quality of the breakfast toast could be used as a yardstick by which others measured the mistress's faithful execution of her duties, and consequently, how worthy she was of her privileged social station.

Alexis Soyer, one of the era's most colorful celebrity chefs, wrote several best-selling cookbooks, including one aimed at the aspiring middle classes: *The Modern Housewife or, Ménagère* (1849). Unlike many cookbooks that are simply pages of recipes with some occasional notes on how to serve a dish, how to use it up for leftovers, or when to purchase a particular food based on season, Soyer created a cookbook that read as an epistolary novel. Through his fictional persona, Hortense B., Soyer championed the middle-class value system and affirmed the importance of the mistress maintaining a smooth-running, tasteful household. As with many domestic authorities of that era, Soyer placed praise or blame for how a household operated solely on the mistress. By setting up his cookbook as a series of advice letters and recipes exchanged between the model housewife, Hortense, and the woefully inefficient housewife, Eloise L. (who is nonetheless eager to reform her ways and has turned to Hortense for guidance), Soyer was also able to work in hundreds of recipes designed to meet the needs of different strata within the middle class.

It is useful to pause at this juncture and explain that historically in England, income alone did not always determine one's class. A bank clerk who made £90 a year did not earn a wage, he earned a salary. His status was the result of numerous factors, including the nature of his job (it did not require physical labor), his education, and his family's background and breeding. A highly skilled cabinet maker who also made £90 a year nonetheless earned a wage, not a salary. Likewise, his social status was based on the fact that he did physical labor, had a rudimentary academic education, and was instead apprenticed. His family was working-class and had probably always been defined as such. These two men thus inhabited different spheres and society judged them by different standards. However, one of industrialization's effects was to create a more fluid society, where a working-class boy might through hard work, initiative, and perhaps just luck end up with a salaried position that now made him a part of what Victorians sometimes called the "new" middle class. Many people did not feel at ease, however, and certainly a middle-class "pecking order" was clearly discernable. Part of Soyer's purpose in the *Modern Housewife* was to help the "new" middle-class wife feel more confident and secure with her status by making visible to her the seemingly invisible codes of conduct and protocols to which she was now expected to subscribe.

Soyer's character, Hortense, was representative of thousands of Victorians who were indeed moving up in social ladder and had to constantly readapt their domestic management and in particular their food expenses to reflect that ascent. Hortense's husband, "Mr. B.," is introduced to readers at the beginning of *The Modern Housewife* as a shopkeeper who, through hard work, talent, and his wife's stunning household management becomes by the middle of the book a prosperous merchant with his own staff of clerks. As Hortense acquires more servants and a growing budget for domestic expenditures, she is constantly challenged with ensuring that the family dining table reflects her husband's prosperity. Hortense takes her role seriously and attempts to impress upon

Table 2.1. Suggested Number of Domestic Servants Per Family Income

| |
|---|
| About £1,000 a year—A cook, upper housemaid, nursemaid, under housemaid, and a man servant |
| About £750 a year—A cook, housemaid, nursemaid, and footboy |
| About £500 a year—A cook, housemaid, and nursemaid |
| About £300 a year—A maid-of-all-work and nursemaid |
| About £200 or £150 a year—A maid-of-all-work (and girl occasionally) |

*Source*: Isabella Beeton, *Book of Household Management* (London: S.O. Beeton, 1864), 8.

Eloise that a woman's discipline, moral fiber, and management skills will either result in her husband's success or bring his failure. Nowhere are her skills and her faults more noticeable than at the table and in her kitchen management, and as breakfast was the first meal of the day, the contest began every morning around 6:00 (and earlier in the summer) and judgment began at 8:00 to 8:30 when the maid carried in the hot breakfast dishes and, also, the plate of hot, buttered toast, neatly wrapped in its white linen napkin.

Recognizing that his reader might likely be starting married life, as did Hortense, with only one general maid and a girl who came in periodically to help with heavy cleaning, Soyer began *The Modern Housewife* with the most basic—and most deceptive—breakfast staple, toast. It was understandable that a young, inexperienced mistress might wrongly assume that the toast would take care of itself, and that her maid could not only prepare the morning's bacon and eggs, a plate of sausages, and a tureen of porridge but that she could also produce a stack of perfectly crisp, golden brown, buttered toast, given that toast took no real skill. Not so, claimed Soyer's Hortense. Because its quality depended absolutely on timing, the right amount of butter, and the tender-crispness of its crumb, toast could be (and too often was) the downfall of the entire breakfast. The mistress's performance was as much at stake as a servant's when it came to food on the table and many authorities would have contended, more so. Bad toast equaled a bad mistress.

To better appreciate this fact as well as the skill involved in getting breakfast to the table every morning, imagine the two key players' viewpoints: the general maid's and her mistress's. Because thousands of middle-class people lived on £150–200 a year, imagine also that this mistress is married to an ambitious London solicitor who currently makes £200, which according to Isabella Beeton's *Book of Household Management* (1861 and 1864 editions) just qualifies them as part of the servant-keeping class (Table 2.1). Our fictional family is thus respectable, but they only have the finances to afford a general maid, or what was sometimes called a maid-of-all-work. As with many in their social stratum, they put a great deal of emphasis on appearances and on ensuring their chances of success by doing precisely what they believed they should be doing to impress their "betters" (employers, for example, who have some determination over the husband's chances in his firm) as well as their social "equals."

The year is 1866, and the family has recently moved into a London middle-class neighborhood where they lease a brick row house, or what the English call a terraced house. The homes in their neighborhood conform to the same floor plan: kitchen and an attached scullery in the basement; a front parlor for company and a private family parlor that doubles as dining room on the ground floor; and on the second floor (what the English call the first floor), three bedrooms and a bathroom (the lavatory is in a separate tiny building out back). The family has no spare room for the maid; she sleeps in the kitchen on a make-shift pallet that she stows away every morning when she rises. Because she is young and relatively inexperienced, the maid earns £6 a year, plus her room, board, her two uniforms, and a pair of shoes.

In spite of having no spare room for the maid, this home has several amenities that working-class families usually did without: more room to define a public and a private space, a separate eating area removed from the kitchen (although in ideal circumstances, the family would not want their parlor doubling as their dining room as it must currently do), and a scullery where the maid does the washing up and prepares the messiest foods such as haunches of beef and large fish. The kitchen also has a pantry for storing dry goods (essentially a cabinet) and a small walk-in larder for storing perishables. Even more significantly, the kitchen is equipped with a moderate-size Leamington Kitchener, the brand name for a coal-fired range complete with water heater and enclosed iron bake oven. And, most significant of all, the house has one indoor water tap located in the scullery, although water service from the city is intermittent at best and the pressure is very low. Nonetheless, they seldom have to leave home and pump water down the street from a communal standpipe—what most Londoners were doing in the 1860s.

While her husband commutes daily to and from his London office, the wife stays at home, managing all domestic affairs, raising three small children, and assisting her maid with light housekeeping. In spite of all her seeming advantages—an attractive home in a respectable neighborhood, enviable modern appliances as well as an indoor water source, the mistress perceives her lot as "quite hard," but she is empathetic enough to realize that what little ease she does gain is purchased at her maid's expense.[7]

## THE EARLY MORNING ROUTINE

### Preparing the Range for Heating and Cooking

The morning of course does not start with breakfast. No one can come downstairs in slippered feet, turn the knob on the stove, and heat water in a tea kettle. Doing last night's dirtiest dishes was the maid's first priority (she did not do them the night before because she was in her clean serving uniform) and so too was preparing the range for the day's cooking and cleaning. Due to the cost of fuel for lighting and heating, a maid might be allowed to sleep as late as five thirty or even six o'clock in winter to save money. When she rose, she did her minimal toilet and cleaned the dirty dishes and then prepared the kitchen range with the light of one candle or a gas jet (if it were later in the century). In summer, she went to work as soon as the sun made it possible for her to see, with five o'clock her usual hour to start the day.

After the dishes, the hardest part of her day commenced with cleaning and preparing the range. To begin, the maid knelt in front of it and opened the firebox. In homes such as this one where thrift and industry were necessities as well as virtues, the maid separated the cinders (fragments of coal that still could be used in a new fire) and ashes (to be collected annually by the dustman) before she laid a new fire. She would then brush the soot and dirt from around and under the range, spreading saved, damp tea leaves on the surface to hold down the dust and make it easier to clean. She proceeded to scrub the steel ornamental parts, removing any rust with emery paper, and then she began blackleading the range. Blacklead came in sticks and she mixed one with turpentine to create what would look like today's black shoe polish. Using an iron bristle bush, she applied the paste-like substance. She then used another brush to rub off excess blacklead and—hoping that the range was still warm from the night before—she proceeded to use a buffing brush to bring the now blackleaded range up to a high shine (a bit of heat from the range facilitated this process).

Once a week (or twice if she were superdiligent and less if she could get away with laziness), the maid had to get up an hour early to clean out the range flues. They became quickly blocked with soot, given the fact that the range was in use from early morning to late at night every day. When blocked with soot, the flues did not allow the air to flow through them and thus heat the oven. An experienced kitchen-maid in a wealthy home could use the blocked flues to her advantage, however. Sometimes, she would deliberately leave one flue blocked up because it worked as a heat control. For the best ranges, those with two ovens, one blocked flue meant that one oven stayed relatively cool (terrific for baking delicate foods or keeping already-prepared food hot), and the other oven became hot by unblocking its flue.[8] But our maid has a one-oven range, and she must ensure that the flues are routinely cleaned. To do so, she takes a long narrow brush with a bent handle, or a long chain attached to a stick, shoves it up into the flue, and jerks the brush or shakes the chain to dislodge the soot. This job was so terribly filthy that after it is done, she has to go and wash (the reason for needing an extra hour of time in the morning to clean the flues), but if the flues were not regularly cleaned, soot would fall into saucepans and food on the stove.

Always trying to economize, the mistress was loath to expend more than the absolute minimum on fuel, particularly candles and gaslight. As a result, many maids started the day in light too dim to see when soot and blacks (coal filaments that stained everything they touched) fell into their saucepans. One of the era's leading domestic and cooking authorities, John Charles Buckmaster criticized mistress and servant alike, noting that as a result of such dim lighting "the ashes and drops of tallow not unfrequently fall into the saucepan" because the maid cannot see clearly how things are progressing. A maid must have inadvertently put many a pan or pot onto her range top, unaware that residing in the bottom were wispy, powdery blacks that would ruin whatever food she might be attempting to prepare.[9] The number of times that cookbook authors such as Soyer and Beeton stressed that the pot must be "scrupulously clean" attests to the frequency of this mistake. As Buckmaster also pointed out (somewhat gratuitously), the ranges were "rather complicated in their construction, and therefore require[d] more intelligence in their management."[10] Very wealthy families who could afford a cook as well as two or more kitchen maids probably ate better-cooked, cleaner food simply because one maid's primary duty was to tend to the range. While she cleaned it, operated it, and maintained it, the cook and other maid could concentrate more efficiently on numerous other requisite tasks.

### Lighting a Coal Fire

We come back to our one maid in her smallish kitchen in the early morning hours. Once the range was cleaned, she had to light the fire and ensure it took. Coal was rather hard to ignite, but once it was going, it produced a steadier and more reliable heat than did wood, a commodity that had largely disappeared by the 1700s. She knelt at the grate with a Lucifer match (the type of wooden kitchen match we are familiar with today) or a lighted piece of paper and ignited the brushwood, cinders, and dry sticks that composed her kindling. On the top of the kindling she carefully began to lay a bed of tennis-ball-sized pieces of coal, making sure that the oven draft was wide open to allow in as much oxygen as possible. Patience was indeed a virtue in the process. Because of the number of other tasks she must see to, she might be tempted to lay on coal too quickly, thus making it harder for the coal to ignite properly. As the fire began to catch, she would move larger pieces of coal and cinders to the back of the grate, and then finally place small coal and more cinders on top of the fire. Assuming that all went as planned and she managed to get it to the point that the flame was burning blue, she could then spare a couple of precious minutes to eat her own breakfast. The typical servant breakfast recommended in guidebooks was a slice of bread topped with butter or dripping. Lilian Westall, a housemaid at the turn of the century who briefly worked for a "very respectable" dentist and his wife, remembered that "there were often mice dirts on the dripping to be scraped off first" before she could eat.[11] After gulping down her meager slice and also a cup of tea, our maid is ready to proceed with her next chores.

## The Early Morning Routine: Procuring Foodstuffs for Breakfast

How much time did it take a maid to clean and light a range and ensure it was in excellent working order for her day's heavy tasks? Her pace would have been frantic, even if she had risen three hours before the master of the house called the family to prayers and breakfast. After all, cleaning and lighting the range were only two duties that she must accomplish before 8:00 (or perhaps 8:30, depending of course on the master's work schedule). Once the range was lit and the flues adjusted to maintain the appropriate draft and heat for any upcoming cooking, the maid was ready to procure the necessary food to make breakfast.

This seemingly simple activity, however, also presented challenges because mistresses did not often trust their maids to take provisions themselves from the larder and pantry; they feared that servants pilfered food, wasted it, or secretly ate more than their allotted share. Such is the mistress's fear in our imaginary family. Up and dressed by 7:00 to see to her children's needs, she is on hand to dole out the day's food supplies. Evenings are too hectic for her to see to this burdensome task, even though she has ringing in her head authoritative instructions from various guidebook authorities that insist that the task should be taken care of the night before. *Cassell's Book of the Household* (1889–1891) for example, summed up the mistress's obligation with these rather terse words:

> In other words, let there be a general rule to—*Look a Day Ahead*. As an instance in point, we should say it would be a sign of bad management if the cook or general servant had to wait till her mistress came downstairs in order to ask the question, "Please, what are you going to have for breakfast this morning?" This should all have been thought of and arranged beforehand.[12]

However, our mistress's system works well enough. Once the day's food supplies are procured and put on the large kitchen worktable, the maid leaves the kitchen temporarily and sees to chores above-stairs.

## The Early Morning Routine: Chores Above-Stairs

The wealthiest middle-class families, like those of the upper class, hired enough domestic servants to divide among them the numerous chores that were to be done before breakfast. In addition to cleaning the previous night's pots and pans, preparing and lighting the range, and cleaning the kitchen floor, a litany of other tasks greeted servants before the cook began the actual preparing of breakfast itself, e.g. setting the dough for breakfast rolls, scrubbing the front steps leading into the house, sweeping the stairs and hallways, twice-weekly washing shelves and cupboards, dressing the nursery dinner and preparing vegetables, meat, and all other foods that would later become the adults' evening dinner. In a more modest home—what the majority of middle-class Victorians lived in—such chores had to be shared between the mistress and her one maid, with the mistress demanding that the hardest and most tedious chores be relegated to the maid. *Cassell's Book of the Household* bluntly laid out her duties:

> The Maid-of-all-Work, or General Servant . . . simply does all the work of a house that there is to do which the mistress does not undertake. Her duties include those of the cook, the housemaid, the parlour-maid, the kitchen-maid, and very often the laundry-maid also; and, in order to do her work properly, she ought to understand cookery, cleaning, scrubbing, sweeping, polishing, waiting at table; and in short, to be acquainted with all the numerous details of which household work is made up.[13]

While our mistress tries to remain upstairs to tend to her children and her husband's early morning demands (particularly for hot water), the maid scrubs, dusts, and polishes. Finally done with those tasks, she now hurries with her heavy basket of cutlery and other breakfast implements to assist the mistress in setting the breakfast table.

### Setting the Breakfast Table and Preparing the Food

Henry Southgate in *Things a Lady Would Like to Know* (1875) recommended that the dining table be covered with a "fair damask cloth." Nothing, he noted, "shows off so sweetly the morning repast with its bright silver, its cheerful china, and the merry, hissing urn. When the months have flowers, by all means have the epergne well filled; for, as the poet beautifully says, 'They are the smiles of God.' "[14] The cloth could then be removed immediately after the meal in order to save it from the soot and dust that constantly settled on all available surfaces. Our maid and mistress place cups, saucers, and teaspoons in front of the mistress's chair, as it is her job to pour and serve the tea and coffee. Stands for the coffee pot and tea pot, a sugar basin, and milk jugs (one for hot milk and one for cold) are likewise placed at the mistress's seat. As our mistress enjoys making tea at the table, the maid ensures that a spirit lamp and small kettle are placed within her mistress's reach as well. Plates, knives, forks, fish-knives (if the mistress has ordered fish for breakfast), and other essentials such as egg cups and glasses are set around the table for each person. Small cruet stands and salt cellars, mustard pots, preserves in cut-glass dishes, a bread and butter knife, as well as a pretty flower arrangement made the breakfast table complete.[15] Satisfied that all is in order and that the mistress can manage the remaining tasks in the dining room, the maid hurries back to the kitchen to see to the cooking.

GENERAL ARRANGEMENT OF BREAKFAST-TABLE.

General arrangement of breakfast-table in *Cassell's Book of the Household* (1889–1891). Notice that the main hot dish sits near the master's place, as he will serve it to the family. Dry toast on a rack sits to the left. Some families preferred the toast unbuttered because it minimized the risk of it becoming soggy.

Middle-class Victorians expanded the continental breakfast of the eighteenth century to include at least one hot dish of meat and/or eggs, often along with a tureen of porridge, a stack of toast, and an array of cold foods to tempt more dainty appetites. The hot dish signified the family's status because its ingredients (in other words, the meat) were expensive. Aside from its symbolism, hot breakfast food was also thought necessary to nourish children for a day of play and lessons, and even more importantly, to prepare the master of the house for a full day's work with possibly no significant lunch break. People today might also think of breakfast, figuratively speaking, as a time to arm the soldiers for battle—that notion was Victorian. Many mothers in the nineteenth century considered the family breakfast with its bacon, eggs, sausages, toast, and porridge in exactly this light.

To vary the monotony of bacon, sausage, and fried eggs, Soyer's Hortense suggested that Eloise show some creativity by serving any of the following alternatives: eggs *au Beurre* (eggs gently cooked in a browned butter sauce), poached eggs served with *maître d'hôtel* or anchovy butter, omelets, herring toast sandwiches, bloated herrings, dried haddock or whiting, soles or sprats, grilled sheep's kidneys, or eggs scrambled with ham. Breakfast and lunch both presented a mistress with opportunities to use up leftovers, so *réchauffé* dishes (the fancy French name for warmed up or rehashed leftovers) were also common on the breakfast table. To round out the selection, the mistress usually ordered fresh bread or rolls as well as hot buttered toast.

As "hot" was key to toast's success, we might be inclined to consider it a hot dish, but it was not substantial like broiled kidneys or eggs and bacon. It must have exasperated maid and mistress alike when the toast sat on the table, perfectly browned with just the right amount of butter spread, and no one thought to eat it. But even more exasperating must have been those unfortunate mornings when the toast was burned and soggy from too much butter and the master then asked his wife to pass it to him along with another cup of tea. When he opened the white linen napkin or lifted the dome to see the charred, soggy pieces, he would have been disappointed, and if he were a normal Victorian man, he would inevitably pass negative judgment on his wife (even if it were a silent one), and she, in her consternation, would take her feelings of ineptitude and guilt out on her maid. As a middle-class breakfast staple, hot toast tested the servant's ability to fulfill her obligations, and it tested the mistress's ability to manage her staff and household efficiently.

For all these reasons, Victorian cookbook authors devoted a significant amount of time to toast, although Soyer was perhaps the most exhaustive on the subject. *Modern Housewife* opened with Eloise's humble request to Hortense to send her "a few receipts for the making of rolls and the other breakfast bread . . . even how to make toast." Hortense enthusiastically responded: "To show my approbation of your idea, I enclose herewith the first receipt, *How to Make Toast.*"[16] In the American edition of Soyer's cookbook, the editor (identified only as "an American Housekeeper") followed up Soyer's initial recipe with this defense of his decision, lest American women should miss the crucial subtext of Hortense's and Eloise's exchange:

> Perhaps some housekeepers may laugh at the presumption of M. Soyer in attempting to give a formal receipt for so trifling a matter as making a piece of toast. But, in Cookery, there are no trifles. Every preparation of food, however simple, requires thought, care, and experience. Among the unpleasantnesses of our breakfast-tables, there are none more common than poor toast.

Eloise, we are given to believe, was no longer laughing. She understood and appreciated that society judged a mistress on the basis of how accomplished she was at preparing the most basic foods. Exotic French sauces will not cover up the terrible flavor of a burned chop; extra sugar will not hide the scorched porridge's foul taste; and extra butter on the toast will merely cause the under slice to swim "in an ocean of butter at the bottom of the dish" at the "peril of its life," as Hortense warned.[17]

The toast exchange between Hortense and Eloise resumed when Hortense outlined her own family's breakfast routine. She wrote: "The cloth was laid by the servant girl at half-past seven precisely; at ten minutes to eight I used to make tea, and at eight o'clock we were seated at breakfast." In the winter, Hortense continued, they frequently had toast "which I never suffered any servant to prepare more than five minutes before we were seated, for, if standing any time, the dry toast becomes tough, and the buttered very greasy, and consequently unpalatable, as well as indigestible." Concerned that Eloise might return to her earlier negligent ways, Hortense reiterated after a couple more exchanges that toast of any kind "that has been made half an hour is not worth eating."[18]

Now consider our maid, who must cook the other food as well as make toast. Among her requisite kitchen utensils was an iron toasting fork. The maid had to slice the bread thinly enough so as not to waste it, but thickly enough to be able to insert the fork tines without tearing through the bread. She then stooped awkwardly in front of the range fire and held the toast to the flame. A careful maid would do as Soyer recommended and warm the bread thoroughly before browning both sides. "Patience!" Col. A. Kenny Herbert (under the pseudonym "Wyvern") cautioned in his classic 1894 cookbook *Fifty Breakfasts*. Echoing Hortense, Herbert lamented: "A very simple thing to be sure, yet how often is it maltreated, scorched outside, spongy within and flabby?" One must stand, Herbert instructed, "a little distance from clear smokeless embers, patiently."[19] However, if the maid was attempting to prepare this dish and in the process allowed the main hot dish to languish because she was fussing over toast, then she must expect other problems and of course reprimands. A large Victorian family probably demanded at least ten slices of toast—the most tedious task, and one that the maid Lilian Westall remembered well when she was employed at Blechingley, Surrey: "I did *all* the washing-up on my own; it took me hours. I remember doing endless slices of toast."[20]

Transporting the toast to the table presented the next challenge for many maids and mistresses. The day's requested hot dish, the porridge, and the toast were to arrive at the table hot. However, Victorians did not heat passageways between their rooms because they believed that cold air was good for health. Except in the warmest summer days, the hot dishes automatically cooled down in the journey from the basement kitchen to upstairs dining table. While some wealthy families had a dumb waiter by which to send the dishes straight from kitchen to dining room, most middle-class Victorians relied on the maid to transport the food. Adding to her difficulty, the maid had to place substantial silver domes over the dishes to help preserve their heat, but then forcing her to carry as much as 40 to 50 pounds over a distance repeatedly during the course of the meal. Although many middle-class Victorians found living in a house with the kitchen next to the dining room to be less than ideal because cooking odors from the kitchen too easily escaped and penetrated the family living quarters, the maids no doubt were relieved with that proximity.

Hot foods could also cool for other reasons beyond the maid's control. Older children who saw to their own toilet and dress could upset the regimental order by daring to arrive at the table tardy—thus postponing the meal and making the father irate. Father had to offer the prayer before the food could be eaten and he might be particularly thankful—and long-winded—on any given day of the week. Of course, the maid herself could easily run behind. In the kitchen, the stove might not heat properly, and as a result the eggs would be underdone. Or, the fire did not burn "clear" and the resulting smoke made it impossible for her to broil the chops without scorching them. And as for scorch, if grease dripped inside the oven and began to smolder, putting forth a putrid odor, then the maid's attention would have to be on how to eliminate the odor. In the process, she could easily burn the porridge.

## THE SYMBOLIC MEANINGS OF THE VICTORIAN BREAKFAST

This illustrative scenario of a general maid seeing to breakfast puts us far away from the days of an eighteenth-century leisurely morning of rolls, breads, marmalade, and newspapers lying about. By the mid-nineteenth century, this leisurely pace and composed attitude no longer characterized many people's households, and the prosperous, rising middle classes in particular adopted a regimen that made breakfast an ordeal for many family members, not just their maids. From the master's point of view, breakfast had to be punctual so that he had time after it to see to his attire, take up his hat and coat, and then head off to work. The general attitude was that no one had the right to keep the master waiting. Victorian novelists could quickly convey a character's standing simply by mentioning what time he appeared for breakfast. Young Fred Vincy in George Eliot's *Middlemarch* (1871–1872) does not make his way to the breakfast table until the shockingly late hour of half-past ten—long after his industrious father has left for the warehouse, and only after his mother has asked the servant Pritchard twice to see to Mr. Fred. Although his mother frets and fusses, she merely excuses her son's laziness and thus directly implicates herself in her son's moral ineptitude. When Fred finally does swagger in, he looks with disdain at the "coffee and buttered toast" that the maid has just prepared fresh. He walks around the table "surveying the ham, potted beef, and other cold remnants, with an air of silent rejection." The maid falters, "Should you like eggs, sir?" With even more disdain, Fred Vincy replies, "Eggs, no! Bring me a grilled bone!" His very proper sister Rosamond objects to his request, "Really, Fred . . . if you must have hot things for breakfast, I wish you would come down earlier."[21] Victorian readers would understand immediately the coming dramatic mishaps involving Fred simply by the clues that Eliot dropped in this one seemingly mundane scene.

Writing in the 1960s, Arnold Palmer recalled that the breakfast of his grandparent's generation was an anxious one: "Anxiety for the lie-a-bed child or guest, anxiety for the hot-faced breathless maid, anxiety even for the amateur reader and hymn-player—all these anxieties led to a rather silent meal, with frequent surreptitious glances at the clock."[22] Industrialization and the laissez-faire capitalism that supported it affected people in myriad ways, with enslavement to the clock chief among them. While enjoyment and good company were the ideal, the real tenor of breakfast was captured not only by Palmer's memories, but also by one of the many pieces of advice on the matter in *Cassell's Book of the Household*, in which the word "punctual" is repeated no less than five times:

> If meals are to be at all comfortable, the servants of the household must be trained to have them ready at the stated hours, and the members of the family must learn to be punctual in observing these hours. There cannot possibly be any comfort at breakfast, for example, if each member of the household appears at the table at a different time . . . For children attending schools, an early punctual breakfast is most necessary; indeed, for every family meal and every member of a family, punctuality cannot be too strictly insisted upon. At the same time, punctuality is a virtue by no means easy of attainment. Servants are rarely punctual naturally, and it often needs long training and much patience to make them so.[23]

Aware of the injunction never to annoy the master, the mistress had the responsibility of being the most punctual of all in order to ensure everyone else's brisk pace. She—not the maid—could expect to take blame from her husband should breakfast be chaotic, the children tardy or disheveled, and she herself not in the best of spirits. This man who presumably bore the ills of the outside world on his shoulders and who was obligated to ruthlessly command, defeat enemies, and triumph over them, could ill afford to struggle and strive within his own home—what was to be his refuge. His wife was to ensure that home remained his refuge; this responsibility induced much anxiety.

Given the serious nature of the wife's role in establishing family harmony and ensuring her husband's good temper, *Mrs Beeton's Every Day Cookery* (an abridged edition of the *Book of Household Management*) offered advice to help the mistress insure a peaceful breakfast. "When it is possible to get the master to enjoy an eight o'clock breakfast, household matters go on charmingly." To "get the master to enjoy an eight o'clock breakfast," *Every Day Cookery* offered the following:

> As soon as The Mistress hears her husband's step, the bell should be rung for the hot dish; and should he be, as business men usually are, rather pressed for time, she should herself wait upon him, cutting his bread, buttering his toast, &c. Also giving standing orders that coat, hat, and umbrella shall be brushed and ready; and see that they are, by helping on the coat, handing the hat, and glancing at the umbrella.[24]

The mistress's duties revolved around her husband's happiness and well-being. She was to accept her husband's blame and criticism and learn eagerly from it, just as she was to gracefully accept his praise and nobly suffer his indifference. She was to do all in her power to show herself serene and unruffled, moving through her day like a virtuoso violinist, handling everything that was thrown at her with expertise and wisdom, and never revealing the true difficulty of her role. Even if she had just one maid, several small children to tend to, accounts to keep, obligatory calls to make and receive, numerous household tasks (including routine drudge work), and of course her husband's own well-being to worry about, she was not to crack, and certainly not to show anger or strain under this pressure.

Frances Power Cobbe, a prominent feminist intellectual who—significantly—did not marry, affirmed that this life was nerve-racking for middle-class women. She shrewdly observed in her 1878 *Contemporary Review* essay "Little Health of Ladies":

> Several of my married acquaintances were liable to a peculiar sort of headache. They were obliged, owing to these distressing attacks, to remain very frequently in bed at breakfast-time, and later in the day to lie on the sofa with darkened blinds and a considerable exhibition of Eau-de-Cologne. A singular immunity from the seizures seemed to be enjoyed when any pleasant society was expected, or when their husbands happened to be in a different part of the country. By degrees, putting my little observations together, I came in my own mind to call these the "Bad-Husband Headaches."[25]

Cobbe's deliberate mention of breakfast as the catalyst of this "peculiar sort of headache" would not have been lost on women readers who understood that no time of the day was more stressful than the early morning. No doubt life became calmer the minute the master put on his brushed overcoat and hat, took up his umbrella, and set purposely out of the door on his way to work. Although left behind, the mistress could at least breathe a sigh of relief that lasted for nine or more hours. She was not to have the anxiety of pleasing her husband and looking after—or worse yet, predicting—his every need.

Did housewives follow all the expert advice rigidly? Did they embrace these values? Did they have the means and stamina to ensure that the toast was not only buttered but also served hot? Did they ensure that the master had all he required nourishment-wise for his commute and long day at work? Clearly, Victorian middle-class people accepted the fact that no household could operate smoothly all the time or along the ideal lines set forth in guidebooks. Thousands of men and women and children modified these social rituals and patterns to fit their own needs and personalities, and certainly their own budgets. Nonetheless, Victorian guidebooks were numerous, and often—as with Soyer's *Modern Housewife, Cassell's Book of the Household,* Beeton's *Book of Household Management,* and *Every Day Cookery*—they were bestsellers. The speed of industrialization had left people with a somewhat shaky sense of their socioeconomic standing and how to keep it. Oftentimes, the rather patronizing and yet forcibly upbeat and encouraging tone in which authorities addressed women readers suggested the degree of anxiety that many experienced when trying to manage their own and their family's lives in the face of erratic and inexplicable economic downturns, the onslaught of new inventions and technologies. We might also assume that many took comfort in the tone and advice both, and applied it when possible to the running of their own homes, and most certainly to the breakfast ritual that started the day. After the rigors of breakfast, luncheon must have seemed a godsend.

# Luncheon or Dinner? The Victorian Midday Meal

> **A Treacle Pudding.** Take a quarter of a pound of suet, half a pound of flour, half a pound of treacle, a teaspoonful of pounded loaf-sugar, and the juice of half a lemon, mix all together in a large basin, with sufficient milk to form a thick batter. Tie it up in a floured cloth with plenty of room to swell, and boil for three hours.
>
> *Precautions.*—It is necessary that the pudding should be thoroughly boiled.
>
> —John Charles Buckmaster, *Buckmaster's Cookery*, 1874

At the end of the Victorian era, author Edith Nesbit produced a series of rollicking adventure novels involving the escapades of five children in a middle-class family. In *Five Children and It* (1902), a magical Sammyadd, or sand fairy, grants the children one wish per day, and Cyril dreamily says at breakfast one morning, "I wish there were Red Indians in England—not big ones, you know, but little ones, just about the right size for us to fight." When the other children recognize Cyril's mistake—that he has inadvertently wished for something that is bound to come true—they are simultaneously terrified and excited. Significantly, several of the children's wished-for adventures occur around the time that their nursery dinner is served. After the cook dishes up minced beef and boiled potatoes, animated talk falters because "there seemed somehow to be something about the food that made the idea of Red Indians seem flat and unbelievable." But after the cook delivers the treacle pudding and exits the nursery for good, the adventure starts: "Peering round the corner of the window, among the red leaves of the Virginia creeper, was a face . . . Every child's mouth in the room opened, and stayed open. The treacle pudding was growing white and cold on their plates. No one could move."[1]

Reheated beef or mutton and potatoes, plain bread, milk, and a boiled pudding were the mainstays of a diet that many well-meaning parents prescribed for their children. For Nesbit, it made the perfect bland backdrop to highlight her young characters' thrilling adventures. Nesbit no doubt was remembering her own childhood foods and meal rituals, including that middle-class dictum: If children are to be healthy and strong, they "must have thoroughly plain and simple food . . . For dinner there should be mutton or beef, with a little fat; also poultry, and a little light soup now and again . . . They should also be trained to take dry bread and potatoes with dinner, and some other vegetable, such as cauliflower, parsnip, broccoli, spinach, stewed celery, peas, beans, cabbage, and tomatoes." So decreed *Cassell's Book of the Household* (1890) and other guidebooks aimed at ensuring that children live to adulthood.[2]

Conveniently, the foods thought most nutritious for the children were also ones that mother needed to use up from the previous night's dinner. Most Victorians believed that fruits, vegetables, and meat should be well cooked, especially for children. It made sound sense to take dinner leftovers, cook them again, and serve them for the nursery meal. Perhaps the whimsical names that the English have given to "cold meat cookery" (what Victorians labeled meat-based leftovers) were to make the foods more attractive to children who faced them. Cold slices of beef or mutton fried up with cabbage became Bubble and Squeak. Leftover sausages, mutton, or beef baked in pancake batter became Toad in a Hole. Cooked, minced lamb piled in the middle of left-over mashed potatoes became Nest of Minced Lamb. Many nursery dinner dishes came with no intriguing name at all, but children were required to eat those up too, just the same.

This chapter explores the Victorian home and workplace at noon and poses answers to some important, interrelated questions: Why did some call the noon meal "dinner" while others called it "luncheon" or "lunch," and why did the name matter? Why was luncheon more associated with women than men? Why did most men pride themselves on missing luncheon, while a significant few indulged in it? How did the noon meal reflect the changing work habits and urban migration that resulted from industrialization? Finally, what did the meal suggest about relationships between men and women, adults and children, rural and urban folk?

## THE EVOLUTION OF LUNCHEON

Because luncheon has never played a fundamental role in English cuisine, it is difficult to pinpoint many universal or widely practiced customs related to the meal. What we can say with some certitude is that luncheon was predicated upon dinner, and dinner's gradual move for the prosperous classes to later and later in the day necessitated eating something around noon. As we discussed earlier, English people up through the 1500s ate their main meal, dinner, from around ten o'clock to twelve o'clock, and by the 1700s, dinner had gradually moved to early afternoon, thus necessitating the addition of a breakfast. For several decades into the nineteenth century, people ate breakfast in the early morning, dinner in the afternoon, and supper in the evening. In all cases, these mealtimes in preindustrial England were based around daylight and people's attempts to accomplish their most important tasks (including cooking and eating) before dark.

Many people craved more than just three meals, however, especially if supper (which meant the last food one ate before bed) were no more than a mug of warm ale and small sandwich. Around the early 1800s when luncheon first began making its formal appearance as a meal, people had been using a variety of words to characterize the snacks that helped them make it between breakfast, dinner, and supper. "Bever," "nuncheon," "nonsenchis," "nonshench," "noonshine" (one of novelist Jane Austen's favorites), "nooning," and also "lunch" were the more common ones. These terms initially characterized the sort of food eaten, but they slowly came to mean the time of day the food was eaten as well. "Nonshench" or "nuncheon" was probably the forerunner of the noontime meal that most Victorians called "luncheon."[3] Composed of two Anglo-Saxon words, "non" (pronounced "known") that meant noon, and "shench" that meant drink, "nonschence" initially meant a hunk of bread and a mug of ale taken a few hours prior to an afternoon dinner. This bread and ale combination was issued for the sawyer's "nonsenchis" at King's Hall, Cambridge, in 1342 every midmorning. The words nonshench and nonsenchis became archaic, replaced in the 1700s by "nuncheon" to characterize a late midmorning snack of bread and ale. In some regions, the word remained in use up through the nineteenth century.

"Bever," another snack word that has a possible connection to the Victorian luncheon, came from the Old French word *beivre* from the Latin *bibere* meaning "to drink." Traditionally a drink taken between meals, by 1500 the word bever was coming to mean a hunk of bread or cake eaten along with a drink. In her semiautobiographical trilogy of Oxfordshire life in the 1880s *Lark Rise to Candleford* ((1939–1943), Flora Thompson depicted a man nicknamed Bavour "so called because when he fancied a snack between meals he would say 'I must just have my mouthful of bavour', using the old name for a snack."[4] The word "Luncheon" was also in use by the seventeenth century, but it meant a lump, typically of meat or cheese, not a meal. The word "lunch" that arrived in the English language around the same time as "luncheon," albeit independently, likewise did not signify a mealtime in early English history, but simply a slice of bread or cake. Thus, for hundreds of years, such terms as bever, nuncheon, lunch, luncheon, along with noonshine and nooning were understood as snacks, with most people settling down to a substantial dinner in the early afternoon.

## LUNCHEON AS AN ACTUAL MEAL IN THE EARLY VICTORIAN ERA

For centuries, one's work and home were usually in the same place, and given their dependency on daylight, it made sense for the entire family to gather in the early afternoon for a large dinner. At the beginning of the 1800s, a doctor spent time in his home office when he was not traveling on his rounds. A solicitor often had his office at home, as did a parish vicar, a dentist, and an apothecary. A dressmaker took her customer's measurements in the downstairs shop and lived above it. Blacksmiths, cabinet makers, coopers, schoolteachers, and grocers likewise worked and lived in the same building or on the same premises. Well into the 1830s and much longer in rural areas, people simply had no need for a luncheon because they were close to home and had no difficulty eating a substantial dinner with their families around midday or early afternoon.

Better transportation and lighting slowly began to alter this work and meal pattern, especially for the middle and upper classes. If they could afford to do so, many began leaving their inner-city locations and moving to exclusive, more isolated neighborhoods by the early 1800s. Some left the cities altogether and relocated to newly planned suburbs such as Edgbaston (a mile outside of Birmingham) to escape the crush of people, noise, air pollution, dirt, crime, and epidemic diseases that characterized early industrialized cities. Commuting took time but prosperous men were willing to give up the convenience of working and living in the same place in order to ensure their family's health and tranquility. The time for the traditional dinner, however, became crunched and inconvenient.

Well before the Victorian era, we see foreshadows of this transition and its effects on a small but growing number of urban professionals. Consider Samuel Pepys' 1660–1669 diary in which this important government official recorded details about his own life as well as the changing tastes and eating patterns of colleagues. Working as a high-level clerk in the British navy office in 1662, Pepys's typical workday went as such:

> September 12, 1662: At my office all the morning—Mr. Lewes teaching me to understand the method of making up pursers accounts, which is very needful for me and very hard. Dined at home, all in dirt and my mind weary of being thus out of order . . . All the afternoon, till 9 at night, at my office; and then home and eat an egge or two, and so to . . . bed.[5]

Such was the hectic nature of Pepys' day, and those of other city and government officials. As his responsibilities grew even more weighty, however, this pattern of rising early, going to the office, returning home for dinner, going back to the office, and finally arriving back home late at night was often detrimental to his work and career. To compensate, he altered his daily pattern when necessary, as this March 1, 1666 entry indicated: "Up, and to the office and there all the morning sitting; and at noon to dinner with my Lord Brouncker, Sir W. Batten, and Sir W. Penn at the White Horse in Lumbard street."[6]

The seventeenth-century coffee house sold coffee, tea, drinking chocolate, and alcoholic beverages, along with sandwiches and other small, convenience foods. A distinctly male institution, the coffee house laid the foundation for the

Victorian era's most popular dining-out options for gentlemen, the club and the chophouse or tavern. In a relatively quiet and inviting atmosphere, men gathered to read newspapers, meet with friends, and more and more, conduct the nation's business. Commerce, shipping, military strategy, and matters of the court were discussed at Lloyd's and the White Horse among others. For the men involved in such weighty affairs, food was secondary to the business at hand.

By the Victorian era, the men following Pepys' routine had become the norm, with increasing numbers giving up an afternoon family dinner altogether. By the 1850s, such a dinner and meal pattern was perceived by the urban middle classes as old-fashioned, quaint, rural, or even backward, and a late evening dinner with a midday luncheon was perceived as cosmopolitan and fashionable. Fiction usefully illustrates some of the subtle messages about one's geographical location and breeding that a meal had begun to convey by this time period. For example, in Elizabeth Gaskell's 1855 novel *North and South*, the Hales live in a country rectory in Hampshire where Mr. Hale is the parish vicar. Their daughter, Margaret, has been raised with her cousin Louisa in London and is well versed in city ways when she returns to the parsonage to live again with her parents. The surprise arrival of Henry Lennox, a London barrister and potential suitor to Margaret, utterly flusters Mrs. Hale. It is ironing day at the parsonage and so that the servants "may get on with their ironing," Mrs. Hale had planned on serving "nothing but cold meat" for the family dinner. Margaret comforts her mother, "Never mind the dinner, dear mamma. Cold meat will do capitally for a lunch, which is the light in which Mr. Lennox will most likely look upon a two o'clock dinner." [7]

As a result of her husband's lengthy daytime absence from home, a wife modified her own schedule and eating times to accommodate his schedule. Significantly, women were among the first to describe an actual meal called "luncheon" in both their novels and letters, and culinary scholars generally agree that women "led the way that men were eventually to follow" in regard to labeling the noon meal "luncheon" and treating it as a special occasion in its own right.[8] Pepys, we might remember, ate at noon when he stayed in the city, but his reasons for doing so most often concerned business deals and transactions; he did not give his noonday meal a particular importance in its own right.

The novelist Maria Edgeworth did, however. She wrote to her half-sister Lucy about a fine luncheon she and her companions had while traveling in Scotland in July, 1823:

> First course, cold: two roast chickens, better never were; a ham, finer never seen, even at my mother's luncheons; pickled salmon, and cold boiled round. Second course, hot: a large dish of little trout from the river; new potatoes, and, as I had professed to be unable to venture on new potatoes, a dish of mashed potatoes for me; fresh greens, with toast

> over, and poached eggs. Then, a custard pudding, a gooseberry tart, and plenty of Highland cream—*highly* superior to Lowland—and butter, ditto. And for all this how much did we pay? Six shillings.[9]

Edgeworth's allusion to her mother's luncheons in the course of describing her own indicates that among prosperous women, this meal was recognized and probably a daily occurrence. Although by our standards the amount of food that Edgeworth described for her luncheon appears enormous, she would not have seen it in that light; the day's large meal would come later in the evening when she sat down for dinner.

Unlike ladies and gentlemen, younger children (no matter what their class), servants in well-to-do homes, and the working classes in general continued for several decades longer to call their midday meal dinner—not lunch or luncheon. Even if at noon the mistress ate the same foods as the servants and her children, she likely referred to her meal as "luncheon" and her children's and servants' meal as "dinner." The difference in these terms had to do with pragmatic as well as symbolic concerns.

## THE NURSERY DINNER

In upper- and upper-middle-class Victorian households, children did not eat most meals with their parents; they ate a nursery dinner around noon and a lighter tea or supper around five o'clock. Their breakfast might be in the nursery or in the family's breakfast or dining room, depending on their parents' preferences and schedules. Customarily, older children made a brief appearance at their parents' dinner table around dessert to greet any guests and to say goodnight, but oftentimes the smallest ones were tucked in bed before dinner even began. Teenagers might eat dinner with their parents on condition that they had learned table manners and were able to follow the established protocol.

"Luncheon," then, was not a children's meal. In another chapter in *Five Children and It,* Nesbit testified to this fact. Unwittingly wishing that their baby brother, "Lamb" would suddenly grow up, the children are dismayed when their wish comes true, and the now-adult Lamb, complete with grey flannel suit and natty mustache, turns to his brothers and sisters and condescendingly orders them to "go home to your lunch—I mean, your dinner"—with his own objective to go into town and take his lunch at the Crown.[10] Given the difficulty of digesting a large meal before bed, it made sense for Victorian parents to keep the children's dinner hour at noon and to feed them a smaller meal in early evening.

Before people understood vitamins and minerals and their role in a balanced diet, they understood good health to be largely a matter of digestion. Victorians praised mutton because they thought it easier to digest than beef, and milk, in Isabella Beeton's words, was "the most complete of all articles of food."[11] Along with well-cooked vegetables and plain bread, meat and milk created a perfect combination of digestible, energy-packed foods thought necessary for growing children. Charles Buckmaster advised his audience that "the diet of children should be a breakfast, with cocoa, milk, macaroni, porridge, or eggs; a dinner of meat, vegetables, and pudding; a substantial supper, like the breakfast, with cocoa or milk. This is the dietary of health, a diet capable, with pure air and exercise, of making a strong body and a strong mind, and a diet which will often improve weakly children and protect them against many diseases."[12]

Fruits posed more difficulty, with the authorities divided on how much fruit was too much. Seldom were children allowed to eat it fresh, and if they did eat it, it was either a special occasion or a sad oversight. Fresh fruit, in other words, was thought of as not only a very sweet indulgence, but it was also thought to cause flatulence, cramps, and other digestive ailments. Some stewed fruit, perhaps a small dish of stewed prunes or rhubarb topped with custard, was acceptable, as was a thin coat of fruit jam on bread, assuming the bread was not also buttered. As these rules about fruit might suggest, more than just digestion was at issue. Food was often used as a means to teach children moderation, discipline, selflessness, and virtuousness in general.

Certain foods, in other words, could pose just as many moral dangers to children as they could pose physical ones, and sweets, along with rich foods such as pheasant, curries, and sweetbreads often posed the biggest dilemma for conscientious parents. "Plain" and "wholesome" came up repeatedly in Victorian-era advice books on raising children. Author Ursula Bloom (1892–1984), remembering life in her grandmother's and mother's generations, put the matter bluntly: "Meals were autocratic. No child could choose what he would eat, but accepted what was put on his plate for him. It was good plain food, and personal tastes meant little, too often if one disliked a dish one received a double portion." In regards to dinner itself, Bloom remembered that no child under ten was permitted to touch any condiments, be they pickles, horseradish, mint sauce, or spicy preserves.[13] Many Victorians also believed that such things ruined digestive systems and—in girls—excited too many troubling passions.[14] Again, well-boiled, plain meat was lauded as appropriate for children, not only because of digestion, but also because of morality. Mrs. Frederick Pedley, author of *Infant Nursing and the Management of Young Children* (1866) put the matter best: "It appears that children who, at a befitting age, are judiciously fed on meat, attain a higher standard of moral and intellectual ability than those who live on a different class of food."[15]

Because adult men were typically scarce around home at midday, a mother often joined her children for their nursery dinner in order to teach them dining etiquette. The nursery table was laid with a tablecloth to indicate that it was now the dining table, and oftentimes, the servants laid extra fabric slips over the cloth to protect it from the children's spills. Mother, along with the nursemaid, governess, and/or tutor, modeled for the children appropriate ways to eat and how to conduct oneself during the meal. Children learned the basics, such as not speaking with food in their mouths, how to hold a fork, how to ask for a second helping (and when it was inappropriate to do so), and how to use a napkin. These meals were practice for the "real thing," when children would be old enough to stay up and take their place at the evening dinner table. Once the nursery meal concluded, the nursemaid or governess escorted the children outdoors for fresh air and exercise while the servants below-stairs sat down to their own midday dinner.

## THE SERVANTS' DINNER

Pragmatically speaking, it made sense for the servants to sit down to their main meal at midday because that was the one lull in their otherwise busy schedule. The kitchen became particularly frantic from five o'clock on as servants prepared the family's evening dinner; time was too precious to allow them a big meal then as well. Instead, servants sat down to what must have felt like a very rushed tea in the early evening. Pragmatics aside, it made sense symbolically speaking, to designate the servant's midday meal their "dinner," because that reemphasized their working-class status. Laborers did not have "luncheon" or "lunch" (the terms were often interchangeable, particularly among men). They ate their dinner at noon, even if dinner came out of a tin pail deep inside a mine shaft. William Taylor, a footman who kept a diary in 1837, recorded many details of his own and his employer's life. Without any seeming awareness of what his rather mundane recordings suggested about his class and breeding, Taylor repeatedly wrote entries such as this one: "I got up at half past seven . . . went to church, came back, got parlour lunch, had my own dinner." The next entry read: "Got home again at half past twelve, got lunch, had dinner, went out with the carriage, went round Hyde Park . . . Got home by 4, had tea, got parlour dinner and tea, spent the evening in writing and reading until twelve o'clock and then went to bed." Taylor's dinner happened after his employer and her daughter had their luncheon in the parlor. He had an early evening tea before helping the maidservants attend to the mistress's later-evening dinner.[16] Taylor might have been unselfconscious about what labels conveyed, or he simply did not care. Status-conscious people did care, however, particularly those who were managing a servant staff and anxious in general to appear as genteel as possible.

Food and mealtimes were used by some employers as a means to train their servants or to "keep them in their place," as distasteful as that might sound to us today. Victorians routinely argued about the quality and quantity of their servants' dinners in particular. Mrs. Eliot James, writing in *Our Servants*, advised that they should be allowed to eat the same meat from the joint that the family itself consumed. Doing so, James contended, will keep down their grumbling and strengthen their morale. She hastened to add, however, that servants should not be allowed on any regular basis to eat game, entrées, or sweets.[17] Plain people did not respond well to fancy treats, she believed. Fancy food made servants irritable because of indigestion or unmanageable because they craved more. (If the reasoning sounds suspiciously similar to what we read above regarding children and diets, that was because many prosperous Victorians saw their servants as little more than large children.) Others disagreed with James. Ursula Bloom maintained that if servants ate what the family itself ate, it "would have been demoralizing for discipline, and might have given them ideas."[18] Regardless of whether the meat came from the family's joint or not, the servants were regularly given plain foods, including boiled, mashed, or fried potatoes, a meat dish that was usually served cold, minced, or hashed (mutton appeared regularly), and sometimes a boiled pudding. Likely they ate vegetables as well, but these would be left over from the family's dinner, reheated or hashed in with the meat. In a bad situation, servants were not given enough to eat. Lilian Westall's employers allowed her only bread and dripping for breakfast (with the dripping covered in mouse droppings as I noted in the previous chapter), herring for dinner every day, and bread and margarine for tea.[19] Most employers stipulated that their servants drink tea with meals, although in the early Victorian era, the cook and upper servants were usually given an allowance of small beer for their meals as well.

Alexis Soyer's fictional persona, Hortense, offered the most popular approach to handling the servants' dinner. Hortense's family and any guests ate luncheon at half-past twelve, incorporating last night's dinner into it and dressing it up a bit with "orange marmalade, potatoes, butter, cheese, sherry and port wines." To control costs, Hortense likewise had last night's dinner served as the children's nursery dinner (minus the fancy additions like butter and cheese), and then, Hortense gave the final remains to her three servants so that they could dine at half-past one.[20] Thus, the servants do eat what the family has eaten, but considering that the adults had it for dinner the night before, the children had it in the nursery at noon, and Hortense and her family had it shortly thereafter as their lunch, we only can wonder what was left by the time it came back to the kitchen.

## USING UP THE LEFTOVERS

Soyer's Hortense was a model middle-class housewife, there to inspire and teach other middle-class women how to run a household in the best of styles, even on a limited budget. As Chapters 6 and 7 will discuss in detail, domestic, or economic, management was vital to a middle-class family's success because a wife had to budget enough money to host a monthly dinner party. This huge expenditure was thought necessary because it would facilitate the family's important social and business connections. To afford the high-quality food and drink that characterized a Victorian dinner party, a conscientious wife did her best to serve relatively plain, inexpensive dinners for the rest of the month and to use the midday meal as a good time for serving leftovers. Oftentimes, dinners were also based around leftovers, simply because meat joints were huge, and it took several meals to work through them. Attempting to help the uninspired housewife, cookbooks such as Soyer's *Modern Housewife* and Beeton's *Book of Household Management* routinely offered not only countless recipes for cold meat cookery, but also upbeat accompanying notes designed to make a bored mistress feel virtuous about her efforts to be a good economist and manager of her husband's limited funds. Here again is Soyer's Hortense:

> For cold meat, I always serve that up which has been left from a previous dinner, if any, or any remains of poultry, game, ham, or tongue. When, however, we have six or eight friends from the country at Christmas, I feel proud to show them my style of doing things well and economically . . . ; but they say, "We do not understand how it is that you make a nice little dish almost out of nothing." For should I have the remnants of any poultry or game not very inviting to the sight, I generally cut it up and show my cook how to hash it in a variety of ways; and I always remark, that they never partake of any cold meat whilst any of the hash remains.[21]

Soyer conveyed a number of messages and lessons in this passage: for one, he implied that it was the mistress's responsibility to pique jaded appetites, even when she must work with little more than an unappetizing hunk of leftover cold meat. Luncheon, Soyer also insisted, allowed the mistress to show off her talent and her creativity more than dinner, even if she might not initially see it that way. To assist her efforts and spark her creativity, Soyer included approximately two hundred recipes in *Modern Housewife* that relied on leftovers and that helped teach young Victorian women what their grandmothers and great-grandmothers would have likely already known: how to use the less attractive remains of meat and to make it both digestible and palatable.[22]

For we see in the Victorian era a paradox. Cookbooks, textbooks, advice manuals, and cookery school instructors lectured constantly on how a family could avoid wasting food, and yet few middle-class families could afford to waste food in the first place. We would imagine that for many, financial straits alone would keep waste from occurring, but it nonetheless did occur, and frequently, if we can trust the period literature on this topic. The farther a person moved from rural traditions, the less she may have understood about how to make efficient use of all parts of an animal, or the purpose or value of whey, or how to make wild greens edible. It takes surprisingly little time for people to forget what previous generations took for granted, especially if one has relocated to a city where space is at a premium, kitchens are no longer outfitted or large enough to handle butchering, cheese- and ale-making, and hundreds of butchers, grocers, costermongers, and bakers suddenly exist to do such work anyway. Offal, for example, could be made into any number of dishes that eighteenth-century people of all classes consumed. But knowing how to treat offal and make it tasty was a skill that many people had lost after moving to cities. A young wife trying to keep house on a husband's yearly income of £100 could not afford many prime joints of mutton and beef, but her ignorance of how to prepare a bullock heart or how to stew mutton neck to make it tender, seemingly limited her to the most expensive foods.

Many families were in debt because mistresses did not know how to cook. While gentlewomen in the eighteenth century still had familiarity with their kitchens and with how to prepare many foods, Victorian gentlewomen were often absent from the kitchen altogether. Soyer, Beeton, Buckmaster, and other prominent cooking authorities bemoaned this situation, but a prevailing social stigma against gentlewomen dirtying their hands with menial chores kept many from exerting any authority over food and cooking, even if they might have had an interest. Compounding the problem was that servants increasingly did not know how to cook, either. Earlier in the century, many girls who entered domestic service came from large rural families where they had exposure to everything from butchering to cheese-making. They had helped their mothers cook, had become used to making substitutions for key ingredients if they were unavailable, and knew how to stretch a morsel of bacon. Of course, country girls from stable families still left their homes and entered domestic service in urban areas, but as the nineteenth century progressed, many servants also came from city slums where food at home had been scarce and home-cooking facilities inadequate. They may never have seen a leg of mutton except those dangling from a hook in the butcher's shop, but now they were being ordered to prepare one for dinner. Some servants also came from the workhouses that were an impoverished family's last choice when it came to survival. The editors of *Cassell's Book of the Household* spoke to the reality, warning middle-class women that a rough "gal from the workhouse" will be apt to waste the family's money due to an early life where she was only "accustomed to see tea bought by the ounce and coals by the half-sack."[23]

Regardless of their class, many urban housewives did not know how to use meat gristle and vegetable parings, whereas many rural people had pigs to feed and knew precisely what to do with scraps, as Flora Thompson detailed it: "The family pig was everybody's pride and everybody's business. Mother spent hours boiling up the 'little taturs' to mash and mix with the pot-liquor, in which food had been cooked, to feed the pig for its evening meal and help out with expensive barley meal."[24] Since pigs consumed scraps and were fattened on the byproducts of food production (such as whey left over from cheese-making) nothing edible went to waste, as the animals themselves became the family's most important food source for the winter.

While the urban middle-class mistress struggled to economize at home, her husband had a number of midday meal options, depending on his mood, work schedule, finances, and location. Because of these numerous variables, no one custom stands out to describe what a gentleman did for luncheon. Those who remained near home or still worked out of it probably ate the meal with their wives and children and continued to call it dinner, especially if they lived in the North. London gentleman, however, usually did not maintain that traditional practice and as the century progressed, a growing number of establishments catered to their inclinations and needs.

## LUNCHEON IN THE CITY

Many Victorian businessmen spoke disparagingly of luncheon, skipping it or partaking of it surreptitiously, as journalist George Augustus Sala observed in *Twice Around the Clock; or the Hours of the Day and Night in London* (1861): "Some I know are too proud to dine." Those who do give in and desire to eat might only do it "after office hours, at Simpson's, at the Albion, at the London, or, save us, at the Wellington." If they do venture out at lunchtime, they might merely skate out for a few minutes to pick up "a snack at the Bay Tree."[25] In other words, most men ate something during the day, but many seemed concerned about the messages that their meals and foods conveyed. Of course, some men did not appreciate the interruption that lunch posed to their workday rhythm. Henry Crabb Robinson, who kept a diary from 1830–1840, only mentioned luncheon twice, both times on days when his schedule was irregular and disarranged. Even then, his lunch was really a snack. Thomas Babington Macaulay desisted from lunch until 1853 and only because his poor health compelled him to stop work to eat and rest.[26]

Hungry but still too busy to leave for a proper meal, some men unwrapped sandwiches and ate at their desks if company policy permitted them to do so; or they opened a pack of biscuits and ate them intermittently throughout the day.[27] American author Herman Melville speaks about that practice in his 1853 short story, "Bartleby, The Scrivener." The errand boy "Ginger Nut" is so nicknamed because he buys gingernuts (or snaps) for the scriveners to munch as they copy away. Biscuits, both sweet (like the North American cookie) and savory (like crackers), were popular Victorian snack foods; they were manufactured commercially from 1791 when the London firm Lemann's produced them to commemorate the Duke of York's marriage.[28] No doubt many city men stashed packs in their desk drawers to stave off hunger.

Nonetheless, most professionals were obligated to work longer hours, not only because the crush of work grew as the century progressed, but also because gas lighting became common and cheap. It was also bright enough to justify keeping clerks at their desks to hand-copy documents, solicitors at theirs to pore over briefs, Members of Parliament and barristers holed up in their chambers to study blue books, and journalists crouched over their foolscap preparing a newspaper report. As a result, a real lunch, as opposed to a meager snack, made sense, and as I noted above in regards to Samuel Pepys, it could also be a convenient way of facilitating business. Bankers, senior accountants, merchants, and businessmen often had lunch catered for their upper employees so that eating and meetings went on simultaneously, just as they do for many professionals today. Those men ("the aristocrats," as Sala called them) also might leave their desks around noon and take lunch elsewhere.[29] Their options were the most wide-ranging and opulent of all.

A fine luncheon for a modest price could be had at one's club, for instance. Depending on his profession or interest, a gentleman could apply for membership in one of the thirty or more clubs that lined Pall Mall in London's fashionable West End. Most were exclusive; one had to have connections and status to be accepted as a member at many of them, and women were not permitted as members and sometimes not as guests even if escorted by a member. Food prices were reasonable and some clubs were internationally famous for their fare. Both Alexis Soyer and Charles Francatelli (who served for a time as chef to Queen Victoria) worked at the Reform Club, where they gained celebrity status.

Next in the hierarchy of luncheon options for the well-to-do were the chophouses. The routine went something like this: A man visited a butcher shop and purchased a steak or chop wrapped in a cabbage leaf to keep it fresh. He proceeded to a baker and bought bread or biscuits. He then went to his favorite chophouse. These establishments differed from today's restaurants in that no extensive menu was available and the table service was minimal. Most patrons sat at long communal tables, not private ones. The patron handed his steak to the grill man who cooked it for a couple of pennies. For a few pennies more, he could purchase ale, cheese, hot roasted potatoes, as well as all necessary condiments—pickles, horseradish, mustard, for example.

Chophouses, like inns and hotel dining rooms, also offered an "ordinary" or fixed-price menu that included a set number of courses but little choice. Roasts, chops, pies, puddings, cheeses, stout, sherry, and Madeira comprised most chophouses' bill of fare. Two of the most famous, the Cheshire Cheese and Simpson's-in-the-Strand, still operate today, albeit on much different standards. From noon until early evening, men crowded into the Cheshire Cheese, where for 2 shillings and 11 pence they could eat their fill of rump steak pudding, stewed cheese (similar to cheese rarebit), and vegetables. Beer was included in the price. Noted in Dickens's *Dictionary of London* in 1879 as one of the most famous "old-fashioned chophouses," the Cheshire Cheese was particularly popular with the pressmen, subeditors, editors, and literary men who worked in Fleet Street, where the Cheshire Cheese was located.[30] Simpson's was likewise old-fashioned in its fare. It started in 1828 as a cigar divan or smoking establishment where for 1 shilling and 6 pence a day, a man would be offered cigars, coffee, and chess. The Grand Cigar Divan, as it was then called, later became a chophouse particularly famous not only for its beef, but also for its fish suppers. Women could not dine at Simpson's alone, but the restaurant did have a dining room upstairs for those accompanied by men.

Many professionals did not have time for such a leisurely luncheon. Instead, they stepped out and ate a quick meal at one of the many oyster bars, shellfish shops, and sandwich shops that catered to them. Garraway's Coffee House, Jamaica Coffee House, and Evett's Ham Shop were all popular. From eleven to one o'clock, these establishments and others like them were crammed with hungry men in a hurry. Garraway's placed its huge trays of ham, beef, and tongue sandwiches on the bar, and men ate these while washing them down with stout, Pale Ale, wine, punch, or sherry.[31]

Lower-middle-class men, including thousands of minor clerks whose salaries were very low (as little as 20 shillings a week), typically brought a wrapped lunch to work. A herring sandwich or a slice of cheese and bread were commonplace items on many desks around noontime. On quarterly payday, however, many clerks frequented Dining Rooms or Eating Houses (the names were interchangeable). They were cheaper than chophouses but still respectable. For 1 shilling and 3 pence or 1 shilling and 6 pence a man could have his fill of meat, vegetable, and pudding, along with beer. If one opted for soup and bread, or stew and bread, the price was roughly 4 to 6 pence.[32] Some of the more notable Dining Rooms included His Lordship's Larder in Cheapside, and Rudkins' Salutation in Newgate.

## A WORKING-CLASS MIDDAY MEAL

Working-class men and women—three-fourths of the English population—also had to find time and a place to eat a noonday meal. Among the working classes, domestic servants often ate better and more regularly than others. Although plain and modest in amount, a servant usually ate breakfast, dinner, and tea every day of the week, and this regularity was considered by many parents to be an incentive to put daughters into full-time service as soon as possible (usually around age thirteen). Most servants could also count on being able to sit down, however briefly, for their dinner. Thousands of urban laborers were not so lucky. For one thing, many employers in the early Victorian period did not schedule regular work breaks to allow laborers to eat meals. For another, they were working too hard to take much time out to eat. Factory and work canteens were a late-nineteenth-century development, with a few notable exceptions earlier in the era. Robert Owen's New Lanark cotton mills, for example, became famous for its treatment of employees. Under his ownership and management from 1800 to 1824, Owen demonstrated to other employers that laborers were more reliable, loyal, and efficient if given necessary amenities. Owen supplied them with decent housing, schools, large kitchens, and a dining room where they could eat their dinners (either brought from home or purchased cheaply) during scheduled breaks.[33]

Most laborers relied on vendors and street stalls that clogged city streets. Carters, cab drivers, dock workers, builders, and casual workers were often compelled to eat meals standing up. However, they did have much to choose from eating-wise, and the street food was cheap, with most dinnertime favorites under 1 penny. Henry Mayhew estimated that in London, 6,000 street traders dealt in readymade food and drink, including ham sandwiches, eel pies, sausages, meat pies with gravy, pea soup (often served with hot eels), sheep's trotters, baked potatoes with butter and salt, fried fish with bread, fresh fruit, roasted nuts, and a variety of boiled sweets, such as plum duff, roly-poly, spotted dick, and treacle pudding.

If laborers were close to home, they might have time to return there for dinner. One Manchester machine operator in 1832 rose at five in the morning, worked at the mill from six to eight, and then came home for a quick half-hour breakfast of tea or coffee, and bread. He returned to the mill and worked until noon. He returned home for dinner and ate potatoes with melted lard or butter, and on some days, accompanied his potatoes with a bit of fat bacon. He then worked at the mill from one o'clock until seven. Before going to bed, he had a supper of bread and tea.[34] This operative's routine resembled that of thousands who lived in cities where the laborers' housing was built close to the factories and mills.

Rural farm laborers often ate their noonday dinner in the fields. Flora Thompson offered a representative description:

> Horses were unyoked, led to the shelter of a hedge or a rick and given their nosebags, and men and boys threw themselves down on sacks spread out beside them and tin bottles of cold tea were uncorked and red handkerchiefs of food unwrapped. The lucky ones had bread and cold bacon, perhaps the top or the bottom of a cottage loaf, on which the small cube of bacon was placed, with a finger of bread on top, called the thumb-piece, to keep the meat untouched by hand and in position for manipulation with a clasp-knife . . . The less fortunate ones munched their bread and lard or morsel of cheese; and the boys with their ends of cold pudding were jokingly bidden not to get "that 'ere treacle' in their ears."[35]

Stories and gossip accompanied the meal, as did moments of relaxing before work resumed, with the laborers often in the fields until sunset in the summer and harvest seasons.

Sundays were the exception for many laborers, with servants often allowed more meat for their dinner as well as one or two Sunday afternoons off a month. Thousands of other laborers were able to splurge and buy a bit of meat, perhaps a neck of mutton, and either expend the necessary fuel to cook a hot dinner at home or pay a small fee to have the corner baker cook it for them. Meat was accompanied by baked, fried, or boiled potatoes. In a prosperous working-class home, where the man was employed full-time and his wife could thus afford to stay at home and tend to children and cooking, the food was better and more plentiful, especially on Sunday. A wife planned the Sunday dinner with her husband's workweek in mind. On Saturday night, she would visit one of the numerous city markets to purchase fish, meat, and vegetables at bargain prices. Her objective was to buy the best and largest joint she could afford so that on Monday, her husband could have the choicest remaining cuts for a sandwich at noon. The mother and children made do with "pieces" if there were any;

usually they ate bread and potatoes and drank tea for all meals of the day except for the Sunday dinner.

Unlike the middle classes, who could afford to think of meals as expressions of their status and values, many working-class people were worried about finding enough food to sustain them for grueling fourteen- to sixteen-hour days. This agonizing search for food and steady work to afford the food was alleviated somewhat as the century progressed, however, because a series of Factory Acts slowly improved conditions and regulated work hours, first for children and then for women. Ultimately, men benefited from the regulations as well. As wages for working-class people slowly increased and national holidays (called Bank holidays) came about in the final years of the nineteenth century, people of all classes gained some leisure, ability to take holidays, and also more money to expend on a noonday meal.

## LUNCHEON IN THE LATE VICTORIAN ERA

Given work patterns and the distinctly urban nature of life for most, late-century Victorians were often not at home come midday. Middle-class women in particular began entering the workforce in large numbers as typists, telephonists, teachers, nurses, bookkeepers, and department store clerks. As so many people entered the workforce, the terminology to define the midday meal became less status-driven or stigmatized as well; "lunch" slowly became the generic term for people of all classes to characterize their noon meal, although to this day, English schoolchildren routinely eat a school dinner prepared by school "dinner ladies." The stigma against women dining alone in public also decreased sharply in the last two decades of the nineteenth century. By 1900, nine clubs had opened that took only women as members, offering them the same amenities as a gentleman's club. Thousands of other hardworking men and women of modest means thronged streets at midday and eagerly patronized a growing number of well-run clean catering establishments that sprang up to meet their needs.

Many of these places, what we now call restaurant chains, were prototypes of temperance "coffee palaces," pub-like establishments that served coffee, tea, and cocoa "on tap," rather than beer and spirits. Although these were not profitable (many were plain and bare with a limited number of food items), they were important for developing a corporate business model that worked. One coffee place that did quite well and began a trend was John Pearce's, located in Farringdon Street in the East End in 1882. Serving 6,000 meals a day, this shop was the beginning of the famous "Pearce and Plenty" chain. Pearce then started a line of teashops in 1892 called "The British Tea Table Company" that catered to a more genteel (and female) clientele.[36] Pearce was only one of the several late nineteenth-century entrepreneurs to recognize the money that could be made by building cheap, clean lunchtime establishments. By 1918, England's largest caterer, Lyon's, operated 250 teashops, 3 Corner Houses (more a restaurant than a teashop), as well as the more exclusive restaurant, the Trocadero.[37] Fuller Tearooms housed in large department stores, ABC Teashops, which grew out of the Aerated Bread Company, and countless other similar chains likewise appeared throughout English cities. The most popular lunchtime dish at a Lyon's teashop, roast beef and two vegetables, cost 10 pence. More prosperous middle-class people or those who wished for a splurge might instead opt for the table d'hôte (the more fashionable French name for an "ordinary") at a Lyon's Corner House, which cost 1 shilling and 6 pence.[38]

The coming of the fish-and-chip shops in the 1880s also helped thousands of working-class people afford a cheap filling meal of 2 to 3 pence. The combination of fried fish and potatoes proved irresistible in the North, with Lancashire and Yorkshire supporting a phenomenal number of shops. For example, by 1910, 133 existed in Preston alone and 317 in Bradford. The number throughout Britain was 25,000, swelled by their growing popularity with middle-class people.[39] So many fish-and-chip shops became possible because of the advanced deep-sea trawlers that caught loads of cod in North Atlantic waters and brought them to market at a cheap price. For that matter, technological advances and wide-scale industrialization of the foods industry resulted in a host of Victorian lunchtime staples that sound quite modern to us today, including canned salmon, corned beef sandwiches, egg salads, green salads, and soup.

* * * *

And finally, back to the children. The Victorians were not able to solve the problem of rampant malnutrition and hunger among its youth, although by the end of the century, social reformers, especially the Fabians, had documented the problem, and the South African (or Boer) War had made it alarmingly obvious that the nation was actually threatened by the inability of its young men to serve as soldiers. By 1870, many children were going to school, and by 1880, elementary school education had become compulsory. It made sense to social reformers to ensure that all children received at least one large dinner a day while at school, but many people believed that the responsibility of feeding children was the family's—not the government's. As plain as it might have been, the children's nursery dinner in *Five Children and It* was at least filling and it fueled the children to make it through their many adventures. It would take the passage of the 1906 Education (Provision of Meals) Act to put into place the process whereby all children would be offered a filling dinner, no matter their class or their family's circumstances.

# 4

# "An Invention of Comparatively Recent Date": Afternoon Tea

**Caraway Seed Cake.** Mix half a pound of sifted sugar with two pounds of flour in a large bowl or pan. Make a hole in the centre, and pour into it half a pint of lukewarm milk, and two tablespoonfuls of yeast. Draw a little of the surrounding flour into this, and throwing a cloth over the vessel, set it in a warm place for an hour or two. Then add half a pound of melted butter, an ounce of caraway seed, a teaspoonful of allspice, ginger, and nutmeg, with milk sufficient to render the whole of a proper consistency. Mix it thoroughly, butter and paper a tin, and pour it in. Let it stand for half an hour at the mouth of the oven to rise; then bake it. Sugar: $\frac{1}{2}$ lb; flour, 2 lbs; milk, $\frac{1}{2}$ pint; yeast, 2 tablespoons; butter melted, $\frac{1}{2}$ lb; caraway seed, 1 oz.; allspice, ginger, nutmeg, 1 teaspoonful mixed; milk, sufficient.

—*The Dictionary of Daily Wants*, Vol. 1, 1858–1861

Victorian and Edwardian authors are famous for depicting cozy tea-drinking scenes, and once more Edith Nesbit in particular stands out. Just as her bland nursery dinners serve as backdrop to the child characters' thrilling exploits, their fireside teas are a release from drama, a return to the comforts of home. In *The Phoenix and the Carpet* (1904) the same children from *Five Children and It* are again treated to fantastic adventures, this time with the assistance of a Phoenix and a magic carpet. After treasure digging in France, they arrive home one "dark, muggy January evening" to an empty house—no servants, no parents. Left to fend for themselves, Anthea and her siblings know just what to do without anyone having to say a word: she lays a fire in the nursery and while it "blazed and crackled so kindly that it really seemed to be affectionately inviting the kettle to come and sit upon its lap," the rest of the children raid the pantry and larder. Without the cook's assistance (or interference), the children find the bread, butter, cheese, a leftover boiled pudding, and cold sliced tongue. Meeting back in the nursery, the children sate their appetites and slake their thirst while the narrator is left trying to define or categorize their meal. It "was not exactly tea," so "let us call it a tea-ish meal," she decides.[1]

Of all the English culinary institutions with which foreigners are familiar, tea probably heads the list, although what exactly the meal consists of and when it takes place is often unclear to them. That is because an English tea is largely based on its specific context. For example, the children in Nesbit's novel do not need to explain to one another what they are about as they gather the food and tea kettle; they do not need to state explicitly, "Let's have tea now instead of dinner or supper." However, outsiders, including the narrator herself, are not so sure what the children are up to because the context is not so transparent to them. The narrator probably calls the children's meal "tea-ish" instead of "tea" proper, because based on her own context, tea is not taken so late in the day, and certainly, a children's nursery tea is never so free-form, so unsupervised.

Given the complexity of what might superficially appear to be a simple meal, it helps to understand some of the many meanings of tea before we turn to the origin and tradition of this chapter's topic, afternoon tea. As with luncheon, afternoon tea was often a women's gathering for reasons that take us back to the reign of Charles II. However, men were by no means excluded, and they were encouraged to participate actively when they were at home. While industrialization sped up the pace of business and life in general, afternoon tea was a bulwark against that speed in two senses. First, it was a stated break in an otherwise busy day, one that many consciously understood as such and appreciated. Second, while industrialization sped up the homogenization of the English diet with many people eating the same foods and using the same nationally distributed cookbooks, the foods that graced tea tables continued to celebrate regions and their ancient customs, particularly as tourism accelerated dramatically in the nineteenth century. But first, some definitions and clarifications.

## THE MULTIPLE MEANINGS OF "TEA"

Confusion about tea starts with the fact that the word for a beverage also means a meal. According to William Ukers, one of the first historians to study the history of tea, "the general term 'tea' was used almost from the first to denote any occasion, like a reception, where tea was served, and 'teatime' connoted the hour for such entertainment." Another meaning of "tea" as an evening meal served with the beverage dates back to the eighteenth century.[2] More confusion can arise when other words preface the word "tea," presumably to describe what kind of meal it is. High tea, low tea, afternoon tea, at-home tea, four o'clock tea, five o'clock tea, meat tea, dining room tea, cream tea, and, just tea: the list is long and some of the prefixes overlap in meaning while others are distinct.

### Afternoon Tea

Many North Americans erroneously think that "high tea" is the name given to a light repast of dainty finger sandwiches, small cakes, and tea. Certainly fancy department stores and tea shops in the United States and Canada will usually bill such an offering as a "high tea" because "high" sounds elite, and for many, "elite" means "English." However, high tea was and remains a substantial, hearty meal, while afternoon tea is a more elegant affair with light foods. Victorians sometimes called afternoon tea a "low tea" because participants sat in the drawing room around low tables (like coffee tables today) rather than at the dining-room table. Afternoon tea was also known as a "four o'clock," "five o'clock," and even "six o'clock tea" because if dinner began as late as eight or eight thirty, it made sense in the early evening to drink a stimulating beverage and eat a snack to tide one over until the actual meal.

### High Tea

"High tea" was what the Nesbit characters in *The Phoenix and the Carpet* were apparently putting together as it included meat, a pudding, as well as bread and butter. Indeed, high tea usually included meat and so some people would call it a "meat tea" to indicate that it was a substantial meal. Middle-class Victorians who had not adopted the fashion of eating luncheon and a late-evening dinner often had a high tea in the early evening. Their resistance to adapting to a late-evening dinner might have come from the expense of conducting such a multicourse affair, or it might have come from a conscious adhesion to more traditional eating patterns. Such was particularly the case in the North, where Yorkshire became famous in the Victorian era for its high teas, complete with steaming tea urns and an abundance of hot foods such as roast beef surrounded by cakes and breads. Northerners were famous for resisting—not adapting—to changes brought about by industrialization. While Yorkshire business and industry magnates made as much money as their cohorts in the South, they still championed many of their region's more simple, plain foods and culinary traditions.[3] As Laura Mason, one of England's culinary history experts, suggests, high tea represented a collision of two worlds: rural/urban, and by implication, traditional/modern.[4] High tea echoed eighteenth-century meal patterns when people ate earlier in the day. A formal evening dinner was a fashionable innovation widely adapted by Londoners and urban sophisticates. Afternoon tea was likewise their innovation—a light snack designed, as I note above, to help tide them over until dinner.

Wealthy Victorians who did not usually eat a high tea might call their meal by that name on the cook's afternoon off, however. Almost like an indoor picnic of the type Nesbit depicts in *The Phoenix and the Carpet*, the participants would bring up from the kitchen and larder cold foods, including meat pies, cheese, bread and biscuits, sliced meats, pickles and other relishes, and some fresh fruit if it were in season. Setting the food out on the dining-room table and sideboard, they would help themselves and sit where they wanted. Tea would of course be included as would spirits such as rum or "hot gin and water with." High teas of this sort were meant to be light-hearted, fun affairs, a break from the usual rigid protocol of formal dinners with the servants standing by to assist. The cook would return in time to see to putting the food away and doing the dishes, of course.

#### Just "Tea"

Labels such as "high," "low," "meat," and otherwise were sometimes attached to tea so that outsiders would understand what the meal entailed and to help initiate strangers to the customs of the place or a family. If a distant niece came to stay with her aunt in Exeter, that aunt might preface tea with "afternoon" so her niece would know better what to expect on the first day of her visit. Even a hostess formally inviting her friends and acquaintances to tea at her house might use a prefix in order to clarify her intentions, as well as stating the time for the gathering to convene (another important clue). Both large and small meals might have been called a "tea" for decades in England, but the affair called afternoon tea was, in the famous surgeon and gastronome Sir Henry Thompson's words, an "invention of comparatively recent date." To understand why afternoon tea became so popular, it is helpful also to know more about the history of the beverage's arrival in England. The fact that meals actually took the name "tea" indicates how essential this drink became to English people's sense of their own well-being.

### A BRIEF HISTORY OF THE BEVERAGE CALLED TEA

One of the first known English references to tea is found in a 1597 letter written by a British sea captain who called tea by its Cantonese dialect name, "chau." However, tea did not appear for sale in England until 1658, when it was sold at Garaway's London coffeehouse. When sweetened with sugar obtained from the Ca1ribbean colonies, tea became palatable to English taste.[5] Common lore has it that tea's popularity was secured for good when King Charles II's Portuguese bride, Catherine of Braganza, brought her love of the drink to England. However, tea's price in the mid-1600s was as much as £4 for one pound—more than what an artisan would make in three months' labor or servant girl make in a year—so, its availability was limited to England's wealthiest citizens.[6]

Recognizing that tea had great retail potential if shrewdly marketed, London merchant Thomas Twining began selling high-quality teas from his Devereux Court, Strand, coffeehouse in 1706. Even shrewder was Twining's decision eleven years later to expand his business to include The Golden Lyon Tea and Coffee Shop—one of the first into which ladies could step to purchase their own tea. Because a woman at that time was forbidden to enter most coffeehouses, she had to send in her footman to make purchases while she waited in her carriage. Frustrated by this service barrier, women started demanding better and Twining obliged them. Larger numbers of women began to patronize Twining's, purchase his teas, and increase their own and their family's consumption of the beverage as a result.[7] Because tea remained expensive, the mistress kept it in a locked caddy and only she carried the key. Likewise, she was in charge of making and serving tea for her family as well as her guests, and this role continued well into the twentieth century among those who "stopped for tea."

Up through the 1700s, most English people drank green tea, prepared by subjecting the leaves to intense heat immediately after picking and not allowing the leaves to then ferment. (Fermentation does not in this case mean to become alcoholic, but rather, to alter the flavor.) The most expensive green tea variety, Finest Hyson, sold for 36 shillings (a little less than half of £4) per pound, retail, according to 1800 figures taken from Twinings. We can see that in the course of 150 or so years, the price of tea per pound had dropped roughly 50 percent. Twinings' Imperial Hyson, a medium-grade tea, sold for 16 to 24 shillings per pound, retail, thus putting it at roughly one-fourth the mid-1660s price. Another popular green tea variety was Bloom Green, which sold for 16 to 26 shillings per pound.[8] The cheapest green tea was Hyson-Skin (composed of inferior tea leaves that were separated from the higher quality Hyson leaves by a winnowing machine). Later in the 1800s, black teas became popular and overtook green tea varieties altogether, although according to the popular Victorian all-purpose reference guide, *Dictionary of Daily Wants*, many people enjoyed a mix composed of "two-fifths black, two-fifths green, and one-fifth gunpowder" [a green tea].[9] Unlike green teas, black teas are fermented. The leaves are wilted and bruised by rolling, and then allowed to ferment in humid, hot air that encourages oxidation. After fermentation, the leaves are dried.[10]

While tea was available at coffeehouses and at home, it received a tremendous boost in popularity because of eighteenth-century pleasure, or tea, gardens. These were often advertised along feminine lines, as the stereotypical language in this 1778 advertisement of Bagnigge Wells Tea Gardens suggests:

> All innocent within the shade you see
> This little Party sip salubrious Tea,
> Soft Tittle-Tattle rises from the stream
> Sweeten'd each word with Sugar and Cream.[11]

The manicured grounds and the wafting music of the string ensembles encouraged strolling and conversation. The eighteenth-century German preacher, Carl Philip Moritz, found Ranelagh Gardens to be especially delightful. In his *Journeys of a German in England in 1782*, Moritz commented that "half a crown [2 shillings, 6 pence] gains one entrance to Ranelagh, and that includes everything—all the refreshments, music, gardens, strolling you want."[12] Londoners likewise loved Vauxhall Gardens, where tea, wine, coffee, bread and butter, ham sandwiches, and various pastries were on sale with plenty of bowers and private alcoves where lovers could confide, families relax, and friends gossip.

The demise of the tea gardens in the late 1700s (too many disreputable types took full advantage of hidden bowers) did not hurt tea's increasing popularity because its taste was addictive and its price dropped due to an 1834 decrease in the tea tax. A year earlier, in 1833, the East India Company lost its trade monopoly. Previously, its ships were the only ones carrying tea from China to London ports. The breakup of the East India monopoly resulted in competition from other trading merchants, a decline in tea smuggling and tea prices that began to fall even more sharply. Equally important to making tea affordable was a discovery of native tea plants growing in Assam, India. Planned tea plantations were established by British colonialists and by 1840 they produced huge amounts of tea for the insatiable British market.[13]

From 1840 to 1853, the flat-rate duty on all grades of tea was 2 shillings, 2½ pence per pound weight.[14] In 1853, immediately after Gladstone's Free Trade Budget, the tea tax again fell, first to 1 shilling, 10 pence a pound and by 1865, to a mere 6 pence per pound. As a result, prices on tea that people purchased in stores likewise fell. By 1859, one could purchase a fair grade of tea for 4 shillings a pound.[15] Tea consumption jumped from 2.31 pounds per person per year between 1851 and 1860 to 3.26 pounds per person per year from 1861 to 1870. By 1891, the number had climbed even higher with average tea consumption at 5.70 pounds per person per year.[16] Two successful Victorian-era tea companies, Lipton and Brooke Bond, pushed Ceylon black teas to the forefront of the market. Wealthy people drank Pekoe and Congo (or Congou) black Ceylon teas, while Bohea was consumed by working classes. Even the poorest people were willing to make whatever sacrifice necessary to procure tea, and no matter one's class, English people demanded reasonable quality. A spokesman for a leading tea firm commented in the *Times* that "it is wrong to assume that the lowest class of consumers use the lowest class of tea ... no class in the community are so particular in having good tea, or are more ready to forego quantity for quality, than the labouring poor—a fact which upsets all theories."[17] As early as 1800, records indicate that a working-class family living on £40 a year spent £2 a year on tea alone.[18]

In spite of tax and price reductions as well as a cheaper source for tea, adulteration plagued this industry up through the 1870s. Mixing the tea leaves with foreign, cheap substances and/or treating tea leaves to make them appear of high quality were so commonplace that most people could not recognize unadulterated tea if they saw it. Green tea was routinely dyed with Prussian blue and magnetic iron to give it a better appearance, so when the Co-operative

Central Agency of London attempted to sell chests of pure, uncolored green tea, co-operative societies in the North and Midlands refused to buy it because it appeared visually "wrong." The agency hired lecturers and took out newspaper advertisements to educate consumers about adulteration and about how green tea was supposed to look.[19] Even wealthy people who could afford premium teas were probably buying an adulterated product because adulteration often began in Canton factories where the tea was processed—and dyed. Unscrupulous English merchants did further mischief by mixing expensive Hyson, Souchongs, and gunpowder varieties with common, damaged green tea. In the 1840s, eight known London factories dried out used tea leaves and resold them. Housekeepers of large estates, hotel waiters, even charwomen were involved in this "trade."[20] Tea adulteration did not end until laws in the 1870s prohibited grocers from tampering with the leaves. By then, Victorians' taste for green tea had diminished as cheaper black tea from both Assam and Ceylon began pouring into the country. The purity of black tea was less questioned; by avoiding Chinese tea and buying only black tea from British plantations in India and Ceylon, people were reasonably assured of an unadulterated product.

Tea's widespread popularity had to do in part with the impurity of most urban water and also with the increasing emphasis among Victorians on sobriety. Impure tea was compromised in taste, but impure water was deadly. Prior to tea usurping it in popularity, people of all classes and both sexes drank routinely small, or low-alcohol, beer for breakfast, dinner, and supper, and many kept it under the bed for a drink in the night. Like tea (and of course coffee), beer was brewed from water that had been heated to a point where harmful bacteria were killed off. Most people did not drink beer to the point of drunkenness; indeed, it was celebrated for its healthy properties, for being a liquid bread. Gin was the poison that most reformers had in mind when the temperance movements began in earnest by the 1830s, not beer. Nonetheless, most people no longer brewed beer because they had little space for the equipment. On the other hand, tea required little equipment and the dried leaves took up no room. It was easier for families to brew tea than to have someone run to the public house (the pub) for beer.

Tea and coffee were championed by temperance advocates as the best solution to working-class drunkenness and unruliness, although others, particularly doctors and scientists, sometimes argued that if taken in too great a quantity, tea had an "excessive stimulant effect on some people."[21] However, taste mattered the most to people and they found tea to be a quickly acquired one. The warmth of the liquid must have been compelling to people who endured cold and damp weather for much of the year, particularly if they lacked the time or proper kitchens to eat the majority of their food hot. Temperance societies, along with Evangelicals who likewise shunned alcohol, created the social imperative to limit alcohol both at home and in public houses, but no doubt the taste and warmth of tea, along with its caffeine, was responsible for the beverage's rise to prominence, temperance advocates or not.

## THE ORIGINS OF THE VICTORIAN AFTERNOON TEA

English lore has it that the woman who invented or at the very least popularized afternoon tea was Anna Maria Stanhope, Seventh Duchess of Bedford and one of Queen Victoria's Ladies in Waiting from 1837 to 1841. Writing to her brother-in-law from Windsor Castle in 1841, the Duchess had mentioned that she often had tea around five o'clock, along with her Ladies in Waiting.[22] Apparently, the Duchess also drank tea when staying at Belvoir Castle in Rutland. Suffering from hunger pains in the late afternoon—still several hours before dinner—the Duchess invited other ladies to take tea in her boudoir. Fanny Kemble, the famous actress, recalled one such gathering during her stay at Belvoir in March, 1842:

> My first introduction to "afternoon tea" took place during this visit to Belvoir, when I received on several occasions private and rather mysterious invitations to the Duchess of Bedford's room, and found her with a 'small and select' circle of female guests of the castle, busily employed in brewing and drinking tea, with her grace's own private teakettle. I do not believe that now universally honored and observed institution of 'five-o'clock tea' dates farther back in the annals of English civilization than this very private and, I think, rather shamefaced practice of it.[23]

Kemble's interpretation of the tea-drinking affairs as "rather mysterious" and "shamefaced" laid the foundation for the dominant impression that culinary historians rely on for detailing the evolution of afternoon tea. [24] Only when the Duchess of Bedford arrived back to her London home and began to host afternoon tea parties did the event lose its tentative overtures and become fashionable as a result of her initiative.

English gentlewomen had been drinking tea with friends and families in their homes for many decades prior to the Victorian era; however, no ritual had been established whereby people stopped their activities around four o'clock and convened for tea and cake. Instead, most well-to-do people had been taking tea and light refreshment after an afternoon or early evening dinner. Jane Austen's novels, which predate the Victorian era and its craze for afternoon tea, are filled with such scenes. In *Sense and Sensibility*, for example, readers feel for Elinor, when after dinner she must endure boring conversation in the drawing room over tea, when what she most wants is an intimate chat with Lucy. Elizabeth Gaskell's *Cranford* (1853), set in the Victorian era but in a fictional village far removed from fashion and new trends, is replete with this type of scene as well. After dining in their own homes in early evening, the Cranford ladies (many on tight budgets but genteel, nonetheless) gather for tea and paper-thin slices of bread and butter afterwards at a hostess's home.

By the 1840s and 1850s, as middle- and upper-class people moved the dinner hour to late evening, it became less practical to follow such a meal with an after-dinner tea, given that the tea typically came with more food along with the beverage itself. Eliza Cheadle wrote in *Manners of Modern Society: Being a Book of Etiquette* (1872) that afternoon tea made more sense when dinner was still at least two hours away and people were hungry. After-dinner tea made less sense as everyone was obviously full.[25] By the 1870s, Cheadle merely validated the practice that was already in place.

Afternoon tea was also influenced by the morning call tradition common among women. "Morning" prior to the twentieth century meant "daylight," and morning calls took place after lunch and before dinner. In the Georgian era, the hostess would offer her guests wine with assorted cakes and biscuits. By the Victorian era, morning calls took place between three o'clock and seven o'clock in the evening, and the hostess offered tea in place of wine. In a time before the telephone, women routinely designated one or two days a week or a month to be at home in order for their acquaintances and friends to drop by and visit. They would often put what were commonly termed their "at home" days on their calling cards so that those in their social circle could note the days. An "at home" became shorthand; it meant that a woman would remain home prepared to receive visitors. By the mid-1800s, morning calls, at homes, and afternoon tea meant virtually the same thing; but by 1882, the term afternoon tea had won out over the rest. As Mrs. Eliot James declared in *Our Servants, Their Duties to Us and Ours to Them,* afternoon tea was by now "an institution."[26]

Etiquette books, conduct manuals, women's magazines, and cookbooks aimed at the servant-keeping classes (clearly a minority in Victorian society) offered extensive, if not exhaustive, detail on how a mistress was to conduct an afternoon tea, and how a guest should respond to the invitation, as well as how to act once she arrived at the hostess's house. It is essential to remember, however, that as with all situations when it comes to etiquette, books themselves can only go so far in revealing to present-day readers how people conducted themselves in the past. Society people typically made the rules, and when they broke them, they often created a new custom—and new rules—as the Duchess of Bedford's initial tea parties suggest. Guidebooks were primarily aimed at lower-middle-class or newly rich people who wanted otherwise silent codes of conduct to be made explicit, so that when out in society, they would not inadvertently commit a faux pas that could have damaging consequences. Thus, guidebooks are helpful, but only to the extent that authorities give their own interpretation of rules and frequently offer ideal scenarios rather than realities.

## AFTERNOON TEA DRESS FASHIONS

Primarily a woman's pastime, afternoon tea was to be in all things feminine, and words such as "pretty," "dainty," "charming," and "soft" came up repeatedly in literature about this ritual, particularly in regards to women's dresses. While those of modest means were advised to wear a "tasteful" morning dress, those with any money to spare were urged to spend it on an actual "tea gown." The Victorian magazine *Beauty & Fashion* justified the expense in this way:

> The first important item with a hostess in regard to afternoon tea is the selection of a becoming gown. The tea will taste sweeter, and the cups will look prettier, if she is robed in some gauze-like fabric of artistic make, and a dainty tea-gown is of just as much consequence to her as the beverage itself, and adds considerably to her good humour. If she knows that she is well-clad, and that the pretty, flimsy lace and soft silk will bear the closest inspection of her particular friends, there is sure to be a charming air of satisfaction pervading her whole conversation, and her manner will be more than usually affable and gracious.[27]

Fashionable tea gowns were designed to allow women relaxed freedom of movement. Looser in the waist than a woman's other dresses, the tea gown was to create flowing, soft movements as she circulated.

Guidebooks also recommended that a woman wear her gloves while taking tea, although if food became difficult to manage, it was permissible to remove them. Hostesses in particular were advised to wear gloves, lest their hands should feel too warm to the touch when they greeted guests. Keeping hats on during afternoon tea was likewise in good form, although men always removed theirs when indoors, tea or no. And, unless one was a particularly close friend and could be urged to remove her coat or cape for a more lengthy, intimate exchange, outer garments likewise could remain on. Once more, however, men were to remove their topcoats, even for a short visit.

## AFTERNOON TEA PROTOCOL

Ideally, the many rules that governed afternoon tea could be disregarded to the point where all participants enjoyed themselves. Such would have been the case when family members convened for tea without any visitors or when the visitors were good friends and thus unconcerned or less preoccupied with "good form." Recollecting a party at the home of sculptor John Graham Lough and his wife where she first met the poet Robert Browning, Camilla Toulmin recalled such *Gemütlichkeit*: "It was not a dinner party for which we assembled, but one of those sociable gatherings very common among people of letters in the early 'forties.' We had tea in the drawing-room, with bread and butter and cake, between six and seven o'clock, but without any attempt to render the meal a 'high tea.' ... About ten o'clock we sat down to a substantial supper, which I believe was thoroughly enjoyed, for surely conversation, or even attentive listening, whets the appetite as much as bodily exercise."[28]

Others would have found afternoon tea to be an ordeal, particularly if they knew few of the people or if they believed themselves socially inferior to those around them. Perhaps explicit rules outlined in conduct manuals were consoling in such cases; people took courage because they had a guide to help them navigate a tricky terrain. The 1889–1891 *Cassell's Book of the Household* might have had such readers in mind for its chapter "The Etiquette of Society." In discussing afternoon tea, the editors also brought in the overlapping topics of "Introductions," "Calls," and "Cards."

To understand better the hostess' duties toward her guests during the affair, imagine a young wife as she sits somewhat nervously in her drawing room awaiting friends and acquaintances to call and take tea. The clock ticks as she occupies her hands with needlework. All is in readiness: The coal fire creates warmth and comfort, the parlor maid is tidy, and the room is pretty. The mistress herself is well-dressed. When the doorbell rings, the parlor maid answers and after taking the visitors' calling cards she escorts them to the drawing room and announces their names. As they are close family friends, they plan to stay not only for the requisite fifteen-minute cup of tea, but also for conversation, and thus, they remove their outerwear. Whether friend or acquaintance, the mistress should allow no more than five minutes to pass before she signals for tea and in a well-run household, *Cassell's* editors hinted, "the tea-things appear, without any apparent sign from the lady of the house."[29] As her guests make themselves comfortable close to the fire, the mistress gives a barely perceptible nod to her maid who leaves to see to the tea.

When afternoon tea was still a very novel practice, *Cassell's* editors allowed that it was "considered sufficient if cups of tea were brought in on a tray and handed round by a servant." By 1890, however, "the most correct thing is for the tea to be made upstairs." Reasons for this change are obscure now and it might seem like an annoying extra burden for the mistress to add to her already lengthy list of rules and obligations; however, assigning the mistress to make and pour the tea was a nod of respect and a celebration of her status within the home. Tea, the authorities agreed, simply tastes better if the mistress makes it. If she expects many guests and has no gentleman or grown-up daughters to help her pass the cups, she was advised by the etiquette authorities to solicit beforehand the help of a close female friend. The office of pouring out tea is too "important" to be "filled by a servant," stated *Cassell's* editors.[30]

## BREWING A PROPER CUP OF TEA

When our mistress signals for the tea-things, the maid brings from the kitchen a tray laden with the essential implements, among them the teakettle of boiling water, a teapot and the cups, a cream pitcher and sugar bowl, thin slices of lemon, and small napkins. She then returns to the kitchen to bring up a second tray of small sandwiches and a cake with serving knife and small plates. Many Victorian cookbooks had instructions on how to brew tea properly, because even though its price had fallen, quality tea was still expensive; thrifty mistresses extracted as much flavor from the tealeaves as possible following the standard guideline: "one teaspoon per person plus one for the pot." Many families owned a plain large kettle for kitchen use and a more elegant one for use at the breakfast and tea-table. These fancy kettles often had an iron heater or spirit lamp attached underneath them to keep the water boiling hot.

Teapots were different from teakettles, even though today some people might use the terms interchangeably. Teakettles were for water only; teapots were for brewing and pouring the tea. They were to be as tasteful as the family could afford, although fine bone china was not recommended; it was a poor heat insulator, as china could not keep the tea at the appropriately hot temperature for long enough to extract maximum flavor. That Victorians took tea brewing very seriously and were troubled about the make of the teapot is best illustrated by the length of this passage from *Dictionary of Daily Wants*:

> It is a well-ascertained fact, that the infusion of tea made in sliver or polished metal teapots is stronger than that which is produced in black or other kinds of earthenware. This is explained on the principle that polished surfaces retain heat much better than dark, rough surfaces, and that, consequently, the heat being confined in the former case, must act more powerfully than in the latter. It is further certain that the silver or metal teapot, when filled a second time, produces worse tea than the earthenware vessel, and that it is advisable to use the earthenware pot, unless a sliver or metal one can be procured sufficiently large to contain at once all that may be required. These facts are readily explained by considering that the action of the heat retained by the silver vessel so far exhausts the herb as to leave very little soluble substance for a second infusion; whereas the reduced temperature of the water in the earthenware pot, by extracting only a small proportion at first, leaves some soluble matter for the action of a subsequent infusion.[31]

In short, silver or polished metal were the best on condition that the pot was large enough to fill everyone's cup a second time. Otherwise, earthenware was best, because the leaves could be infused twice and still give an adequate flavor from a second infusion.

To ensure further the fullest extraction of flavor from the leaves, the mistress first warmed her pot using one of the many suggested options, the most common of which tea drinkers today will recognize: Pour scalding hot water in the teapot and empty it just before adding tealeaves and fresh boiling water. To neglect this step and simply pour hot water into a cold pot would result in poorly steeped tea, as the water would be too cool to do its job. Alexis Soyer recommended another approach, more common in the Victorian era than now: Put tealeaves into a dry teapot, warm the pot by the fire for fifteen minutes, and then pour boiling water over the now-hot tealeaves. Alice Ellis, author of *Fish, Flesh and Good Red Herring* (2004) humorously noted that the tea would be steeped in the time that it took a person to slowly recite the *Misere* (Psalm 67).[32] The need to infuse the leaves twice or to extract full flavor from the leaves is significant, as is the is sometimes made with a rising top, as shown in the annexed figure, and the various canisters are arranged within.

TEA SYRUP.—Pour a quarter of a pint of boiling water over three ounces of young hyson tea; let it stand an hour, then add a pint of brandy; cork it up well, let it stand for ten days, shaking it frequently; then strain it, sweeten with clarified syrup, and bottle it. A teaspoonful of this in a glass of water makes a very refreshing drink.

TEA URN.—The tea-urn is the most elegant mode of supplying water for tea. It is made in the form of a vase, but in a great variety of patterns. The accompanying engraving represents one of the usual

kind. In the centre there is a vertical tube, into which a cylinder of iron heated red hot is slipped down, and covered by a small lid, and that by the lid of the urn. This keeps the water in the urn at a boiling heat. Some tea-urns have lamps beneath them, instead of iron heaters, which have the advantage of keeping the water hot any length of time.

TEA URN, TO CLEAN.—In an earthen gallipot put an ounce of bees-wax, cut up in small pieces; set it by the fireside until perfectly melted and quite hot, very near boiling heat; remove the jar from the fire, and stir into it rather less than a tablespoonful of salad oil, and rather more than a tablespoonful of best spirits of turpentine, continue stirring till well mixed and nearly cold; fill the urn with boiling water so as to make it thoroughly hot, apply a thin coating of the above mixture, and rub with a soft cloth till all stickiness is removed; then polish with a clean rag and a little crocus powder. The crocus powder must be very fine, so as to sift through muslin.

TEAL.—A bird which is a great favourite with sportsmen. About April, these birds collect a quantity of grass and rushes, and make a covered nest, the opening for the most part to the south; in this they lay from ten to fourteen eggs, of a dirty white,

and as big as those of a pullet. The nest of the teal is never placed in such a situation as to rise and fall with the water. It is found on all the grassy lochs of the north, and sometimes some hundred yards from the water's edge, and at others, close by; but at all times a dry spot is selected, where it deposits its eggs. Teal shooting bears a certain resemblance to some of our inland shootings which are neither common nor within the reach of every one; and it is a most amusing sport when pursued on the banks of a small river or even a large brook, well sheltered by bushes. When hunted up, a teal seldom rises in the air, but usually skims along the stream, and presents a fine shot. If it cannot be got at through the interception of trees or large bushes, one of the party should run forward so as to circumvent its entire escape out of reach. It is not often, however, that a teal flies away altogether. The teal will also frequently swim down stream the moment after it drops; so that if the shooter does not cast his eye quickly that way, instead of continuing to look for him in one spot, the bird will probably catch sight of the sportsman and fly up, while his attention is being directed to the wrong place.

TEAL, TO DRESS.—Half-roast them; when they come to table slice the breast, strew on pepper and salt, pour on a little port wine, and squeeze the juice of a lemon over; put some gravy to this, set the plate on a lamp, cut up the bird, let it remain over the lamp till done, turning it.

TEETOTAL DRINKS.—As there are many persons who wholly abstain from alcoholic liquors, the following collection of recipes for unintoxicating beverages are herewith given under a general head, for the purpose of easy reference:—

*Apple Baked Drink.*—Bake half a dozen apples without peeling them, put them into a jug, and pour half a gallon of boiling water over them whilst they are hot, cover the whole up until cold, then sweeten with honey or sugar.



Tea Urn in *Dictionary of Daily Wants* (1858–1861). Notice the vertical tube that runs up the middle of the urn. Into this tube a red-hot iron rod would be slipped, and the small cap placed on top. Illustration courtesy of the Morse Department of Special Collections, Hale Library, Kansas State University.

exhaustive detail on warming the pot. Many people today do not practice such frugality, taking tea much more for granted than even the wealthy Victorians did.

Our imaginary mistress is not of the most fashion-conscious or wealthy set. If she were, then a tea urn would have replaced her teakettle as an urn was considered "the most elegant mode of supplying water for tea." It "is made in the form of a vase . . . In the centre there is a vertical tube, into which a cylinder of iron heated red hot is slipped down, and covered by a small lid, and that by the lid of the urn. This keeps the water in the urn at a boiling point."[33]

While perfect from the family's perspective, imagine the servant's nightmarish job of trying to insert a red-hot iron rod into the vertical tube and then also trying to pour thirty-two cups' worth of boiling water into the urn from her kettle. No doubt the family using an urn would also have had a footman nearby to lift the urn for the maid. A slightly safer option was an urn with spirit- (or paraffin-) lamp attached underneath. Regardless of their heating mechanisms, urns were often of polished metal with silver preferable. They held more water than kettles and had a spigot handle that allowed the mistress to fill her teapot more easily. (The urn held only boiling water—not tea.) For more modest families without an urn, *Cassell's* editors advised a stand for kettle and spirit-lamp, as it, too, was "very convenient. They stand on the floor, about as high as the afternoon tea-table. They give more room on the table, and are more easily get-at-able than the ordinary table-stands; but they are rather expensive." The mistress's china cups, saucers, and tea plates were to be "dainty, and the tea-cozy should be pretty and handsomely decorated with embroidery."[34]

Our young mistress's demeanor, like her china, is pleasing and delightful. However, her teatime duties secretly challenge her patience and nerve because of the many roles she has to play. After she pours the tea and makes it to all her guests' specifications, she then sees to it that all are supplied with sandwiches and cake or both, if they are particularly hungry. She is then allowed (according to *Cassell's* editors) to "provide herself with a cup of tea, which she can enjoy until the time arrives to once more assist her guests by offering second cups." At this point, hosting the tea must have become particularly trying:

> During the whole process of making and pouring out of the tea, the conversation must not be allowed to flag for one instant, and no guest must be permitted either to engross too much attention or to be neglected. Tact, practice, and some skills are needed to accomplish these various duties successfully; but on the whole the process of the tea-making and tea-drinking will be found much more of an assistance than a hindrance.[35]

The "Tea and Chatter" column in the magazine *Beauty & Fashion* put the matter this way: The mistress "breathed a sigh of relief" before hurrying upstairs at the conclusion of tea to dress for a dinner party or the theater.[36]

Kettle and stand in *Cassell's Book of the Household* (1889–1891).

## FORMAL TEA RECEPTIONS

Just as people today might have a reception to celebrate an important landmark in their own or their family's life, so too did Victorians. A graduation for a young man from university, a couple's engagement, an ordination, the birth of an heir: all called for celebration, and by the end of the Victorian era, well-to-do people often hosted a tea reception for a special occasion of this nature. Unlike a woman's "at home," a tea reception was formal and costly. A family might invite upwards of one hundred guests, all of whom would have been sent a formal invitation by post. Tea receptions were supposed to be lavish; a simple seed cake and cup of tea did not suffice. While tea was offered to guests, so too were champagne punches, sherry, wine, effervescent water, and cocktails. With the food laid out on a long table in the drawing room or dining room, guests were to be awed by an elaborate display as they entered. Most certainly, they would see a large trifle, which is a dessert of sherry-soaked cake layered with jam, fresh berries, custard, and whipped cream in a stunning crystal bowl. Surrounding the trifle would be numerous fancy cakes and pastries, probably prepared by a French-owned confectionary, and beautifully molded ice creams (or ices, as they were called). Given the number of guests, the mistress was not expected to make tea and serve the food; servants saw to that. However, she was expected to pour the tea or relegate that important duty to a close female friend or family member.[37]

Tea receptions were not limited to the wealthy. At the end of the century, entire towns and villages might throw the rough equivalent of an outdoor tea reception to celebrate a monumental event or passing. Thomas Jordan, a coal miner who recalled his youth in Usworth Colliery outside Durham, noted one such tea reception: "In 1897 was the Diamond Jubilee of Queen Victoria and the villages of Usworth and Washington celebrated it in grand style. We, from the various schools, assembled on the village green. . . . Each of us was presented with a cup with the regal image of the Queen stamped upon it. Our teachers led us into a large field where we sat down and were given a large paper bag packed with food and fruit. They filled our mugs with tea and we ate to the sound of the colliery bands playing nearby."[38]

## THE CASUAL NATURE OF A DAILY TEA BREAK

However, Victorians did not need the Queen's Jubilee as an excuse to drink tea. At all levels of society, an afternoon tea break had become an ordinary occurrence by the 1880s and 1890s. Flora Thompson's account of rural life in the 1880s is helpful for illustrating its pervasiveness. "Those of the younger set," Thompson recalled, "would sometimes meet in the afternoon in one of their cottages to sip strong, sweet, milkless tea and talk things over." She continued:

> These tea-drinkings were never premeditated. One neighbour would drop in, then another, and another would be beckoned to from the doorway or fetched in to settle some disputed point. Then someone would say, 'How about a cup o'tay?' and they would all run home to fetch a spoonful, with a few leaves over to help make up the spoonful for the pot. . . . This tea-drinking was the woman's hour. Soon the children would be rushing in from school; then would come the men, with their loud voices and coarse jokes and corduroys reeking of earth and sweat. In the meantime, the wives and mothers were free to crook their little fingers genteelly as they sipped from their teacups.[39]

With little money to spare, these Oxfordshire village women nonetheless gave a few extra leaves for the pot's spoonful; for this small sacrifice, a few minutes' leisure and entertainment could be had by all before the evening meal (called in that part of the country a "supper-tea"). These impromptu afternoon teas testified to what teatime ideally was: convivial and pleasurable, a time where community goodwill and friendship outweighed whatever rules and decorum appeared in etiquette guides. Because such books concentrated on the afternoon tea as a rule-laden social occasion, we might mistakenly believe that this event did not go on everyday among family members. However, most women, especially the countless numbers of the lower-middle-class women, did not often go out calling at teatime or expect callers. They nevertheless took an afternoon tea break but with less ceremony and fuss. Usually around four o'clock, household members paused in their routines, convened in the drawing room, parlor, or kitchen, and had a cup of tea with a slice of cake or a toasted muffin; they then returned to their routines. Sometimes small children were a part of this affair and sometimes they were not. It depended largely on the family's income and social status. Wealthy families likely had the nursemaid see to the children's nursery tea above-stairs, but the casual and comfortable nature of the break did not necessarily call for the children's exclusion.

## POPULAR TEATIME FOODS

Industrialization resulted in a national cuisine that began to replace regional food traditions. Trains made it possible to transport food anywhere easily and quickly, and as a result, the same name-brand, factory-produced biscuits, jams, tinned meats, canned fruits and vegetables, and custard powders thus made it to grocery shelves nationwide. But at the same time that manufactured jams and potted meats became commonplace in Victorian pantries, a surge in tourism, an expanding middleclass, and the nature of the afternoon tea helped ensure that some regional traditions and foods would not entirely fall out of popularity; indeed, some of these foods are still being produced today on a small regional scale by bakeries and teashops throughout the United Kingdom.

Places such as Yorkshire, Cornwall, the Lake District, and parts of the Peak District were removed geographically and/or culturally from London's sphere of influence and its new culinary fashions, and yet, they absorbed record numbers of tourists in the Victorian era. Visitors to the Lake District enjoyed Grasmere gingerbread and Borrowdale tea bread. Devonshire became known for its buns (called Devonshire splits by around 1905) and its exceptional clotted cream. Whitby, a tourist resort on the Yorkshire coast, sold dozens of its distinctive lemon buns and its still-famous gingerbread. Likewise, Ashbourne gingerbread gained fame in the Peak District. Wiltshire lardy cake, Banbury cakes, Northumberland stotty cake, Shrewsbury cake (immortalized in the 1840 *Ingoldsby Legends*), Staffordshire oatcakes, and Suffolk cakes all became sought-after treats among tourists and locals alike.[40] As afternoon tea was a crucial part of many tourists' daily agenda, bakeries and teashops did brisk business in such goods, and they often promoted their locale's specialties and distinct, cherished regional identities.

Some foods became so famous that they were eventually claimed as national treasures. Before the 1800s, Chelsea buns, Yorkshire pudding, and Bath buns had lost their attachment to specific locales to become defined as traditional English foods. During the Victorian era, the same thing happened to Yorkshire tea cakes. They became so popular that the Finchley manual, *Cooking, or, Practical and Economical Training for Those Who Are to Be Servants, Wives, and Mothers* (1851) used a catechistic approach to teach a servant how make these requisite treats:

> Q. How do you make Yorkshire tea cakes?
> A. Mix 2 lb. of flour with ¼ lb of butter melted in 1 pint of milk, 2 eggs well beaten and 3 tablespoonfuls of fresh yeast. Having left the mixture to rise I knead it, and make 4 or 5 cakes. These cakes I place on a tin, and leave to rise fully. When risen, I put them in a slow oven and bake them.
> Q. Would they not be lighter made without butter?
> A. Yes ma'am, but most prefer them made with butter as they eat shorter.
> Q. How do you send them to table?
> A. They should be buttered hot, or if cold cut in two and toasted brown and buttered."[41]

"Shorter" or "Short" are terms that describe the crumbling or brittle texture of baked goods. Some people preferred their teacakes to be crumbly and rather dry; others preferred a softer, more muffin-like crumb.

While many people have heard of Yorkshire tea cakes, few are familiar with the most ubiquitous Victorian teatime staple, the seed cake; nor are they familiar with its regional identity and rise to national fame. Seed cake apparently originated in East Anglia in the sixteenth century, although versions of it were known elsewhere as well, perhaps at an earlier date. However, East Anglia was famous for wheat fields and it makes sense that many specialty cakes and breads originated in that area. As with Bath buns, Mothering buns (a traditional Mid-Lent Sunday treat that I will discuss in the final chapter), and Hawkshead Wigs, seed cake depended on caraway seeds for its signature taste—a surprising flavor for sweet goods by today's standards. The seed cake was traditionally served at harvest and at seeding time in East Anglia, where farmers treated their laborers to large feasts. The sixteenth-century Essex farmer and poet, Thomas Tussar, stated the farmer's wife's obligation this way:

> Wife sometime this week, if the weather hold clear,
> an end of wheat-sowing we make for this year:
> Remember thou therefore, though I do it not:
> the seed-cake the patties, and the furmenty pot.[42]

This "cakes and ale" meal, as Tusser described it, included a sweetened wheat porridge (frumenty), patties that, according to Elisabeth Ayrton, were probably made of fresh farm cheese (versions of which existed in Huntingdon and Cambridge as well as Essex), and the seed cake itself.[43] Thus, not only did the cake's name possibly derive from caraway seeds, but also from its association with planting and harvest.

As with many English cakes prior to the introduction of chemical leavening (baking powder) in the 1850s, seed cake was rich and heavy; it was called a "keeping cake" because it did not easily spoil and its flavor was enhanced with aging. Aside from caraway seeds, it was flavored and moistened with fortified wine such as Madeira, spirits such as brandy, or occasionally with rose water or milk. Its leavening from the sixteenth to the early nineteenth century was yeast or eggs, depending on what was available. Nutmeg or mace, ginger, and allspice also flavored the cake.[44] By the 1860s, some Victorians began replacing the caraway seeds with currents, an option that Isabella Beeton offered in her 1861 seed cake recipe in *Book of Household Management*.

While the seed cake remained a teatime staple into the early twentieth century, some Victorians nonetheless treated it with ambivalence, perhaps as North Americans might treat Christmas fruitcake (another English "keeping cake" that resembled seed cake). That ambivalence was crystallized in Elizabeth Gaskell's humorous depiction of the seed cake's prominence on a tea table in *Cranford* (1853):

> The tea-tray was abundantly loaded—I was pleased to see it, I was so hungry; but I was afraid the ladies present might think it vulgarly heaped up. I know they would have done at their own houses; but somehow the heaps disappeared here. I saw Mrs Jamieson eating seed-cake, slowly and considerately, as she did everything; and I was rather surprised, for I knew she had told us, on the occasion of her last party, that she never had it in her house, it reminded her so much of scented soap. She always gave us Savoy biscuits. However, Mrs Jamieson was kindly indulgent to Miss Barker's want of knowledge of the customs of high life; and, to spare her feelings, ate three large pieces of seed-cake, with a placid, ruminating expression of countenance, not unlike a cow's.[45]

Covert, class-conscious messages are flying around the table as the daughter-in-law of a baron condescends to attend the tea party of Cranford's retired milliner, Miss Barker (whose sister, incidentally, was Mrs. Jamieson's lady's maid). Gaskell meant to convey a good deal by mentioning that Mrs. Jamieson serves the fashionable light-as-a-feather Savoy biscuits, while Miss Barker serves what she perceives to be the height of solid respectability, the seed-cake.

* * * *

As the pace of living accelerated throughout the nineteenth century, and as women's opportunities outside the home expanded, the ability for many people to pause around four o'clock and take tea was increasingly challenged. By the twentieth century, tea merchants became rarer because fewer people understood or cared enough about fine tea to seek it out, and the cost and trouble of expertly blending teas became prohibitive as a result. Loose-leaf tea was slowly replaced by the tea-bag in part because people at work wanted a fast means of brewing tea a cup at a time, with no ceremony, no second infusion—and no company. It should not surprise us that today the afternoon tea ritual is the stuff of holidays and tourism. Victorian tourists expected an afternoon tea with various cakes along with a steaming pot, as do many tourists in England today. They work hard for their leisure and when leisure comes in the form of a touring holiday, they manage once again to find the time to sit, wait for the tea to brew properly, and enter into conversation with friends.

# 5

# "The Chief Meal of the Day": The Victorian Working-Class Tea

**Red Herrings.** The cheaper sort of red herrings are always too salt [sic], and unpleasantly strong-flavored, and are therefore an indifferent form of food, unless due precaution is taken to soak them first in water for an hour before they are cooked. First, soak the red herrings in water for an hour; wipe and split them down the back; toast or broil them on both sides for two or three minutes, and having placed them on a dish, put a bit of butter and some chopped onion upon each herring; pour a little vinegar over all, and this will make a cheap and savoury dish to be eaten with well-boiled potatoes.
—Charles Francatelli, *A Plain Cookery Book for the Working Classes,* 1852

While genteel people in urban areas took afternoon tea and sat down to a late evening dinner, working-class people all over England sat down to what they often called their "tea" (a meat tea) as soon as the dayshift ended. Flora Thompson described one such meal from a farm laborer's family in Oxfordshire in the 1880s:

When the men came home from work they would find the table spread with a clean whitey-brown cloth, upon which would be knives and two-pronged steel forks with buckhorn handles. The vegetables would then be turned out into big round yellow crockery dishes and the bacon cut into dice, with much the largest cube upon Feyther's [sic] plate, and the whole family would sit down to the chief meal of the day. True, it was seldom that all could find places at the central table; but some of the smaller children could sit upon stools with the seat of a chair for a table, or on the doorstep with their plates on their laps.[1]

As Thompson remembered, meals were typically silent. "Father and Mother might talk if they wanted to; but usually they were content to concentrate upon their enjoyment of the meal."[2] Followed by a few hours of relaxing or gardening for father and mending and knitting for mother before bed, the evening meal for most families was the only time of the day when all could be together.

This chapter brings together several related themes: the role of the main meal in working-class homes, the foods that workers could afford and that they most enjoyed, the events that led to acute hunger and malnutrition for thousands of English people up through the 1840s, and the limited improvements in people's diets by 1900. Given the numerous ambiguities and complexities that immediately come into play when we consider one's socioeconomic class rather than just economic standing, I will concentrate in this chapter primarily on economics alone. I am concerned with the diets of approximately fifteen million men, women, and children in England, and how they managed to survive on a minimal amount of food and yet still do the physical work of a nation.

## WORKING-CLASS EMPLOYMENT AND WAGES

In the Victorian era, three-fourths of the population was working class and well into the 1800s, three-fourths of that 75 per cent earned just enough to pay rent, buy fuel, and eat. For many families, buying clothes, boots, and even soap was a weekly challenge, and an unexpected cost, such as a funeral or medical bill, could throw a family hopelessly into debt; moreover, if the primary breadwinner lost his or her job, hunger and severe malnutrition was an immediate reality. These grim truths affected all working-class people, although the unskilled, displaced, infirm, or physically handicapped were clearly the most vulnerable and as a result, the most likely to be institutionalized in a workhouse.

Just as the upper and middle classes were composed of various strata, so too were the working classes, and to understand working-class diets and culinary traditions, it is important to recognize those gradations and have an overview of each stratum's general earnings per week. Because many workers were subject to the constant threat of injury or even death on the job and because the nature of physical labor was as such that a worker could easily sicken and have to quit, it makes more sense to look at how much workers earned weekly instead of yearly. An elite 15 percent included highly skilled artisans such as cabinet makers, compositors (typesetters), experienced metalsmiths, and those who could repair and maintain sophisticated machines and engines. Also included in the working elite were factory and mining supervisors, policemen, omnibus and train conductors, and small shopkeepers. Some expertly trained workers such as cabinet makers or a mill worker who specialized in "fine counts" could earn up to 36 shillings a week, thus putting them at par income-wise with those in the lower middle classes.[3] With few exceptions, working-class people making this much a week were men, seldom women, never children. Men were presumed to be supporting families and thus in need of a higher wage. Women doing the same work were usually paid significantly less, and children, the least of all.

Most working-class people were semiskilled; they learned on the job rather than in a formal apprenticeship, and their wages were often around 20 shillings a week, although in some occupations such as mining, wages became better as unions became stronger. At mid-century, hewers, or those miners who with picks and shovels manually removed coal from seams, made a weekly wage of 18 to 23 shillings, based on how much coal they extracted. Because industrialization depended absolutely on coal, miners generally shared in the prosperity that characterized the middle decades of the nineteenth century. On average, miners' wages rose roughly 20 percent between the 1850s and 1880s, and because they had started from a higher wage scale than many working-class people and also were increasingly unionized, their standard of living was considered relatively high.[4] Agricultural laborers often fared the worst wage-wise in Victorian England; a labor surplus in the South continually depressed wages in that region where work was seldom guaranteed. A single man might earn as tiny a wage as 3 shillings a week, according to a Parliamentary Report published in 1824, while a married man might only earn 8 to 12 shillings a week, depending on the area, the season, and the labor supply.[5]

Semiskilled men and women working in factories, fishing, and tailoring likewise earned low wages until unions became stronger (or came into existence). In one of the fastest-growing industrial occupations, textiles, an adult male spinner might earn 14 to 22 shillings a week; a woman of roughly the same skill set might earn between 5 and 10 shillings a week. Unlike coal miners and agricultural laborers, factory laborers were subjected to strictly regulated work hours, with most averaging around seventy hours a week in the 1840s. Children, however, were always the most easily exploited, and even when the Factory Acts came into existence, they still often worked hours that put them well beyond the legal limits. A fifteen- or sixteen-year-old male who had started in a textile mill when he was eight could expect to earn roughly 10 to 12 shillings a week by the time he could work two looms.[6]

The lowest paid were itinerant workers, or those who moved from place to place looking for whatever work was available. Joining them were general laborers, a term used to characterize people who had either no particular experience in any one area or whose work demanded little more than physical strength—a washerwoman, water carrier, charwoman, chimney-sweep assistant, a van or omnibus washer. Many street-sellers also struggled daily to survive, with their earnings contingent upon competition and weather. Match and watercress girls, women hawking oranges from a barrow, rag-and-bones men, and knife grinders comprised part of this work category, because many had to move from place to place and endure spates of no work at all. Weekly earnings could be as little as 6 to 10 shillings a week for the most destitute. At the bottom of the social scale were the unemployed, people who often because of injury, infirmity, or small children and in some cases laziness or alcoholism, did not or could not keep a job and were thus institutionalized in workhouses if family members could not afford to care for them. Oftentimes, Victorians would lump the unemployed with what they called the "criminal classes," or those who made their living by prostitution, thievery, and other crimes. The thinking was that having no regular employment tempted one to a life of corruption.

## RURAL WORKING PEOPLE: THEIR FOODS AND MEALS

In spite of significant changes in agriculture that often reduced wages and jeopardized an age-old standard of life for millions, many rural people nonetheless continued to labor for farmers and wealthy landowners up into the twentieth century, and they maintained a quality of life that they appreciated and were hard-pressed to give up. Rather than turn immediately to the destitute, I would instead like to focus first on the average cottager's diet and food customs. I have already mentioned in previous chapters the importance of the pig to a rural laborer's way of life. A family might go into debt in order to ensure that Piggy (as he was affectionately called) did not himself go hungry and thus produce less meat. Most cottagers kept a pig or pigs "and the pig ruled the diet all the year round," as Dorothy Hartley put it in *Food in England* (1954). In other words, if the cottagers were not eating ham, sausage, bacon, and lard off the pig, they were eating a diet that would facilitate the pig's putting on weight before slaughter. Rural people typically raised pig breeds that would produce quantities of cured meat (ham, bacon, and sausage), given that cured meat was less likely to spoil.

Once autumn slaughter was over and debts were paid with meat, the first parts of the pig that the family used were entrails and joints (knuckle bones, for example). November 11, known as Martinmas, was not only the traditional day to slaughter animals such as pigs, but was also a rural community holiday of sorts. Families worked together at the butchering, and then in Scotland and throughout rural communities in the North of England, the women mixed huge batches of mealie (the oats) with the blood, internal organs, and entrails of the pig to create black puddings—sausages that were boiled first to set them and then fried as needed. By winter when the puddings and other offal had been consumed, the family turned to the saltings (what we today might call salt pork or fat pork), ham, and bacon.[7] According to the memories of Tom Mullins, a Staffordshire farm laborer in the 1870s, many families would hang their hams to dry for two or three weeks, after which they were "put in the 'meal ark', a great oak chest nine feet long and a yard wide, in which the oatmeal was kept. The hams were buried out of sight in the meal, and were thus kept airtight until required."[8] The Scots and the Welsh stored their hams in meal arks as well.

Flora Thompson noted that most laborers started their day with thick slices of bread smeared with rosemary-infused lard. They had the same food for their dinner break, and then a flitch, or unsliced hunk, of bacon with potatoes and greens for their tea. Most rural people, even as late as the early 1920s, did not have coal-fired ranges or access to gas appliances. Their cooking methods were preindustrial and they worked fine, as Thompson made clear in her description of how wives prepared their families' teas. Around four o'clock "smoke would go up from the chimneys, as the fire was made up and the big iron boiler, or the three-legged pot, was slung on the hook of the chimney-chain. Everything was cooked in the one utensil; the square of bacon . . . cabbage or other green vegetables in the net, potatoes in another, and the roly-poly swathed in a cloth." By "timing the putting in of each item and keeping the simmering of the pot well regulated, each item was kept intact and an appetizing meal was produced. The water in which the food had been cooked, the potato parings, and other vegetable trimmings were the pig's share."[9]

The greens that went into the net were either from the family's garden allotment or they were gathered wild. Indeed, rural people foraged year-round for whatever foods they could find that grew in nearby hedgerows, forests, and copses. Bilberries and high-bush blueberries flourished in the hills and heathland, and inhabitants picked them as well as wild blackberries for pies, tarts, and preserves. Dock pudding made of the earliest spring greens and oats was considered by those in South Yorkshire and the Lake District to be a blood purifier, or in other words, a purgative. After a long winter of surviving on salty preserved foods, rural people must have felt that fresh greens, even bitter ones, aided their health.[10] In the East Midlands, people gathered Good King Henry—also called "poor man's asparagus," given that its young shoots were eaten like asparagus and its leaves boiled to make pottage.[11]

In the summer when they were cheap, cheese, eggs, and butter rounded out the rural family's diet, but milk for many was a luxury. Although it was cheap at a penny for a jug, it still had to be fetched from the farmhouse dairy, and the weight of the jug was a deterrent to many who were already compelled to haul water home from a communal pump or well. "A few families fetched [milk] daily; but many did not bother about it. The women said they preferred their tea neat, and it did not seem to occur to them that the children needed milk," recalled Thompson.[12]

One was lucky to live on the seacoast or near a river where fishing rights were not heavily restricted. Villagers in the North, in Scotland, and in Wales foraged for seaweed (called sea vegetables), scallops, shrimp, crabs, cockles, whelks, and mussels, all of which formed the bulk of many subsistence diets well into the nineteenth century. Freshly dredged cockles (a shellfish) were boiled in the open air. Fishers placed them in large pans in a little water over the fire and they cooked quickly. Women stood by to remove shells and then wash them in spring water before putting them in baskets or wooden tubs to take home for the family and/or to sell in local markets.[13] Marsh samphire, a plant with fleshy bright green spears that grows in the marshes around the coast, was a common food of rural poor. They collected it by hand from the edges of tidal creeks, washed it, and blanched it in water.[14]

Bread, be it baked in an oven or cooked on a griddle, was the staple food. To save money, many rural women and children participated in "leazing." After the grain had been harvested, they were allowed by the farmer to comb his fields for missed grain: "At the end of the fortnight or three weeks that the leazing lasted," Thompson wrote, "the corn would be thrashed out at home and sent to the miller, who paid himself for grinding by taking toll of the flour. Great was the excitement in a good year when the flour came home—one bushel, two bushels, or even more in large, industrious families."[15] In most of England "corn" meant wheat, but in the far North "corn" meant oats or barley as well as some wheat. For families who could not leaze or where the collected grain amounted to little, the village baker supplied the rest of the family bread, or if the family had a large brick or beehive oven, they purchased flour from the miller and made the bread themselves. This custom of home baking survived in the North much longer than it did in the rest of England. Elsewhere, the baker would drive his horse-drawn cart through the hamlets on the outskirts of the market town, delivering the large loaves to his customers.

While two of the day's meals were usually sparse (bread or potatoes, a bit of meat or cheese) tea was a substantial one, with as much hot food on the table as the family could afford. While middle-class people were often concerned about the negative social connotations of some foods and thus avoided them regardless of taste, rural folk ate with more abandon. Greens, either cooked or fresh, lots of onion, leeks and garlic, and raw and cooked fruits and vegetables were eaten when available. Children were given leave from school (after school became compulsory in 1880) to gather mushrooms, nuts, apples, and whatever other wild food was in season that their mother could use.

Several varieties of herbs flavored foods and created any number of teas. Thompson's depiction of women's herb gardens in Lark Rise attest to the beauty and the usefulness of what women grew:

> As well as their flower garden, the women cultivated a herb corner, stocked with thyme and parsley and sage for cooking, rosemary to flavour the home-made lard, lavender to scent the best clothes, and peppermint, pennyroyal, horehound, chamomile, tansy, balm, and rue for physic. They made a good deal of chamomile tea, which they drank freely to ward off colds, to soothe the nerves, and as a general tonic. A large jug of this was always prepared and stood ready for heating up after confinements. The horehound was used with honey in a preparation to be taken for sore throats and colds on the chest. Peppermint tea was made rather as a luxury than a medicine; it was brought out on special occasions and drunk from wine-glasses; and the women had a private use for the pennyroyal, though, judging from appearances, it was not very effective.[16]

People relied on wild herbs as well; many gathered yarrow in large quantities to make "yarb beer," a thirst-quenching, highly nutritious drink that when ready, men took in their tea cans as a change from the typical barley water, ginger beer, or cold tea, and that mothers and children drank whenever they were thirsty.

## URBAN WORKING PEOPLE: THEIR FOODS AND MEALS

While Thompson chronicled the lives of an agricultural community and the importance of cured pork, bread, and fresh foods to their diet, other Victorian and Edwardian writers focused on the urban working classes. As migration accelerated and more people relocated to cities, writers detailed their experiences in both fiction and nonfiction. Along with Charles Dickens' novels such as *Oliver Twist* (1837–1839) and Elizabeth Gaskell's *Mary Barton* (1848), journalists wrote about the daily experiences of factory workers, miners, street sellers, carters, navvies, artisans, and the masses whose lives were largely invisible to the well-to-do. Henry Mayhew's *London Labour and the London Poor,* first published serially in the *Morning Chronicle* newspaper from 1850–1851 and George Augustus Sala's *Twice Around the Clock* (1861) are two of the most famous journalistic accounts of working Victorians, and as with Thompson's trilogy, food and cooking figure prominently in both. Once more, pork was an essential food for urban laborers as well as cured fish, particularly herrings, and up through the 1850s when overharvesting made their prices skyrocket, oysters and other shellfish.

In "London Street-Folk," Mayhew interviewed a ham-sandwich seller whose comments regarding his evening tea are indicative of many laborers who lived on 6 to 10 shillings a week. The vendor admits to Mayhew, "Ah, sir! I live very poorly. A ha'porth [half-penny worth] or a penn'orth [penny worth] of cheap fish, which I cook myself, is one of my treats—either herrings or plaice—with a 'tatur, perhaps"[17] Herrings come up again when Mayhew described the lives of the boy street sellers. Two informed Mayhew that they were of course as fond of good living as anyone else, and when settled in business "they always managed to have what they called 'a relish' for breakfast and tea, a couple of herrings, or a bit of bacon, or what not."[18]

The word "relish" comes up frequently in other accounts of working-class diets. For example, George Augustus Sala used the word when describing the diet of workers in "Dock London," a "vast, yet to thousands unknown and unrecked of city" unto itself.[19] At one o'clock, the dock workers rushed back from their twenty-minute meal break, one that likely consisted of nothing or at most a "fragment of hard, dry bread, and the bibulous solace of the nearest [water] pump." Their evening tea, Sala speculated, would likely be "a mess of potatoes, with one solitary red herring smashed up therein, to 'give it a relish.'"[20] Maud Pemberton Reeves noted in *Round About a Pound a Week* (1913) that when the baby is weaned, it, too, gets its share of the family diet, and "if its father be particularly partial to it, a mouthful of fat bacon once or twice a week, spared from the not too generous 'relish to his tea.'"[21]

The urban worker needed a relish. An 1840s Factory Commissioners' report noted that most could only afford the plainest foods; namely, bread and potatoes. Depending on one's wage, the following foods made up the rest of the diet in this order: cheese, butter (or beef fat or lard), sugar, tea, salt, and a tiny amount of bacon or other cheap cured meat such as fish to be used for flavoring. Even in the final decades of the Victorian era when the harshest effects of industrialization were somewhat mitigated and the cost of living had fallen, working-class families had added little to these earlier, bland staples, although processed foods such as condensed milk, canned mutton, margarine, and jam figured more prominently. A highly flavored food like a cured fish made teatime more appetizing and substantive than what it would have seemed otherwise.

## THE DAILY STRUGGLE TO AFFORD MEAT

I began this discussion of laborers' diets with meat not because it was their most common food but because it was the most essential for helping people make it through long days of hard labor. Victorians did not understand fully the science of vitamins and minerals, but they did understand the importance of protein and how to use calories as a unit to measure food's energy. In his groundbreaking study of poverty in York in 1899, one to which I will return in detail in the conclusion of this chapter, Benjamin Seebohm Rowntree (1871–1954) argued that for a man to do a day of "moderate" work, he required 3,500 calories and 137 grams of protein. Women required 2,987 calories and 115.5 grams of protein. To meet those needs, Rowntree calculated that the minimum expenditure that a man had to make for his weekly food was 3 shillings, 3 pence and a woman 2 shillings, 9 pence. Wages for all but the most elite working families however, failed to provide that minimum once lodging and coals for heat were covered. Many hardworking, regularly employed men supporting families consisting of a wife and five children made less than 17 shillings a week, falling short of what was required to keep the family fit.[22] Nonetheless, these families understood that meat was the most important food in the diet and they did everything possible to purchase some meat, even if it were only a "relish" to flavor potatoes and bread.

Indeed, one could gauge a Victorian family's overall health and prosperity by observing how much meat they ate in a week. For example, if a family sat down to meat at every meal and could afford the best cuts of beef, mutton, game, as well as poultry and fresh fish, that family was undoubtedly rich. If the family could afford to sit down to meat at four to eight meals a week, with much of it coming in the form of leftovers from Sunday's roast, the family was likely middle-class. If the family could sit down to meat less than three or four times a week, and the majority of it was bacon, offal, cheap sausages, or cured fish, then the family was likely working-class. If there was no meat or if meat were limited to rancid dripping to flavor the water in which the potatoes were boiled, the family was in poverty.

Most working-class wives, even if they too were employed, reserved the meat for their husbands; they also ensured that no matter what their tea might consist of food-wise, their husbands received the biggest portion of it. Their reasons were not sentimental. Reeves observed that "the father of the family cannot eat less. He is already eating as little as will enable him to earn the family wage. To starve him would be bad economy . . . The rest of the family can eat less without bothering anybody—and do."[23] Most working families rarely, if ever, could afford the choicest cuts of beef or mutton, and so in cities, their most important protein source was fish, particularly cured herring.

Most of the herring came from Yarmouth where the catch was harvested and cured in autumn and from Northumbria and Scotland where the catch was harvested and cured in the spring; herring's importance to the English diet in general takes us back at least as far as Elizabethan times.[24] Thomas Nashe, born in Lowestoft, a fishing port in eastern England, wrote in his last work *Lenten Stuffe* (1599) that the curing method for red herring was discovered when a Yarmouth man hung his excess catch from the rafters where, in the smoke of the fire, they turned from white to red. Bloaters, or herrings that were left whole instead of being split before curing, were equally popular. While the first herring customers may have been English folk looking to buy fish for their fasting days, trade never fell away with a change in religion or politics; new buyers continually appeared.[25] By the Victorian era, cured herring had become even more common in a laborer's diet because the salt tax was abolished in 1825, thus making the fish cheaper.

In capturing the cacophony of Lambeth's New Cut market on Saturday night when poor people shopped, Mayhew drew out the voices of Yarmouth bloater vendors:

> "Buy, buy, buy, buy, buy—bu-u-uy!" cries the butcher. "Half-quire of paper for a penny," bellows the street stationer. "An 'aypenny a loting-uns!" "Two-pence a pound grapes." "Three a penny Yarmouth bloaters." "Who'll buy a bonnet for fourpence? . . . " "Here's ha'p'orths," shouts the perambulating confectioner. "Come and look at 'em! here's toasters!" bellows one with a Yarmouth bloater stuck on a toasting-fork. "Penny a lot, fine russets," calls the apple woman: and so the Babel goes on.[26]

Three bloaters for a penny was a splurge for Saturday night tea or Sunday breakfast.

Whenever possible, working-class people also ate fresh fish, particularly plaice, eel, and mackerel. In the early Victorian era, oysters were extremely cheap and thus the most popular shellfish among the urban laboring classes. They were harvested very close to London, with easy water transport to Billingsgate, the main fish market. They were in unlimited supply until the 1860s when beds were developed off the coasts of Sussex. The price fell due to oversupply, the beds were soon exhausted, and then disease and bad weather combined to make what had been a limitless food very rare and thus extremely expensive. Literally overnight, oysters became the food of the wealthy, along with turtle, lobster, and salmon.

Urban workers also ate pork because it took less salt than other meat to cure, and thus it was cheap. As with cured fish, bacon was especially popular because it imparted a lot of flavor for little price. Popular foods based on pork scraps included spicy sausages called saveloys and faggots. Sometimes called "savoury ducks" in the North, faggots were made of ground pig liver, breadcrumbs or oatmeal, grated suet, onion, and typical sausage spices such as sage, mace, thyme, salt, and pepper. The mixture was formed into "fingers" to make a link-sausage shape, or it was patted into a baking pan, cut into squares to be used later as sandwich filling, and baked. For her husband's tea, a wife would reheat the faggots in a frying pan and serve them with gravy alongside a mound of potatoes. Cured fish, sausages, faggots, and bacon were all "fast food" for those who had limited time, inferior cooking equipment, and little money to expend on fuel.

Working-class people sometimes could afford cheap cuts of mutton, such as the scrag (neck meat), and cheap beef, called "pieces"—the leftover tough bits. Both scrag and pieces demanded long stewing to make them tender. As a result, a mutton stew or steamed beef pudding were typically reserved for Sunday dinner when people had more time to make their food and either had enough money to pay a baker to cook the finished product for them (a couple of pennies at most) or had the appropriate cooking utensils and equipment at home to see to it themselves. A cheap knuckle joint from a cow or sheep and ox-cheek soup were also common Sunday dinner foods that many enjoyed.

The price of meat began to fall in the 1850s, and by the early 1870s, canned meat was a cheaper alternative to fresh. Fray Bentos' Corned Beef (still remembered by Britons who grew up in the 1940s, 1950s, and 1960s) was shipped from a canning factory in Uruguay to England and became a working-class staple; like faggots and bacon, it was easily sliced and made into sandwiches. Canned mutton, imported from Australia, cost between 5 and 7 pence for a half-pound— half the price of fresh. In 1876, Frenchman Charles Tellier built a ship equipped with a refrigeration system and it was only a matter of three or so years before England began to import fresh meat from the United States and Australia. The meat's quality was consistently low if not bad. It was generally bargained for at street markets catering to the poor, but for those with no alternative other than to go without, the meat was seen as necessary and sales in it were brisk.

If meat was more often a relish or a flavoring than a source of food in and of itself, we must ask, what was it flavoring? Bread and potatoes constituted the bulk of the urban worker's diet, and such was more the case for women and children than it was for men. Even when the working-class food budget dropped by 30 percent in the 1870s, bread still remained the chief article of diet in a 20 shilling weekly London budget, followed by potatoes, and then as pennies were available, meat and fish. Potatoes and bread touch on the two most significant events in English culinary history as it relates to the laboring classes: land enclosure, and Corn Laws in effect between 1815 and 1846.

## THE EFFECT OF LAND ENCLOSURES ON WORKING-CLASS DIETS

Laborers never enjoyed a rich, plentiful diet, but for many centuries they had recourse to one essential advantage that was a distant memory by the 1880s: access to common land. These untenanted expanses had allowed people to graze some livestock if they had it, forage for wild food and fuel, and in some instances, grow enough of their own grain to supply them with bread. Heavy, dark, and coarse, homemade bread was filling, and when spread with butter or lard and topped with farmhouse cheese, it made a highly nutritious meal. Bread, butter, and cheese eaten along with cabbages or other greens kept laborers from going hungry, and many lived to old age without debilitating diseases. Enclosure of common land, which began in earnest in the eighteenth century and accelerated in the early nineteenth, had a dire effect on thousands of workers' diets and well-being. The reasons for land enclosure were complicated and based on a number of interrelated factors, some of which are briefly outlined below.

In 1751, the population of England and Wales was just under six million, and by 1801, it had risen by 50 percent to roughly nine million. In the next fifty years, the rate of growth doubled, putting the population at almost seventeen million by 1851.[27] At the same time that the population was exploding, wars were breaking out across Europe, and the Napoleonic Wars directly involved Great Britain. Both factors—war and an exploding population—were serious threats to national security, particularly because famine could result from both as well as a revolution. Land enclosure that was carried out quite literally by enclosing vast acres of common land with stone fences and high hedgerows was partly the result of agricultural reform designed to allay the fear of a famine and partly the result of economic greed.

To understand better the effect that came from land enclosure, it helps to recall how English land had traditionally been distributed and worked. If we remember back to the first chapter in this history, most English people, including the middle classes, had always been "landless." In *The Landed Interest and the Supply of Food* (1878), James Caird set out how the system worked. Approximately 180,000 people possessed "the whole of the agricultural land from 10 acres upwards," wrote Caird. These aristocrats and gentry rented their land to a class of tenant-farmers "whose business [was] the cultivation of the land, with a capital quite independent of the landowner."[28] The most powerful and successful of these tenant-farmers were often called gentlemen farmers or squires; they did not actually do physical labor but instead hired others to work on their farms in exchange for a wage, housing, and usually an allotment on which to grow food and keep some livestock. Other tenant-farmers were not so rich and powerful; they worked alongside their hired laborers in order to bring in the harvests, and they lived humble lives. Many rural people, including small farmers, laborers, and people who lived in villages and hamlets relied both on their gardens and on neighboring common land to supplement their food supply and thus, kept from going hungry or malnourished.

This intricate system where the well-being of the laborer was in part contingent on the well-being of the tenant-farmer and so on up the socioeconomic scale was ultimately destroyed by land enclosure, although in some regions such as Oxfordshire, the breakup of the system was slower than in others. Wealthy tenant-farmers had traditionally been obligated to their laborers. They provided cheap or free housing, paid them a yearly wage (even when weather did not permit or demand a lot of work), and also gave yearly bonuses of food, beer, and monetary gifts at harvest time and Christmas. Laborers likewise had obligations to the farmers, including their commitment to work very long hours especially during sowing and harvesting. This sense of mutual obligation had its roots in feudal times.

By the late 1700s and early 1800s "land hunger," or a drive on the part of investors to make larger profits off the land, translated into sharply increased rents on property and hundreds of tenant-farmers who had worked and lived on the same land for generations were now being evicted by landowners interested in greater profit. Some landowners would buy and join adjacent farms and they in turn would be financed by outside investors—at the expense of the tenant-farmers who ran farms on that land and hired laborers to work for them. Farmers still farmed, of course, but they were paying higher rents to do so, and fewer farmers were needed if the stretches of land were consolidated. To afford higher rents, many farmers abandoned yearly hiring practices and instead employed laborers on a seasonal basis, or in the worst times, a weekly or even daily basis. Laborers' wages as well as job security decreased, particularly in the South where a surplus of laborers drove wages down to less than subsistence level. Where industry was competing with agriculture in the North and the Midlands, laborers fared better.

Exacerbating the problems associated with this new way of managing farmland was some landowners' decision to claim to what had before been considered marginal (or unprofitable) acreage and turn it into grazing pasture to support an increasingly profitable sheep industry. Because of their vast stretches of unarable or hard-to-farm land, Scotland and Wales would likewise feel the harsh effects of these enclosure policies. Sheep had to be contained, so fences were built. By 1850, over six million acres of English common land had been enclosed and turned into private holdings.[29]

The result of such enclosures can be glimpsed in the statistics of rural-to-urban migration. In 1801, there were only five towns aside from London with over 50,000 inhabitants: Birmingham, Bristol, Leeds, Liverpool, and Manchester. By 1851, these were joined by seventeen more.[30] By that same year, roughly half the population was located in urban areas. During the first part of the nineteenth century, Leeds, an important center of cloth weaving, grew from 53,000 to 172,000 people. Sheffield, center of the steel industry, saw its population quadruple in the same time-span.[31] London, always England's largest city, likewise experienced rapid growth with its population quadrupling in just over a century.[32] Industry and technological advances were creating jobs for thousands of these displaced rural workers, and some of them found more independence and better employment in factories and various industries, including rail and ship building, construction, and mercantile trades. Others had a much more difficult transition. Crowded into cities where land for growing food was sharply curtailed and where living quarters were cramped, people who only a generation (or less) before had been able to grow and produce much of their own food, now no longer had the room, equipment, time, or money to do so.

Enclosure was not simply about capitalist greed. The threats of war worsening and of the nation being underequipped to withstand consequent hardships were also important catalysts to agricultural reforms. Napoleon's policy of achieving victory over England by starving the nation was a serious threat. The Berlin and Milan decrees of December 1806 and December 1807 forbid first the French and then neutral ships from entering British ports. Although the decrees were never fully enforced, the English government and farmers accelerated aggressive agricultural reforms as a result of the war.[33] By consolidating properties and using advanced crop rotation techniques, reformers argued, much greater crop yields would result. Furthermore, it was more rational, many experts argued, to consolidate scattered, common fields and turn them into huge, uninterrupted ones that could then be more efficiently worked. The complexity of this situation—attempting to feed the nation by displacing a large number of its most vulnerable workers—is summarized best by historian John Burnett in his classic study *Plenty and Want: A Social History of Food in England from 1815 to the Present Day*:

> The ability of English agriculture practically to keep pace with a population growth of unprecedented speed and size was a remarkable achievement, made possible by more intensive methods of farming, the employment of new rotational systems and the cultivation of wide areas of formerly waste or common land. The disappearance of the commons was the hard price the labourer had to pay for the maintenance of his dietary standard at something like a constant level at a time when the growing pressure of population upon the land could have been as disastrous for England as it was for Ireland.[34]

Burnett recognized that thousands suffered initially as a result of enclosure and agricultural reform, but farmers were for the time able to produce larger grain yields. The average annual import of wheat between 1801 and 1810 was a mere 600,000 quarters. It did rise to 1,900,000 in the 1840s and varied from year to year, depending on harvests, but nonetheless, England's grain imports were only large when harvests were bad; otherwise, until the 1840s and 1850s, the nation could essentially supply itself.[35]

## THE CORN LAWS AND THEIR EFFECT ON THE WORKING-CLASS DIET

When the Napoleonic Wars ended in 1815, the nation had to adjust to peacetime—itself a potential threat because people had become used to a wartime world where food shortages and erratic prices were explainable, no matter how hard to live with. The same year that the war ended, the British Parliament passed a series of protectionist measures known as the Corn Laws. Although not new to England (Corn Laws of one sort or another had been used since the 1300s to control the export and import of grain), the ones passed in 1815 were meant to ensure the strength of the English wheat market and to prevent the nation from slipping into an agricultural depression. Designed to tax imported Continental wheat and thus keep it out of the market when English harvests were sufficient, the Corn Laws allowed the landowners and wealthy tenant farmers to make a high profit from grain sales and, equally important, let the English government stabilize and perhaps increase its national revenue by collecting tariffs on imported wheat, along with its tariffs on other staples such as sugar, tea, and coffee.[36]

From their inception, the Corn Laws were unpopular with working-class consumers because the cost of living remained high. While grain prices were protected, laborers' wages were not; they were paid what the market would bear. Increasing numbers of people were forced to live on a subsistence diet because the price of bread and flour were higher than many could easily afford, even though for middle-class people, bread was so cheap that it was treated as a negligible expense. Such hardship was particularly the case in urban areas where people were more dependent on bakers to supply bread for them, as well as in rural areas where wheat, rather than oats or barely, was the staple grain. Budgets collected by Parliamentary committees investigating rates of agricultural wages and conditions of laborers bore out the fact that most laborers did not make enough money to save anything, no matter how careful they were. The Poor Law Commissioners on women's and children's employment in agriculture in 1843 offered as representative the weekly budget of Robert Crick, his wife, and their five children. Crick's wage of 9 shillings went entirely to buying bread; his wife and three of the children (the three old enough to work, with the youngest of that three only eight years old) had to work to buy everything else. The family's total earnings per week amounted to 13 shillings, 9 pence; the family's total weekly expenditure was likewise 13 shillings, 9 pence.[37]

As a result of workers having to spend the majority of their food budget on bread, their diets lacked adequate protein, fat, vitamins, and minerals; many were consuming up to 70 percent carbohydrates a day. Bakery bread by this time, be it for rich or poor, was typically white and adulterated by alum, a harmless chemical, but one whose weight replaced that of flour and which contributed to making the bread nutritionally unsound. David Davies, Rector of Barkham, Berkshire, commented angrily that a day-laborer was forced on his wage to choose between "the daily bread which is to sustain" his children's bodies and "that other bread, which is to nourish their souls, and prepare them for a future state of being." His account of a family having just enough money to eat but not enough to send children to school or pay for them to enter an apprenticeship was illustrative of other families' despair and frustration during the early decades of industrialization. Schooling for all children in England and Wales was not available for free until 1891. The cheapest schools cost 2 pence or 3 pence a week, and although to middle-class families such a fee was a "pittance," in working families, Davies argued, that "pittance is wanted for so many other purposes that it would be missed in the family."[38]

Of course, not all working people were adversely affected by Corn Laws, enclosure, and urban industrialization. In the strata between the unskilled, displaced laborer and the increasingly powerful middle-classes were those whose expertise was in demand. Some earned enough money to raise them financially to a living standard comparable to that of lower-middle-class people. Among the highest paid of all artisans, the London compositors, for example, made as much as £2, 9 pence a week.[39] On this wage, a compositor with a wife and two children could afford to buy bread and flour, vegetables, 14 pounds of meat at 9 pence a pound, vinegar, salt, pepper, 2 pounds of sugar, butter, cheese, and three pints of porter a day. He could clothe his family, and most significantly, send his children to school, which in 1810 cost him 1 shilling, 6 pence a week for two. When his sons were old enough, he could pay the fee to have them apprenticed and thus ensure to the best of his ability that when they were trained, they would have work and a modicum of respect. If he had social ambition, he could opt to continue his sons' and daughters' schooling in hopes that such a path would offer his children better prospects.

Because urbanization resulted in both competition as well as social imitation among all classes, prosperous working people routinely purchased and enjoyed using such goods as coal-fired ranges, modern cutlery, and other tableware: the "fruits," so to speak, of industrialization. They ate foods that suggested their modest prosperity (particularly mutton and beef) and they applied the same etiquette and manners that made them comparable to middle-class people. However when a job disappeared or a breadwinner was injured and unable to work, poverty could set in quickly, eating up any small savings, forcing children to quit school and go immediately to work, and bringing a family into debt or worse, the workhouse.

Several first-hand accounts detail how an untimely misfortune could ruin a working-class family's aspirations. A widow, for example, remembered that before her husband's death, they and their young son enjoyed a diet that included "four gallons [roughly 32 pounds] of bread a week, 1 lb or 1½ lb of cheese, bacon, salt beef, butter, tea, sugar . . . and soap, with beer on Saturday night." She continued: "Since my husband's death, the [Poor Law] Guardians allow 1s 6d [pence] a week for the child, and I earn 4s 6d a week." This sharply reduced allowance thus resulted in their diet changing from 4 gallons of bread per week to 1½ gallons, butter and sugar reduced to ¼ pound each, a mere 1½ pence-worth of tea, and no meat or cheese. The widow was luckily able to maintain the rental of their garden allotment, thus allowing her to produce potatoes and "also this last year, three bushels of wheat." She noted that each week she had left over from all of her food costs 1 shilling, 8 pence "for firing [fuel], shoes, which cost a great deal, etc."[40]

The widow's mention of potatoes supplementing her and the child's diet leads us to the second staple food of the working classes. A seemingly innocuous food, the potato was lauded by some as the most valuable food source in keeping people from starving and simultaneously damned by others for encouraging laziness on the part of workers, for demoralizing them, even for turning them into brutes. No discussion of early Victorian cuisine would be complete without an assessment of the potato's introduction to Europe and particularly the British Isles. At the very least, the potato was a catalyst to Prime Minster Peel abolishing the Corn Laws in 1846.

## THE POTATO'S IMPORTANCE TO THE WORKING-CLASS DIET

The most ominous obstacle to working people maintaining a healthy diet was the price of food. Between 1836 and 1841, food prices turned sharply upward while wages remained stagnant or fell. Working people turned to potatoes as the most reliable, cheap food available. While potatoes never matched bread's popularity in England, they were eaten by working people because they could be easily stored, were convenient, simple to cook, easy to grow on limited land, and filling. Prosperous people also came to appreciate and love the potato; it was the most popular starch on any Victorian family's dinner table, regardless of class. Wealthy Victorians typically ate expensive new potatoes, while poor people purchased inexpensive older ones.

The potato controversy had to do with society's debate on how to react to and address increasing poverty. It also concerned the anger and desperation of the laborers themselves. As widespread malnutrition and even starvation began to manifest itself during the late 1830s and 1840s, many people initially blamed the poor's condition on the poor, arguing that if they would stop relying on potatoes as their main food source and return to baking their own bread, brewing their own beer, and eating pottages and soups as they used to eat in the "old days," then they would have more money and thus, be less hungry.

However, as this history has tried to make clear, one of industrialization's effects was to increase people's reliance on others to procure and prepare their food, irrespective of whether they were satisfied by that outcome or not. Nonetheless, many well-meaning authorities, including Queen Victoria's former chef, Charles Francatelli, and the journalist and social reformer William Cobbett, persisted in arguing that if poor people would cook their own food, they could cut significant expenditure out of their limited budget, improve their diets, and improve their work ethic. Such was Francatelli's rationale in *A Plain Cookery Book for the Working Classes* (1852). He addressed his working-class readers in this fashion:

> And now a few words on baking your own bread. I assure you if you would adopt this excellent practice, you would not only effect a great saving in your expenditure, but you would also insure a more substantial and wholesome kind of food; it would be free from potato, rice, bean or pea flour, and alum, all of which substances are objectionable in the composition of bread. The only utensil required for bread-making would be a tub, or trough, capable of working a bushel or two of flour. This tub would be useful in brewing, for which you will find in this book plain and easy directions.[41]

Francatelli, an Italian-born chef who trained in Paris and was considered one of the era's most important innovators when it came to cuisine, had seemingly little understanding of the living and working conditions of those he was trying to address. Along with the purchase of a tub or trough for making bread, Francatelli listed what he believed to be the minimum number of utensils that a housewife must possess in order to prepare nutritious and economical food. The total expenditure amounted to £6, 12 shillings, 4 pence—savings he imagined to be within the means of those who, because of "industry, good health, and constant employment," have been able to "lay by"[42] (see Table 5.1).

Many working-class families subsisted on budgets that might net them annually as little as £20–40 at mid-century, and as we have seen above, few had any means, no matter how much they economized and no matter how hard they worked, to save that much extra money. Buying cooking equipment, no matter the soundness of Francatelli's rationale, was almost always an impossibility for many working families, and if Reeves' *Round About a Pound a Week* is a reliable indication, such remained the case into the twentieth century. Poor urban people usually had two saucepans—both burnt—a tea kettle, and a frying pan. Furthermore, Reeves continued, "the certainty of an economical stove or fireplace is out of the reach of the poor. They are often obliged to use old-fashioned and broken ranges and grates which devour coal with as little benefit to the user as possible."[43]

Earlier in the century, Cobbett had likewise contended that the poor were culpable in their plight because they did not economize by growing their own vegetables, baking their own bread, and brewing their own beer. Cobbett believed that homemade beer and bread were the most wholesome foods available. Brewing and baking went together, after all. A housewife collected the barm, or foamy yeast, which appeared on the top of the malt liquor as it fermented and

Table 5.1. List and Cost of Items Deemed Essential to a Kitchen

| | £ | s. | d. |
|---|---|---|---|
| A cooking-stove, 2 ft. 6 in. wide, with oven only | 1 | 10 | 0 |
| A cooking-stove, 2 ft. 6 in. wide, with oven and boiler | 1 | 18 | 0 |
| A three-gallon oval boiling pot | 0 | 4 | 6 |
| A one-gallon tin saucepan, and lid | 0 | 2 | 6 |
| A two-quart tin saucepan, and lid | 0 | 1 | 6 |
| A potato steamer | 0 | 2 | 0 |
| An oval frying-pan, from | 0 | 0 | 10 |
| A gridiron, from | 0 | 1 | 0 |
| A copper for washing or brewing, 12 gallons | 1 | 10 | 0 |
| A mash-tub, from | 0 | 10 | 0 |
| Two cooling-tubs (or an old wine or beer cask cut in halves, would be cheaper, and answer the same purchase), each 6 s | 0 | 12 | 0 |
| *Total* | £6 | 12 | 4 |

*Source:* Charles Francatelli, *A Plain Cookery Book for the Working Classes* (London: Routledge, Warne, and Routledge, 1852), 10.

used it for making her dough rise. Cobbett argued that not only was it cheaper for housewives to do both baking and brewing themselves but the finished products would also be vastly superior to the adulterated, filthy stuff one bought from bakers and publicans. However, Cobbett went further than Francatelli by declaring that the potato was fundamentally at the heart of poor people's plight. In the late 1700s and early 1800s, many people—not just Cobbett—were adding their voices to the potato debate, one that began shortly after wrecked Spanish ships spilled potatoes onto Irish shores in 1588, the year that England defeated the Spanish Armada.

Possibly, the Irish were among the first after the Spanish to see the advantages of growing potatoes. It quickly proved its value as a food crop because unlike grains that could be easily destroyed (particularly in wartime and skirmishes when Irish fields became battlegrounds), potatoes remained hidden under soil and humus and could be raised on tiny allotments and still produce a prodigious amount of food. The English, however, associated the vegetable with the Irish and therein lay the first problem: English people did not wish to see themselves on the same level as the Irish. By 1663, Mr. Buckland, a Somerset gentleman and member of the Royal Agriculture Society, had argued that if the potato could save thousands from starving in Ireland, it could do as much in England.[44] The English stigma against potatoes remained entrenched until a series of disastrous harvests in the 1790s made them a necessity in most workers' diets from that point on. Although many authorities continued to resist the potato, the British Board of Agriculture convincingly argued that people could be nourished completely on potatoes, water, and salt alone—and that such a diet would even enhance human enjoyment of eating.[45] Adam Smith agreed, noting that an acre of potatoes produced as much food as three acres of wheat, and as a result, potatoes could maintain a larger population.[46] Slowly, the stigma against potatoes dissipated and it was accepted throughout England as a cheap and filling food, the easiest to grow and cook.

That was precisely the problem for many critics, particularly Cobbett. Growing potatoes was a stop-gap measure; it filled people's bellies certainly, but at the loss of what? Some politicians believed that poor people's reliance on this "lazy man's vegetable" would continue to hold them down, making it impossible for them to improve their lot through the natural medicines of hard work and discipline. Eating potatoes, Cobbett concluded in *Cottage Economy* (1835), engenders among the poor "slovenly and beastly habits." All a man must do, he indignantly continued, is lift the potato to his mouth without even having to use any "implements other than the hands and the teeth." By "dispensing with everything requiring skill in the preparation of the food, and requiring cleanliness in its consumption or preservation," entire families devolve into brutes. In regards then to nourishment, work ethic, and common manners, Cobbett reiterated, "bread is the preferable diet."[47] However, baking bread was impossible for many working people, and Cobbett's and Francatelli's laying out directions in laborious detail as well as itemizing how many pennies might be saved from baking as opposed to buying bread was tragically irrelevant for the reasons we have thus far examined, i.e., no room, no equipment, no adequate cooking facilities, and no time.

Added to these reasons, increasingly, was no knowledge. Charles Dickens was one of the few famous authors to speak publicly about the realities that urban laborers faced rather than ignoring them or blaming them for their hunger and despair. In his weekly magazine *Household Words*, he and his contributors informed a reform-minded middle-class readership about the challenges that sober and hardworking people endured when it came to preparing wholesome food. For example, in 1852 the journalist and economist Harriet Martineau described for *Household Words* readers a Birmingham school open to all working-class women who desired to learn writing, arithmetic, reading, sewing, and cooking. Martineau recognized that working women had little choice but to rely on others for prepared food and she endorsed the idea of teaching them how to cook. More importantly, she argued persuasively that even if they had the knowledge to cook, time was their main problem, and she condemned factory owners who made it impossible for women to undertake some of their work at home and thus allow them to let the baby sleep in the cradle while the "stew is simmering on the fire."[48]

As the negative effects of industrialization reverberated throughout communities, social reformers and average citizens alike grew appalled and ashamed by the number of gaunt, haggard people—particularly children and women—in their midst. Manuscript cookbooks of the 1830s and 1840s suggest how surrounding poverty affected many middle-class families; their recipes and descriptions echo those of Agnes Beaufoy's manuscript cookery book that I discussed in the first chapter of this history. The Willis family in Brace-boro', Lincolnshire, kept a cookbook from 1833 to 1861, some of the hardest decades for many laborers because of Corn Laws and the Irish potato famine. Like others of its time, the Willis's cookbook contained recipes that call for ingredients beyond the budgets of the working class: meat, butter, eggs, loaf sugar, citrus fruits, spices, and delicacies. Alongside such recipes, however, are lists of what to distribute to the poor in the area, including yards of calico and flannel as well as food. The Willis family also recorded the names of suffering families in their vicinity. Many had between five and eight children with fathers out of work and mothers too sick to take care of children.[49]

A similar manuscript cookbook kept in the 1840s by a Dr. and Mrs. Smith of Bathhampton included several recipes designed to feed the area poor. One soup made fifty gallons; another, also designed to feed many people, included these directions for how to distribute the soup:

> Subscribers should give tickets to those whom they wish to have soup and also send a list of their names to the person who gives it out—if any should be too poor to pay [for] a quart, subscribers might give free tickets equal to the value—taking care that the person supplying the soup should be told the names both of subscribers and of the person who had received a free ticket—this might prevent the tickets being sold which should in some cases probably be the case . . .[50]

As complicated as it might sound today, the system was designed to reserve poor people's sense of self-respect. Although a pint of soup cost a penny and a quart two, the price allowed a family to feel as if it were paying and not merely taking charity. The system also accommodated the worst off or those who could not spare even a penny, and it also allowed better-off people to contribute to the cause by purchasing tickets and distributing them free of charge.

The spirit of reform for which the Victorians are often recognized took place on the national level as well. In 1847, the Ten Hours Act limited women's and children's work in textile factories to 56½ hours a week—what seems an unacceptable number of hours to many today, but which was the first of several reforms that by the end of the century would regulate the number of hours a person could work and also bar young children from working at all. While Parliament was debating working conditions, powerful industrialists joined forces with members of the Anti-Corn-Law League to demand a repeal of the Corn Laws; not only did the laws harm the nation's most vulnerable workers, but they also interfered with the workings of a free-market economy.

As the horrific effects of the European potato blight spread to Ireland by 1845 and resulted in what the Irish call *An Gorta Mór*, the Great Hunger, pressure against the Corn Laws mounted in intensity and potential for violence escalated. From 1845 through as late as 1851, potato crops throughout Ireland, the Scottish Highlands, and also some of northern England turned black and rotted on the ground, starving to death unprecedented numbers of people, mainly Irish laborers whose sole food had often become the potato. In 1846, Prime Minister Sir Robert Peel succeeded in abolishing the Corn Laws, a move that enraged many of his Tories colleagues who represented the landed aristocracy's interests, but also initiated economic reforms that began to result in lower food prices for the nation's poor.

## AT CENTURY'S END

As the century progressed, tariffs that kept up the price of other staples such as sugar and tea also declined or were abolished altogether, and partly as a result the standard of living by the end of the century was better than it had been during the 1830s and 1840s. A number of industrial and technological innovations also helped. By 1900, better-off working families (those living on roughly £2 a week) often had gas cookers in their homes. Attached to the cooker was a penny-in-the-slot meter that allowed people to use only the gas necessary to cook a hot meal; many found this system economical and convenient. Indoor water for many families, better lighting, and sewage disposal also made people's lives easier than they had been, cutting down the risk of infectious diseases and also making it easier for families to cook more of their own food. However, in spite of lower tariffs and food prices in general and in spite of the innovations that new technology brought, the working poor still usually went to bed hungry at night and children were ill equipped for school because of insufficient diets. From 1886 until World War I, roughly 60 percent of a working-class man's income still had to be spent on food, and thus, the difficulty of raising a family out of poverty remained entrenched.[51] Two wars—and the nation's ill-preparedness to fight them—were perhaps the greatest impetus to abolish hunger, along with sustained efforts on the part of social reformers.

The Boer War was the first of two wars that drove home the seriousness of the food problem. When men volunteered to enlist in 1899, roughly 40 percent had to be rejected on grounds that they were physically unfit to serve. Malnourished, stunted, suffering from vitamin deficiencies, and nervous, these men alarmed authorities and validated the findings of three pioneering sociologists who worked on the question of poverty, Charles Booth (1840–1916), Beatrice Potter Webb (1858–1943), and Benjamin Seebohm Rowntree, discussed previously.

Booth, with Potter Webb's assistance, created a comprehensive study of the lives of the London poor and eventually he published his results in a seventeen-volume series entitled *Life and Labour of the People in London* (1891–1903). Influenced by both his father, Joseph Rowntree, and Booth's work and methodology, Benjamin Rowntree decided to study the life of people in York. Gathering data from a sampling of 11,560 York area families in 1899, Rowntree published *Poverty: A Study of Town Life* in 1901 to great critical acclaim. He was interested in the "wage earning" or "working" classes and in particular, whether or not the food the families ate gave them sufficient calories or energy to perform their jobs.

Rowntree determined that 9.9 percent of York's population lived in "primary poverty" where the family's total earnings were "insufficient to obtain the minimum necessaries for the maintenance of merely physical efficiency."[52] Of York's population, 17.9 percent lived in what Rowntree classified as "secondary poverty" where a family's total earnings could have covered the essentials—adequate food, housing, and clothing—but did not because "some portion of [the wage] was absorbed by other expenditure either useful or wasteful."[53] These families' diets were as monotonous and protein-deficient as they had been for much of the Victorian era. Breakfast was bread, butter, and tea. Dinner was bread, butter, tea, and sometimes a cheap meat such as bacon. Early evening tea consisted of (again) bread, butter, and tea, and the last meal, supper, was tea, bread, and sometimes a bit of meat—cured fish, or bacon.[54] If money were too scarce, then supper was no more than one cup of tea with no food. Well into the twentieth century, meat remained the chief expenditure in a working-class family's budget with women and children receiving the smallest amounts. Many families of three to six children only had enough money to feed the children a pound of meat a week between them, usually in the form of cheap stewing pieces served with plenty of potatoes so that mothers could make "great show with the gravy," as Maud Pemberton Reeves expressed it.[55]

That over a fourth of the population in a typical English city such as York suffered from such deprivation was particularly alarming as England prepared to enter World War I. The minister for munitions and soon-to-be prime minister, David Lloyd George, had good cause for alarm. Once again, the world's first industrialized nation discovered on the eve of the war that 41 percent of the 2.5 million eligible men, those theoretically in their physical prime and from all classes of society, were in poor health and unfit for service. It was evident that undernourishment was the reason in most of the cases. "Nutrition," as culinary historian Reay Tannahill put it, "became a political issue."[56] David Lloyd George demanded that munitions workers must have enough food to keep healthy and fit and thus help protect the nation. Factories opened canteens where three-course meals cost as little as 4 pence, meat stews 2 pence, meat pies or mince and potatoes 3 pence.[57] However, these facts and actions belong to the twentieth century. We must conclude this chapter by admitting that the problem of widespread hunger was not solved during Queen Victoria's reign and that it took military conscription to compel the government to institute widespread social programs aimed at raising the nation's standard of living.

# The Effects of Industrial and Technological Innovation on Dinner *à la Française*, 1830–1870

**Plain Family Dinner (January)**
**Sunday.** *1. Boiled turbot and oyster sauce, potatoes. 2. Roast Leg or griskin of pork, apple sauce, brocoli [sic], potatoes. 3. Cabinet pudding, and damson tart made with preserved damsons.*

**Dinner for Ten Persons (January)**
**First Course.**
*Soup à la Reine.*
*Whitings au Gratin. Crimped Cod and Oyster Sauce.*

**Entrees.**
*Tendrons de Veau. Curried Fowl and Boiled Rice.*

**Second Course.**
*Turkey, stuffed with Chestnuts, and Chestnut Sauce.*
*Boiled Leg of Mutton, English Fashion, with Capers Sauce and Mashed Turnips.*

**Third Course.**
*Woodcocks or Partridges. Widgeon.*
*Charlotte à la Vanille. Cabinet Pudding. Orange Jelly. Blancmange.*
*Artichoke Bottoms. Macaroni, with Parmesan Cheese.*

**Dessert and Ices**

—Isabella Beeton, *The Book of Household Management,* 1864 edition.

"Man, it has been said, is a dining animal. Creatures of the inferior races eat and drink; man only dines," began Isabella Beeton in "Dinners and Dining," a chapter in her *Book of Household Management*. Before proceeding to list out eighty-one recommended dinner menus for every month of the year, Beeton continued her reflections: "Dinner . . . is a matter of considerable importance; and a well-served table is a striking index of human ingenuity and resource."[1] We examined in the last chapter how industrialization affected the working classes in regards to their main meal of the day, but how did it affect prosperous people when they sat down to dinner? For Beeton and her readers, dinner epitomized what it meant to live in the world's most powerful nation. Her observation that the meal was a "striking index of human ingenuity and resource" echoed many well-off Victorians' own sense of how industry and technology were transforming cooking and dining into something quite different from what previous generations had known.

These next two chapters explore that transformation: why dinner *à la Française*, the style of dining popular in the eighteenth and early-nineteenth centuries, gave way to dinner *à la Russe* in the latter decades of the nineteenth. Predicated on the traditions and values of preindustrial, agrarian England, dinner *à la Française* celebrated English country cuisine and the values of landed gentry. Dinner *à la Russe*, in contrast, was predicated on new-fashioned values of industrial urban England. Published in the 1860s, Beeton's *Book of Household Management* fell at the crossroads of that transition from one mode to the other, and by focusing loosely on the menus printed above, we can examine the degrees to which industry and technology were responsible for the transition.

## THE ORIGINS OF DINNER *À LA FRANÇAISE*

Dinner *à la Française* is thought to have originated in seventeenth-century France during the reign of Louis XIV. This style of service was a refinement of what prosperous English people had been doing at their banquets as far back as medieval times: serving several dishes of food in two and sometimes three courses. By the eighteenth century, English gentlemen and women continued to serve food in two or three designated courses, but they were also keenly interested in symmetry and beauty of arrangement and the *à la Française* mode captured that sense of elegance and style. However, beyond the number of courses and the symmetrical laying out of dishes on the table that characterized the French formal dinner, the food and the spirit in which it was consumed remained English. Indeed, the heightened sense of patriotism that characterized England during the Napoleonic Wars had an effect on dinner, and the English often rejected French words such as *menu*, *entrée*, or *relevé* in favor of the more prosaic "bill of fare," "side dish," and "remove." The food itself could become, and often was, a patriotic gesture. Spit-roasted joints of British-raised beef, mutton, and pork cooked plainly but expertly; large pies stuffed with quail and duck; tarts full of English fruits such as apples, blackberries, and gooseberries; sweet boiled puddings spiked with dried fruits and swimming in brandy; aged farmhouse cheeses such as Stilton and Cheddar; the sharp accent of homemade pickles to complement the roasted meat; fruit preserves spread thickly on white cottage loaves of bread; and when in season, fresh vegetables and fruits to garnish the roasted joints and adorn the dessert offerings: these were the foods that Georgian and early Victorian gentry most enjoyed.

## THE ORGANIZATION, FOODS, AND VALUES ASSOCIATED WITH DINNER *À LA FRANÇAISE*

French in name but English in spirit, dinner *à la Française* also captured the essence of what the gentry valued about their society and culture prior to full-scale industrialization. Hospitality, conviviality, goodwill, and a celebration of seasonal bounty were all implicitly at the heart of dinner *à la Française,* although from a technical standpoint, dinner *à la Française* in England simply meant that the host carved the meat, the side dishes were placed on the table so that the guests and family could help themselves, and the meal was done in a series of courses. Beyond these basics, variations regarding this style and the types of food people served were numerous and so describing exactly what transpired during the meal is difficult. The service was often modified to fit the needs of a particular family and its tastes, and thus, what follows below is only a guide to how a dinner might have progressed. Meg Dods (the pseudonym for Christian Isabel Johnstone) put the dinner's complexity best when she wrote in *The Cook and Housewife's Manual* (1856): "Bills of fare may be varied in endless ways,—nor can any specific rules be given for selecting dishes for the table, which must depend wholly on fortune, fashion, the season of the year, local situation, and a variety of circumstances."[2]

In the early Victorian era, many prosperous people continued the tradition of their Georgian predecessors by sitting down to dinner in the afternoon in the winter and early evening in the summer. Such a schedule allowed people to make full use of daylight hours and thus conserve fuel. This concern was more typical on nights when the family dined alone and often retired to bed shortly after darkness fell. When the family planned to entertain, they scheduled their dinner parties during a full-moon phase, thus helping to ensure everyone's safe passage home along unlit, often rough roads. Dinner parties of five to six hours were not uncommon because this lengthy timeframe suited the lifestyles of gentry and gentlemen farmers who had the leisure to devote to long meals and a firm enough sense of their social footing to be expansive and generous toward friends and acquaintances. Over the course of an afternoon and evening, the family had time to demonstrate their hospitality and goodwill. Nothing was rushed and guests were made to feel welcome.

On ordinary nights, the family often limited their meal to a fish or soup to start, and then a more substantial course of meat, one or two side dishes, and

Table 6.1. Suggested Family Dinner Menus, Early Victorian Era

**Menu One**
Knuckled of Veal stewed with Rice.
Apple Sauce. Bread and Butter Pudding. Potatoes.
Loin of Pork Roasted.

**Menu Two**
Peas Soup
*(Remove—Boiled Fowl.)*
Oyster Sauce.
Potatoes. Broccoli.
Apple pie.
Roasted Beef.
Benton Sauce.

**Menu Three**
Pig Souse fried in Butter.
*(Remove for Yorkshire Pudding.)*
Potatoes. Peas Soup. Salad.
Roast Veal.

**Menu Four**
Hessian Ragout.
Stewed Beet. Hessian Soup of the above. Potatoes and Onions.
Leg of Lamb roasted.

**Menu Five**
Beef Podovies.
*(Remove—Curd Puddings.)*
Mashed Potatoes. Mutton Broth. Carrots and Turnips.
Neck of Mutton.

*Source: The New Female Instructor; or, Young Woman's Guide to Domestic Happiness* (London: Printed for Thomas Kelly, 1824), 486.

bread. Modest middle-class families incorporated leftover meat from a previous night's joint for their main dish a couple of times a week in order to economize and use up leftovers. If there were a joint, the father carved it while the rest of the family members helped themselves to the remaining dishes (see Table 6.1). After all had eaten their fill, a servant removed the plates, distributed clean ones, and the family finished dinner with a sweet such as a pudding or fruit tart. An evening of relaxation and entertainment followed with cards, games, reading, music, and needlework customary activities. Before retiring, many families ate a small supper, perhaps a sandwich and a mug of ale in summer, or in winter a hot drink such as negus. By the 1830s and 1840s, however, many concluded their day as they had started it, with a cup of tea.

On nights when the family entertained, dinner was more intricate and involved more protocol. Arriving guests mingled with the host, hostess, and their grown-up children in the drawing room for half an hour or so before a servant (in very wealthy families a footman) quietly informed the host that "dinner was upon the table." Isabella Beeton offered the standard procedure from there:

> The host offers his arm to, and places on his right hand at the dinner-table, the lady to whom he desires to pay most respect, either on account of her age, position, or from her being the greatest stranger in the party. If this lady be married and her husband present, the latter takes the hostess to her place at table, and seats himself at her right hand. The rest of the company follow in couples, as specified by the master and mistress of the house, arranging the party according to their rank and other circumstances which may be known to the host and hostess.[3]

No matter if the family dined alone or entertained guests, servants had already placed covered food dishes up and down the table in neat symmetrical lines. A dinner party was designed to showcase and celebrate the abundance and variety that came with each season, and that abundance further reinforced the hospitality and goodwill on which the meal was based. Although the dishes were symmetrically arranged, the table appeared crowded with plates, food, and cutlery. A good hostess, John Trusler advised in *Honours of the Table* (1803), commenced the meal by acquainting her "company with what is to come; or if the whole is put on the table at once, should tell her friends, that they 'see their dinner.'" She should also point out that wine, other beverages, cold meats, and salads were available at the sideboard.[4] In describing the amount of food placed before guests, François de la Rochefoucauld exclaimed in his 1784 book, *A Frenchman in England,* that he did "nothing but eat" from the time that he sat down until the time when he got up from the table.[5] An English host and hostess believed that a lot of food slowly eaten over several hours was essential to showing their hospitality and generosity. These values had been a part of English gentrified culture at least since Norman times.

Dinner commenced with soup or soups, depending on the number of guests and the formality of the occasion. A fish often "removed" the soup. During a course, whenever a main dish was taken away and replaced by another, these dishes were called the "removes." So when the guests were done with the soup, it was removed by the fish. The hostess served the soup; the host carved and served the fish. Servants supplied the diners with bowls and plates that were being kept warm in the plate warmer, a device similar to an elegant bookshelf that stood before the dining-room fireplace or in the kitchen. As each new food required a clean plate or bowl, the amount of porcelain the family had to have on hand could be enormous and its finest pieces were displayed on a large sideboard for all to admire.

PLATE WARMER.—A useful apparatus for warming plates and dishes, either in the kitchen or the dining-room. Those used in the kitchen may be fitted up on the fire-screen on a small scale; these are made of wood lined with tin, and may have a door in the back to take out the plates and dishes. The kind of plate warmer, however, which is most generally used is the one seen in the engraving, and which is both useful and ornamental.

PLEURISY. — Inflammation of the lining membrane of the chest, or the *pleura*, as it is called. This disease is so analogous to inflammation of the substance of the lungs, or pneumonia, as to be a matter of difficulty for medical men sometimes to detect the difference; and as the treatment is almost the same, the two diseases will be treated under one head: see PNEUMONIA. The only special peculiarity in pleurisy is, that being an inflammation of a serious membrane, the pain is more acute, and the pulse harder and sharper than in the corresponding disease of the substance of the lungs, where the pain is deeper, the breathing more oppressed and the pulse fuller and softer, than in pleurisy.

PLOUGH.—In this well-known agricultural implement, various improvements have been from time to time introduced. In Kent the turn-wrist plough is common, and is considered superior to all others for its particular purposes. It is intended for under-surface ploughing, so as to clear the ground from grass and rubbish, as well as to loosen the soil. It is adapted for crossing the ridges, as well as for ploughing in a line with the common furrows, and it may be used so as to lay the stitches on lands rounding or flat, as desired. This implement lays the furrows all in the same direction from one side of the field to the other, and this is effected by the alteration of the wrist, which occupies to a considerable extent the place of the ordinary mould-board, laying over the seam in the same way. In Howard's Prize Plough the improvements consist in greater elegance of design, more equal proportions, and the furrow-turners being made particularly tapering and regular in their curve, and formed upon exact geometrical principles; the furrow-slice is thus made to travel at a uniform rate, from its being first cut, until left in its final position, the power required to work the implement is considerably lessened, and the furrows are laid more evenly and in the best form to receive the seed, as well as working much cleaner upon land inclined to adhere or load to the breast or furrow-turner. The shares are fixed to lever necks of wrought-iron, made upon an improved principle, the raising or lowering of which gives the point greater or less "pitch," or inclination, as the share wears or as the state of the land may require. The superiority of this lever neck over others is its great simplicity, and its being tightened at the end instead of by a bolt through the side. When raised or lowered (which can be done instantly) it is secured in a series of grooves; the iron is thus brought into a state of tension, ensuring firmness as well as increasing strength. The centre pin upon which the lever works is a fixture to the neck, and takes its bearing close to the head or socket of the share, so that the top of the share is not raised above or below the point of the breast when moved into higher or lower grooves. The lever neck has another great advantage over any other, the accumulation of earth inside the plough, in most instances, renders the lever useless, as it cannot be moved without a great deal of trouble, but in this arrangement by simply taking off the end next the neck, it may be at once disconnected from the plough, and any obstacle preventing its free action removed. The axles of the wheels are upon a new principle, and are made so that no grit can enter, nor any oil or grease escape. The wheels, therefore, wear much longer, the axles require little or no repairing, and the friction is considerably reduced. The mode of fixing the wheels is also peculiar. The holdfasts, or clumps securing them, are made to slide



Plate warmer in *Dictionary of Daily Wants* (1858–1861). This ornamental plate warmer would have been a tasteful addition to the family's dining room. The inside is lined with tin to help retain heat, and the cabinetry would have been of wood, perhaps walnut. Illustration courtesy of the Morse Department of Special Collections, Hale Library, Kansas State University.

Once diners had taken their fill of fish and soup, the servants again distributed clean plates and guests turned to a variety of tempting foods set out on the table, many of which were meat-based or "made up" with sauces and gravies. Fashionable people were also calling the dishes entrées by the time that Beeton was writing but many continued to call them "made" or "side dishes" as they had called them earlier in the nineteenth century. They might include curries, fricassees, oyster patties with gravy, or croquettes composed of minced meat and egg and fried in clarified butter or beef dripping. While a man might take as much food and drink as he desired (as long as he stayed within the bounds of decorum and did not keep the others waiting for the next course) women were to demur politely to second helpings and were to take only small servings. John Trusler wrote that "as eating a great deal is deemed indelicate in a lady" because "her character should be rather divine than sensual," it would be "ill-manners to help her to a large slice of meat at once, or fill her plate too full."[6] However, the extensive number of dishes on the table for an elegant party meant that no diner, male or female, was expected to eat everything.

Fish, soup, and side dishes were designed in part to make a dent in the guests' appetite before servants brought in the *pièces de résistance,* or the main joints, such as a roast leg of mutton, a roast sirloin of beef, or a boiled beef knuckle. Sometimes, the roast was called a remove, as it was technically removing the fish and/or soup; sometimes it constituted the second course, as it does in Beeton's menu at the beginning of this chapter. Once more, the host was in charge of carving the meat. Because it was difficult to be both efficient and artful, carving was considered a challenge and some culinary historians suggest that it was probably one of the reasons that the *à la Française* mode fell out of fashion. Dinner *à la Russe* relegated carving to servants who did it at the sideboard or in the kitchen, thus saving the master the challenge of trying to accomplish it while people patiently waited for him to finish. An incompetent carver jeopardized the pace of the meal; if he were slow, those served first would find their meat cold by the time the others were served. Meg Dods stressed that carving is in fact "a test at first sight of the breeding of men, as its dexterous and graceful performance is presumed to mark a person trained in good fashion."[7]

Along with the various dishes of food, diners also chose from a variety of drinks. Up through the first half of the nineteenth century, only the most ostentatious and wealthy hosts offered guests French Champagne. It could be either red or white and typically it was not effervescent. More traditional and patriotic hosts stuck to port, mainly because it was relatively cheap due to the 1703 Methuen Treaty between Britain and Portugal. Britain's oldest ally could ship port and other fortified wines, such as sherry, to England with only a nominal duty attached. In the early nineteenth century, claret (what the English called French Bordeaux) had not yet gained popularity, in part because of its expense and also because it was French. Samuel Johnson's contempt for claret was famous, with him remarking in April, 1779 to Sir Joshua Reynolds that "a man would be drowned by it before it made him drunk. . . . No Sir, claret is the liquor for boys; port for men," Johnson concluded.[8] Writing in 1856, George Dodd noted that "so much encouragement has been offered to the drinking of heavy port, in comparison with light French and German wines, and so much does this port undergo sophistication to adapt it to the popular English taste, that foreigners are prone to deny to us any power of really appreciating good wine . . . Four fifths of all the wine we drink are port and sherry."[9] Fortified wines lost in popularity when in 1861 Prime Minister William Gladstone imposed a duty on alcohol that was based on the product's strength, not its country of origin. French and German wines then rose in esteem and claret became a dinner-party requisite. If ill-will toward the French waned by the 1860s, no doubt lower prices on their wine helped.

Because diverse dishes constituted each course, no one was required to drink a particular wine or ask specifically for beer or wine at any point. Insisting on the importance of generosity rather than the importance of one's personal tastes, Trusler cautioned the host and hostess:

> If any of the company seem backward in asking for wine, it is the part of the master to ask or invite them to drink, or he will be thought to grudge his liquor; and it is the part of the mistress or master to ask those friends who seem to have dined, whether they would please to have more. As it is unseemly in ladies to call for wine, the gentleman present should ask them in turn, whether it is agreeable to drink a glass of wine.[10]

After the diner selected his beverage, the servant chose the appropriate glass at the sideboard and proceeded to fill it three-quarters full. He placed the glass on a small tray called a "waiter" to present it to the diner. When one finished his or her drink, the servant removed the glass and placed it on the sideboard so that it could be used again if the diner requested the same kind of drink. If a different one were requested, the servant produced the requisite clean glass and repeated the procedure.[11] Families drank home-produced beer, cider, or fruit wines such as elderberry or gooseberry on ordinary nights. Imported mineral water and effervescent water were popular nonalcoholic offerings. Adding to dinner *à la Française*'s convivial spirit was the relatively limited role that servants played. While they were present to announce dinner, supply plates, and assist the master and mistress with passing soup and meat, they were dismissed at key points in the meal. In some families, wine bottles were placed on the table during all courses so that diners could help themselves, thus eliminating even more need for servants and allowing diners opportunities to speak openly.

When guests had taken their fill of meat and side dishes, the servant cleared the table, brushed off crumbs, and laid the table for the next course, using the indentations from the previous dishes to know where to place the new ones. Rich game often came at this juncture in the meal, along with more savory side dishes such as a baked macaroni and parmesan or cheddar cheese, a fricassee of mushrooms, scalloped oysters topped with breadcrumbs, or maybe "asparagus pease," asparagus cut to resemble peas, boiled, and topped with butter. Sweet dishes as well as savory ones might appear for all the courses, but by Beeton's time, the hostess often saved sweets for the second or third course. Baked custard, cakes, fruit pies, and a fancy pudding were typical dinner-party fare.

People today call the sweets that come at the end of dinner "dessert" (or in England, the "pudding," no matter if it be a pudding or not), but to Victorians, dessert was technically what came after the final course—when the table was deserted of its white damask cloth to show the polished beauty of the (preferably) mahogany dining table—a sight calculated to awe guests as much as the previously loaded table of food had done. La Rochefoucauld was duly impressed, perhaps because he had recovered from his astonishment over the amount of food that he had just consumed: "The cloth is removed and you behold the most beautiful table that it is possible to see . . . [T]heir tables are made of the most beautiful wood and always have a brilliant polish like that of the finest glass."[12] Dessert plates, silverware, wine glasses, finger bowls, and a dessert doily (a fancy finger towel) were passed around by the servants before they retired for good and the dining room doors were shut.

As much as the dinner did itself, dessert gave families an opportunity to present guests their finest foods, in this case, exotic fruits they raised in greenhouses, including grapes, apricots, pineapples, even avocados. These exotics, however, were usually secondary in importance to native English fruits, most importantly, apples. Many country gentlemen and women enjoyed cultivating new varieties, often working with knowledgeable head gardeners to develop hundreds of new types. Many of England's famous apples were nineteenth-century products, including Bramley's Seedling, a cooking apple, and Cox's Orange Pippin, a dessert apple served with port because the flavors complemented one another.[13] Along with fruit, a hostess served nuts, and if it were a fancy occasion, iced puddings, or what we would think of as molded ice creams. The most fancy parties might warrant a third, distinct course, composed of such sweets, thus pushing the dessert later in the evening.

After her glass or two of wine, the hostess rose from her seat, the women from theirs, and they proceeded to the drawing room for coffee or tea while the men again shut the door, reached for the stronger liquors and the finer vintage ports, and drank at their leisure. De la Rochefoucauld observed for his French audience that this was when "real enjoyment begins—there is not an Englishman who is not supremely happy at this particular moment." De la Rochefoucauld continued:

> Conversation is as free as it can be, everyone expresses his political opinions with as much frankness as he would employ upon personal subjects. Sometimes conversation becomes extremely free upon highly indecent topics—complete licence is allowed . . . Very often I have heard things mentioned in good society which would be in the grossest taste in France.[14]

As conversation grew raucous and the men bolder due to drinking, the more delicate among the crowd would have become uncomfortable. De la Rochefoucauld's goodwill again was compromised when his jubilant host opened a sideboard cabinet and took out a chamber pot so that all could relieve themselves—with "no kind of concealment"—de la Rochefoucauld indignantly recalled.[15]

But in this early era, the women were probably carrying on intimate and lively (perhaps scandalous) conversations themselves around the tea urn in the drawing room. In the many small towns and villages that dotted an English county, wealthy families knew one another well and they were on secure social footing. This sense of common ground and interest made it easier for many people to feel comfortable, less stilted and formal. When each sex grew bored with its own company, men and women reconvened for cards, music, charades, and perhaps dancing. That entertainment and fellowship were as important as the food is suggested in Agnes Beaufoy's manuscript cookery book, where the first entry is not a food recipe but instructions for a charade.

Now called "English country cooking" by culinary historians and best exemplified in Eliza Acton's popular *Modern Cookery* (1845), the foods that graced an early Victorian dinner table testified to the importance of seasons and geographical region when it came to eating and entertaining. Given the difficulty of keeping perishables fresh and the near impossibility of eating foods out of season, cookbook authors created detailed charts to indicate what was seasonable in any given month. Some fabulously wealthy (and, their neighbors might whisper, foolishly extravagant) persons liked to showcase spring peas in January and strawberries in February but these gourmands were exceptions to the rule. Furthermore, families usually relied on their large gardens, orchards, poultry yards, and dovecotes for the bulk of their food, or if they were in an urban area, they sent experienced servants to city markets to shop daily, and they developed relationships with a host of purveyors who worked with the cook and mistress to ensure that the freshest seasonable meats, vegetables, and dairy products were delivered to the house. Even winter had its own abundance and anticipated specialties, with much game at its best and thus able to compensate for the lack of fresh foods. The temporal nature of many vegetables and fruits made their appearance in any given season something to look forward to and remember when the season ended and the next began.

John Trusler summed up the spirit of dinner *à la Française* best when he proclaimed that "a gentleman and lady never shew themselves to more advantage, than in acquitting themselves well in the honours of their table; that is to say, in serving their guests and treating their friends, agreeable to their rank and situation in life."[16] By the 1860s and 1870s, prosperous Victorians were not often so willing or able to spend three hours at the table; their meals and the times before and after became more choreographed. Few chamber pots came out of storage from sideboard cabinets, men did not linger so long over their port, and the constant presence of servants that dinner *à la Russe* required stymied free conversation. But for those living in the decades just before Victoria's reign and up through the 1840s and 1850s, the rituals associated with "serving guests and treating friends" added several minutes to each course at dinner, and this fact did not disturb most English gentry; rather, it gratified them.

## THE EFFECTS OF TECHNOLOGY AND INDUSTRIALIZATION ON DINNER *À LA FRANÇAISE*

Initially, industrialization and new technologies did not challenge the customs associated with dinner *à la française,* but by the 1860s the wealthy elite had abandoned it and the middle classes were soon to follow. Part of its falling out had to do with the amount of time the meal took and the shifting priorities of the people who both hosted and attended dinner parties, and part of its waning was also the result of changes to cooking and food technology. We might not think about it, but technology plays a fundamental role in dictating dining fashion, just as it does in dictating food preparation. From around 1860 to 1880, middle-class Victorians were living with both old-fashioned cooking tools and dining modes as well as new-fashioned ones. In a sense, mid-century Victorians might be defined as "a generation apart": they were usually familiar with older ways of doing things but they were not yet at a time and place where new technologies and fashions could be taken for granted. Some might be living in the first homes to have indoor plumbing—and yet, the city water supply was not pressurized nor service guaranteed. Even when the water gushed out, it was unsafe to drink until it was filtered and boiled. Others might have had money to buy canned apricots and jars of pickles, but they detested canned and bottled food because they feared that it was spoiled or adulterated (and much of it was). Still others might have purchased a new Leamington coal range only to discover that to use it properly they needed to hire another kitchen servant, one who understood range technology. They might not be successful in this quest for such a servant, or if they were, the wages they would need to pay her were more than they could easily afford.

During this rather rocky transition from old, traditional ways to new, modern ones, dinner *à la Française* remained largely the norm. But as cities began to grow and improve their infrastructure and as previously novel technology became mainstream, the mode lost its relevance, particularly among people who were attuned to fashion and conscientiously building a social identity that in many ways put them at odds with those of their parents' and grandparents' generations. Beeton's menus and her *Book of Household Management* in general speak to that transition, including its technological and culinary innovations. In this 1,112-page volume we can see what remained popular in the 1860s, what was becoming obsolete, and what new trends were just beginning to manifest themselves among the middle classes at whom it was aimed.

## The Challenge of Stove and Range Technology

The first difficulty that many mistresses and their servants encountered when attempting to prepare all the requisite dishes for a dinner *à la Française* concerned the cooking technology itself, particularly trying to adapt to use of a closed range—the status symbol of the Victorian middle class. Charles Buckmaster addressed this challenge in *Buckmaster's Cookery* (1874) where he explained that the range

> depends on management. If a cook were taught, as she ought to be taught, the elementary principles of heat and the construction of ranges, she would be able to manage her range more economically . . . If a closed range be used, as only an educated scientific cook can use it, it is economical, when you remember the variety of work you can do with it. But if a cook does or will not understand the use of the dampers, and the fire is frequently and freely stirred, then a kitchener becomes a furnace, and is much more oppressive than an open range.

Worse than that, Buckmaster concluded, food is cooked improperly and is most often wasted, thus costing the master of the house money for his wife's ineptness as much as for his cook's.[17]

Ranges presented one of the biggest problems that mid-Victorians were likely to confront when it came to updating a kitchen (to use modern parlance) and installing what advertisers and the store owners purported to be century's most important advance in terms of cooking technology and fuel efficiency. We examined the difficulty a general maid experienced when using one of these coal-fired ranges to make breakfast, but as we explore the mid-Victorian era in regards to cooking, it makes sense to discuss as well the transition from open hearth to range cooking and the various headaches it was bound to cause.

Preparing a dinner *à la Française* worked best when a family had a large kitchen fireplace: one equipped with enough space that the cook could use part of it to spit-roast ducks, pigeons, as well as a sirloin of beef; another part of it to boil and simmer stews and whole fish; and yet another part to keep already-prepared foods warm. In this same kitchen another servant was busy using the built-in brick oven, where she prepared the pastries, cakes, and breads that the family required. She heated the oven by building a blazing fire on its capacious brick floor and when the fuel had burned down to ash, she swept it out completely and then proceeded with her baking, starting first with items that demanded a very hot oven, and proceeding all the way to the point where the residual heat could dry out damp feather pillows and even make potpourri.

As thousands of families relocated to cities in the 1830s and 1840s and as their houses became smaller and space more cramped, such a kitchen, let alone a large fireplace, was seldom possible for anyone but the most wealthy. Furthermore, fuel was expensive. To solve the problem of cost and to also make it easier for a cook to bake, fry, poach, and boil all at the same time on the same machine, Thomas Robinson in 1780 created the first open range that could rely on one batch of fuel for all cooking procedures. It was designed with the fire itself exposed (hence the word open), but with a large enclosed oven attached to its side and with a convenient flat top. Because the early oven models often caused the breads and pastry to burn on their sides nearest the fire, Robinson's rudimentary model was refined and flues were invented to carry heat around the oven and thus make baking more reliable. In spite of the rather tricky oven, many cooks appreciated the open range because it was not a great deal different than open hearth cooking, given that the fire was still almost entirely exposed and they could continue to spit-roast meat (the preferred way of preparing meat in England). A cook simply put the joint or bird on a standing roaster spit in front of the fire or she suspended the meat from a dangle-spit over the fire as she had done previously. The meat was rotated either mechanically or manually.

Considered even more productive was the closed range, patented in 1802. It was called a closed range because an iron plate kept heat from going up the chimney and instead diverted it to a series of flues that went behind and warmed the oven or ovens. The cost of a closed range and its maintenance demands put them beyond the reach of average middle-class consumers until the 1850s and 1860s, when cheaper, smaller models were produced and competition among various manufacturers became keen. Although initially billed as using less coal, Jennifer Davies has pointed out in *The Victorian Kitchen* (1989) that they actually consumed more because air from the kitchen had to pass through the fire before it passed into the chimney.[18]

Nonetheless, these Cadillacs of cooking became hugely popular because they could save kitchen space, presumably keep the kitchen cooler than the open range, and if it came with an attached boiler, store many gallons of hot water to be immediately ready for cooking, bathing, and cleaning. One drawback, however, was its limited amount of exposed fire for spit-roasting meat. To compensate, the cook used a screen called a "hastener." Like a plate warmer, the hastener looked somewhat like a semicircular bookshelf made of highly polished tin to help reflect the heat. Attached at the top of the hastener was a bottle jack from which the cook suspended her meat, or a horizontal spring jack (a spit) on which she secured the joint or bird. In the back of the hastener was a door that she could open and thus reach inside to baste the meat as it roasted. A metal cylinder contained the mechanism that caused the jack to rotate automatically.

However, many closed ranges, particularly the cheaper models in lower-middle-class houses, had no exposed fire at all, and here was a serious dilemma for those who had been used to the flavor of a spit-roasted joint with its crackling crust and juicy interior. With these cheaper models, the cook had no choice but to try and bake the meat in the oven, even though she feared to do so because she believed the noxious fumes could not escape from it, and the meat would be

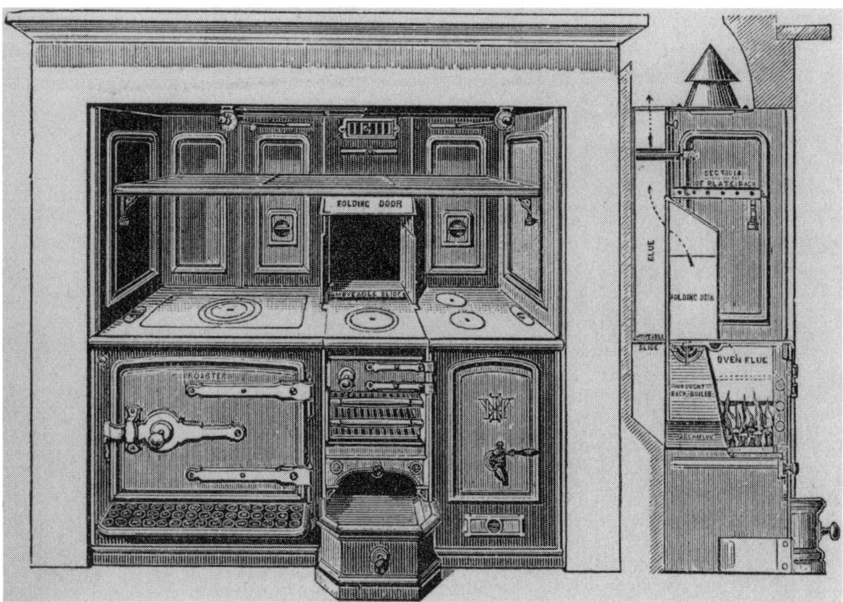


Kitchener with oven and side boiler from *Cassell's Book of the Household* (1889–1891). The enclosed oven sits to the left of the firebox, and the water boiler, complete with spigot, sits to the right of the firebox. The rack above the hotplate was the most convenient place to keep dishes, breads, pies, and other previously prepared hot foods.

contaminated. To counter this dilemma, Count Rumford developed a "roasting oven" that heated the air by passing it along the hot base of the oven and then causing it to rise up through an outlet behind.[19] By the 1860s and 1870s, most ranges incorporated Rumford's technology, and by the close of the nineteenth century, these closed kitcheners were being fitted in 90 percent of all new houses.[20] The spit-roasted joint that generations of English people had taken for granted was fast becoming a luxury for all but the most wealthy because the range fire was now enclosed.

During the time when these transitions were occurring, many Victorians who were familiar with old-fashioned cooking technology found the new ranges confusing and frustrating. A competent cook born in 1800 understood how to work with an open fire, operating the various dangle spits, standing roasters, weights, chimney cranes, and trivets, but she was a novice at operating flues and working effectively with coal; she found that cooking was even more contingent on the weather than it had been when she used an open fire; she hated having to make accommodations to the range, instead of the range making accommodations to her. When Charles Dickens moved his growing family from Devonshire Terrace to Tavistock House in 1851, he and his wife Catherine desired to remodel this 1801 mansion and they made the kitchen a priority. Along with

JAC DAILY WANTS. JAM

JACK SALAD.—Cut the remains of a cold jack into pieces, and mix with it gherkins, capers, and anchovies, and some herbs shred; serve the jack, garnishing the dish with lettuces and hard-boiled eggs. Mix oil and vinegar at table.

JACK, FOR ROASTING.—This culinary implement has been introduced in a variety of forms. The best kind is an improved spring jack as shown in the engraving, and in which the article to be roasted is fixed on a spit lying horizontally in the usual manner. A box on the top contains the spring, which causes a wheel to revolve in front; round

this, an endless chain passes over two pulleys to the spit, which goes through on the side of the tin screen. By means of a series of holes, and shortening or lengthening the chain, the height of the spit can be adjusted; and there is a fly-wheel to regulate the motion.—See BOTTLE JACK.

JACKDAW.—A well-known bird of the rook genus. The bill and legs are black; the claws strong and hooked; eyes white; and the hinder part of the head and neck silvery gray; the rest of the plumage is of a

fine, glossy blue-black above, and dusky beneath. The jackdaw may be easily tamed; it is an amusing bird, and may be taught to imitate the human voice in speaking, singing, &c.

JALAP.—A medicinal agent derived from a root indigenous to South America. It is a stimulant cathartic, performing its office briskly, and safe and efficacious, although occasionally griping severely. It is a good medicine in the torpid state of the intestines; and for children who are troubled with worms. A drop or two of some essential oil, as the oil of carraway or aniseed, should be added to each dose of jalap, to prevent griping. The dose is from ten grains to half a drachm, given in the form of pill or powder.

JAM.—Fruit boiled down with sugar to the consistence of a paste. Jams form valuable domestic stores, supplying us the flavour and essences of fruits at such times as they are no longer in season. In the preparation of this confection, some little care and nicety are demanded; ordinarily

they are prepared in stewpans lined with enamel, and placed over the fire of the kitchen. An improved method of preparing jams, however, is through the medium of the small portable French stove or furnace in the accompanying illustration; this is furnished with a trivet and stewpan, and is exceedingly convenient for the purpose intended. By this furnace all smoke is kept away, and the heat can be regulated at pleasure. There should always be a free current of air in the room in which it stands when lighted, as it is lighted with charcoal, that being the only fuel suitable to it. To kindle it, two or three pieces must be lighted in a common fire, and laid on the top of that in the furnace, which should be evenly placed between the grating and the brim, and then blown gently with the bellows until the whole is lighted; the door of the furnace must in the meanwhile remain open, unless the heat should at any time prove too fierce, when the door must be closed for a few minutes to regulate the heat. To extinguish the fire entirely, the cover must be pressed closely on, and the door be quite shut; the embers which remain will serve to re-kindle it easily, but before it is again lighted, the grating must be lifted out and all the ashes cleared away. It should

579

Spring Jack and Hastener from *Dictionary of Daily Wants* (1858–1861). The large wheel on top of the hastener was used to wind the spring jack and thus allow the meat to rotate mechanically. Illustration courtesy of the Morse Department of Special Collections, Hale Library, Kansas State University.

whitewashing the walls to give it more light, they ordered a kitchen range to be installed. As weeks went by and the range was still not installed, Dickens became irate: "'O the perjured, beastly, odious, and incompetent Burton! The Imbecile pretender!!' Charles raged at the contractor."[21] Without a range, the family could not cook its meals, and the moving day was approaching quickly. Just as people today grow dependent on electricity to the point that life comes to a standstill when it goes out, so must it have felt when a kitchen range took the place of the traditional fireside.

In its section "Roasting in an Oven," *Cassell's Book of the Household* presented a scenario that exemplified the middle-class mistress's dilemma. A young couple who has grown up in "the grander style" than what they can currently afford on the husband's salary, now live in a pretty, albeit small house in the suburbs where they commence to "keep house," along with their live-in cook and waiting maid. Enjoying their home and one another's company in their first weeks of married life, the husband turns enthusiastically one afternoon to his wife: "Oh! let us have a plain dinner and good. A little clear soup, a haunch or leg of mutton, and a pheasant." The husband is excited by the prospect, but his bride is stricken with anxiety: "If you say it cannot be done" (*Cassell's* was now speaking directly to the bride), "he may think it is all nonsense. Yet with a little oven and no open fire-place, how are you to roast both mutton and pheasant for the same dinner?" *Cassell's* advised the mistress to take the mutton round to the baker and concentrate on the pheasant, the soup and gravy, the bread-sauce and the vegetables.[22] That the baker was an imperfect solution was made clear by Meg Dods when she wrote that the "meat is seldom got home in season" from the baker, who cooks on his own schedule and who forces the customer to bend to his own schedule." Dods ruefully continued: "What dismay is often created by the face of the maid,—"[?]

> Who comes with most terrible news from the baker,
> That insolent sloven!
> Who shut out the pasty when shutting his oven.[23]

In other words, the mistress had asked the maid to take the pasty to the baker, and in his haste to finish his baking, he neglected the mistress's pasty.

Not only was the typical range too small, it remained tricky to heat in spite of improvements made to the flues and dampers. To return to *Cassell's* scenario: Even if the pheasant were small enough to fit into the oven, the cook and mistress might both be inexperienced with how to use a range and thus underheat it, or even more often, overheat it. *Cassell's* again offered some advice, in a rather stern, fatherly sort of voice, perhaps calculated to bolster the mistress's or cook's failing spirits. First, "exercise your common sense." Second, prop an old plate up against the side of the oven that burns red hot, as it will act as a heat diffuser. Then, one will need to turn the fowl occasionally, and right before it is cooked, take the plate out and turn the fowl "over on its side towards the hot part to brown." *Cassell's* admitted that "all this is very troublesome," but the book's editors were "not writing only for people with first-class kitchen-ranges and ovens."[24]

*Cassell's* scenario was for a small, intimate meal; what was one to do for a dinner party to be carried out in the *à la Française* style and which demanded so many dishes for each course, as well as the *pièce de résistance* and the traditional roast fowl? A country estate kitchen or city mansion with a large open range or fireplace made such meals possible. With millions of people now living in cities and suburbs, space was at a premium, and the mistress was increasingly stressed from trying to prepare dinner on a small range. The *à la Russe* style, which might have appeared to be at the apex of elegance and refinement, could craftily be made to overcome some of this space and equipment crunch, as we shall see in the next chapter.

Although not explicitly, Beeton's 1860s-era menus take into account that many readers were struggling to work simultaneously with both old- and new-fashioned kitchen implements, and that they were coming from a wide range of incomes, from those who could afford the £23, 10 shilling Improved Leamington Kitchener to those who lived with a modest £5, 15 shilling version of the same.[25] Take, for example, the predominance of boiled meat in Beeton's suggested menus. When all else fails, Beeton seemed to imply, just put the meat in a pot and boil it. One can put a pot on top of the range, or one can suspend the pot over the fire with a chain, or one can put the pot on a trivet. The cooking technology is not sophisticated and it can be used regardless of the kitchen limitation. Boiled turbot, boiled haddock, boiled leg of mutton, boiled rabbit, boiled turkey, boiled capon, and lots of curried dishes that are made from first boiling the meat figure prominently in Beeton's menus. Furthermore, if the main dish can be boiled, then the cook is free to use her range oven to bake a smaller joint or to bake a tart. Beeton leaves unspecified in numerous instances how the meat is to be prepared. For example, instead of directing that the woodcocks, the turkey, or the haunch of mutton be roasted, stewed, or boiled, she leaves the mode of cooking to the discretion of the mistress who understands her kitchen's limitations, be it in terms of equipment, size, a servant staff, or all three.

### The Problem of Spoiled and Adulterated Food

Spoiled food was a reality of life in mid-Victorian England, especially in cities where ice sold at a premium and was considered a luxury. In the transitional decades of the mid-nineteenth century, obtaining ice was difficult for many city residents because there simply was not enough of it. Wealthy country families harvested ice on their own ponds and stored it in underground ice houses in the summer. City people depended on ice stores but there were not many of them prior to the 1880s. Up through the 1830s, farmers harvested ice in England by flooding their fields in the winter, cutting ice into large blocks, and selling it to companies that put it on barges and floated it to cities and towns. By the Victorian era, the United States began exporting ice to England. A £5 entry in Charles Dickens's 1850 account book included a notation for ice purchased at Wenham Lake Ice Company. This company harvested ice in Massachusetts, shipped it to London, and sold it at its store starting in 1846.[26] Dickens was quite prosperous by 1850; lower-middle-class people living on a salary of roughly £4 a week could not afford such an expense and thus did not often keep large iceboxes. If the kitchen servants and mistress were careless in hot summer months, their perishables spoiled and money was wasted. Only when Norway began competing with the United States in the last decades of the nineteenth century did ice become more abundant and cheaper. By 1899, some 500,000 tons were being shipped to England via Scandinavia.[27]

Not only did mid-century Victorians contend with spoilage and inefficient refrigeration, they also worried about adulterated products. Much of the food that had traditionally composed the *à la Française* dinner menu had been home-produced, from the cottage loaves of bread to the beer. But as middle-class families relocated to cities for better economic opportunities, they had no choice but to purchase many items readymade, and time itself was now at a premium. As families lost self-sufficiency and became dependent on others to supply food, their risk of buying adulterated products increased. As people lost knowledge of how to cook competently, they also lost a sense of how food should taste, how it should look, even how long it should last. Underhanded purveyors eagerly took advantage of such ignorance because they suffered no harmful consequences and they usually increased their profit margin.

Beer, wine, coffee, tea, bread, pickles, spices, confectionary, and milk were routinely adulterated. Wine was extended by adding spoiled cider to it. Crooked vintners lined their port bottles with supertartrate of potash to make the product appear like an expensive crusted port. Beer was adulterated with cocculus indicus, liquor ice, salts of steel, or molasses. Blackthorn leaves replaced tea leaves, cheese was dyed with red lead, bread made whiter by alum or even arsenic, and candy colored with poisonous salts of copper and lead. Cheap, spoiled butter could be "revived" with a washing in milk and then sweetened with sugar. Cocoa was extended with brick dust—as was cayenne pepper. Black pepper was often mixed with sand, while mustard powder could be more flour and turmeric than actual mustard.[28]

Murderous or not, the rampant cheating in the food and beverage industry alarmed many chemists who understood adulteration's potential harm to people's overall health. Efforts to stem such practices began early in the nineteenth century when chemist Frederick Accum published his *Treatise on Adulterations of Food and Culinary Poisons* in 1820. Accum detailed the adverse effects of adulteration and the "misdeeds of manufacturers" and then created a scandal by publishing a list of English druggists, grocers, and brewers who had already been convicted of food adulteration and fined for it. But the backlash against

Accum was intense and resulted in his indictment on a trivial and never-proven offence of defacing some Royal Institution books.[29]

Many politicians and government officials hesitated to pass stricter pure food laws or enforce existing ones because they contended that a lassiez-faire economy would keep food adulteration in check. Inferior goods would not attract buyers, the thinking went, and thus their manufacturers would go out of business. The theory did not play itself out in this way because people were ignorant about adulteration and because the poor—the majority of the English population in the 1850s and 1860s—had no choice about where to shop and what to buy: they were limited to the cheapest, and thus, the most heavily adulterated products. Many bakers, dairymen, publicans, as well as dry-goods grocers argued that if they did not add fillers, they would not make enough profit to stay in business. If anything, adulteration only grew more rampant in the mid-Victorian era. A raft of books were published on how to successfully adulterate products, including *The Guide to Trade* (1841) by Anon. and Samuel Child's *Every Man his own Brewer*, published in 12 editions from 1790 up through the first half of the nineteenth century.[30]

Physician Arthur Hill Hassall was the most important catalyst to reform; his comprehensive reports on adulterated foods published in the *Lancet* alarmed the public and government officials. Between 1851 and 1854, Hassall and his team analyzed thousands of household products that they suspected of adulteration. With no exception, all the bakery bread that they analyzed contained alum and all but one of the twenty-nine coffee tins had been bulked out with chicory, ground-up acorns, and/or mangel-wurzel. In 1855 Parliament appointed a commission to look into the *Lancet*'s claims, and by 1872, the Adulteration of Food, Drink, and Drugs Act was passed and real enforcement began. Public food analysts were appointed and put under the control of local police forces. It became a criminal offense to sell goods that contained ingredients adding weight or bulk unless specifically declared to purchasers. By 1875, the Sale of Food and Drugs Act further tightened regulations, and by the 1890s the practice had virtually been eradicated. But until then, cookbook authorities such as Beeton routinely published directions for detecting adulteration as well as tips for how to avoid purchasing adulterated products. That fear and anxiety ran rife among middle-class housewives in the 1850s and 1860s is evident from *Book of Household Management* itself where Beeton's biographer, Kathryn Hughes, suggested, "Mrs. Beeton would make the household safe by putting it in a tin, soldering the covers and exposing it to boiling water for three hours." Unfortunately, Hughes continued, Mrs. Beeton was forced to acknowledge that tragically, adulteration began before the goods were even put into the cans.[31] As housewives turned to canned and bottled foods, factory-made breads, biscuits, and candies, they remained the victims of adulteration. Many suffered the slow effects of malnutrition or food poisoning.

### Impure Water: The Biggest Industrial Challenge

Even more serious than rampant food adulteration was impure water. Water is the basis of all cooking, and historically speaking, it posed the first urban problem. In preindustrial England, people had obtained water by collecting it from rivers, streams, local wells, and sometimes via a public fountain or conduit in the village or town center.[32] That water could pose health risks had been clear at least as far back as biblical times when Paul counseled Timothy to "stop drinking only water, and use a little wine because of your stomach and your frequent illnesses."[33] Although people did not fully understand the relationship between dirty water and fatal disease, they had enough common sense to recognize that their drinking water had to be filtered and boiled before it was even near a safe enough level to drink. It took repeated typhoid and cholera outbreaks to force the government to take seriously the scientific findings on the correlation between dirty water and disease and begin to clean up the nation's water and its sewage systems.

Because water was hard to obtain and too dirty to drink, the amount that Victorians used in comparison to people in more recent times is significant. In the 1830s, a person used on an average four imperial gallons of water a day for drinking, cooking, washing, and cleaning, whereas by the 1970s, that number had jumped to ten imperial gallons of water a day.[34] Industrialization exacerbated already-existent problems with both the water supply and its safety by causing extensive pollution of rivers and streams and by attracting thousands into cities that had not been built to house them. Water became a scarce and expensive commodity to the point that people in Liverpool in the early nineteenth century took to the streets begging for water rather than money. In the mid-1840s, only five thousand wealthy Bristol residents had piped water.[35] Londoners preferred the taste of well water to that of the Thames, but in the 1860s, scientific assessments revealed that most of the well water was contaminated by cesspool soakage, and London's 250,000 cesspools still drained directly into the Thames—the main source of the city's water supply. [36]

Middle-class Londoners sometimes had well water brought into the house via their scullery pump, or Thames water brought into their house via a city water pipe and tap. They also collected rain (soft) water in a cistern to use for washing fine linens, hair, and china, as well as for use in cooking. Piped or well water was "hard"; it contained high levels of iron and other minerals that made it difficult to remove soap, and that clearly could destroy the taste of more delicate foods, including sauces in which water was an important ingredient. For middle-class urban and suburban people who did not have a well or piped water, a waterman in a horse-drawn cart made regular deliveries and filled the family cistern. The maid or children would then cart that water into the home to distribute it as need be.[37]

In 1866, only half of London households had piped, indoor water, but it was an intermittent, expensive luxury at 3 shillings a week.[38] Private water companies would not supply water on Sundays or during all twenty-four hours on other days. Low pressure made collecting any meaningful amount from the pipes a tediously slow operation.[39] In Manchester, the progress of supplying houses with water was likewise slow and complicated. By 1846, 23.4 percent of residents had indoor water pipes, and by 1879, 79.4 percent did. Poor Mancunians continued to rely on communal standpipes up through the 1870s, and in London, up through the 1890s.[40]

Successive cholera outbreaks in London impressed upon the wealthy and poor alike that one's location in the city was no safeguard from this disease. In 1832, 5,000 died of cholera; 14,000 perished in 1849, and 10,000 in 1854. A final major attack in 1866 forced authorities to take seriously John Snow's groundbreaking *On the Mode of Communication of Cholera* (1849 and 1855). They abandoned their reservations about the linkage of water to the disease and began modernizing city water supplies.[41] Substantial improvements began in the 1870s when water was taken out of private control and given over to municipalities. The next improvements involved finding clean water for city use and making water constantly available. To these ends, aqueducts that spanned as much as 35 miles were approved and built in the second half of the nineteenth century, and Manchester, Liverpool, and Birmingham developed long-distance gravitation works that allowed water from artificial dams to flow into these cities at high pressure.[42] Not only was piped water now increasingly available throughout the cities and suburbs of England, but by the 1890s, the application of chlorine to water and also experimental work with rapid sand filtration (first initiated in the United States) made water purer to drink. But in the 1860s when Beeton was writing, this modernization was in its infant stages, and the beverages that she deemed appropriate for meals, quenching thirst, nursing invalids, and caring for children were almost all alcoholic (even if slightly so), or based on boiled water.

## THE WANING POPULARITY OF DINNER *À LA FRANÇAISE*

While most of Beeton's suggested menus were based on service *à la Française*, she covered briefly the rudiments of service *à la Russe* and offered two suggested menus for it as well. First, Beeton explained, "Dinners *à la Russe* differ from ordinary dinners in the mode of serving the various dishes. In a dinner *à la Russe*, the dishes are cut up on a sideboard, and handed round to the guests, and each dish may be considered a course." Second came Beeton's qualification: "Dinners *à la Russe* are scarcely suitable for small establishments; a large number of servants being required to carve, and to help the guests; besides there being a necessity for more plates, dishes, knives, forks, and spoons, than are usually to be found in any other than a very large establishment."[43]

Given the convincing nature of Beeton's comments regarding dinner *à la Russe*, why would the majority of middle-class Victorians—most of whom were in "relatively small establishments"—begin to abandon dinner *à la Française* in order to adapt to this new mode that appeared to be best suited to the upper classes? Of course, not all middle-class Victorians did abandon the *à la Française* style; many found the alternative cumbersome and if they used the *à la Russe* service at all, they limited it to rare formal dinners. But the thousands who did adapt the *à la Russe* service managed it in part because by the last decades of the nineteenth century, the technical glitches that I have detailed above had been largely eliminated, or even better technology, such as gas ranges, had replaced the earlier versions. The modern kitchen did not facilitate an *à la Française* dinner, but it could be made to facilitate an *à la Russe* one.

Furthermore, as technology changed, so too did people's priorities. The waning of dinner *à la Française* suggested a slow but evident shift in middle-class social attitudes that simply made the traditional style irrelevant or even antithetical to its modern values. In his account of the transition from one dining style to another, Arnold Palmer wrote nostalgically about the "old fashioned" professional men in the 1840s and 1850s who continued to leave work and return home to an early dinner that was unchanged from what their parents and grandparents had known. Families passed evenings "with chess or backgammon, needlework and reading aloud, solos and duets and choruses." This class of people, Palmer continued, was "steady-going, comfortably well off, pursuing a sedentary calling" and thus resembled Londoners who had "existed for many generations." Dinner *à la Française* suited them. But the class usurping these families in influence and power, Palmer continued, were those best represented by Mr. B. and Hortense in Soyer's *Modern Housewife*: "the prosperous, scrambling, climbing world of merchants, manufacturers, financiers, and politicians" who had no time for leisure, no desire to share the abundance of a groaning table, no need to celebrate seasonal abundance when it came to food. Rather, they wished to show off their status, exclude those who did not belong, and in many regards reject their parents' values.[44]

The abundance of food and drink at a dinner *à la Française* facilitated conversation and congeniality. Diners were by and large serving themselves, passing dishes, talking as they did so. They worried less about eavesdropping servants and less about the meal's pace if they desired to eat slowly or carry on a conversation. A table crowded with good food, the master carving the joints, the wife passing the soup, all spoke of an intimacy and harmony that increasingly clashed with the concerns and the values of later Victorian urban society, and as the technology itself altered by the 1870s and 1880s, the justification for dinner *à la Française* was further jeopardized.

# The Multiple Meanings and Purposes of Dinner *à la Russe*, 1880–1900

**Menu du Diner.**
(For 10 to 12 persons.)

**Hors D' Oeuvre.**
*Caviar sur Croûtes.*

**Potage.**
*Croûte au Pot.*

**Poisson.**
*Saumon bouilli, Sauce Ecrevisses.*

**Entrée.**
*Côtelettes de Pigeon à l'Américaine.*

**Relevé.**
*Poulet à la Valencienne.*
*Pommes de Terre à la Maître d' Hotel.*
*Epinards à la Crème.*

[**Sorbet**
*Sorbet à la Américaine*]

**Rôt.**
*Bécassines sur Croûtes.*

**Entremets.**
*Petits Pois à la Française.*
*Abricots à la Condé.*
*Croûtes à la Neuvaine.*

—Agnes B. Marshall, *Mrs. A. B. Marshall's Cookery Book,* 1885

In the dinner-party chapter of *Cassell's Book of the Household* (1889), editors offered readers exhaustive advice on how to plan and execute a dinner *à la Russe*. Along with step-by-step instructions for folding dinner napkins, placing wine glasses, and arranging the centerpiece, the editors offered numerous asides calculated to encourage the timid, bolster the spirits of the weary, and needle those who might be inclined to cut corners. That *Cassell's* approached a dinner party defensively (in our time, we would expect a guidebook to be neutral) is revealing. Instead of assuming that a family might actually want to invite people over to dinner for pleasure, *Cassell's* assumed that "many people nowadays look upon a dinner-party as an expensive and troublesome mode of entertainment, and prefer an 'at home' or a 'reception.'" Lest a husband and wife should allow that reasoning to dissuade them from hosting a dinner party, *Cassell's* cautioned: An "'at home' is looked at in a very different light, and regarded as much less a of compliment, than is an invitation to dinner."[1] Shortly thereafter, *Cassell's* editors offered a reflection that indicates how far society had moved from the days when dinner *à la Française* was at its apex:

> It is a great pity that the extravagant ideas of the present day deter so many from daring to ask their friends to dinner. There is a feeling that a dinner-party must of necessity be very elaborate and very costly, and that such a luxury is only within the reach of well-to-do people, and quite beyond those who have only moderate incomes. If we were more courageous, more simple and honest, and less pretentious, there would be more dinner-parties to enliven winter evenings, and pleasant social intercourse would not be so rare as it is.[2]

In spite of this wishful thinking, *Cassell's* was as guilty as the rest of late-century guidebooks in making the fashionable dinner *à la Russe* out to be anything less than an ordeal.

What was it about a dinner party that raised so much anxiety, to the point that by 1900, most prosperous Victorians were abandoning the practice? This chapter, along with going into detail about the format and organization of dinner *à la Russe*, explores where that anxiety might have come from and what it suggested about life for professional urbanites at the turn of the century. Just as dinner *à la Française* had been based partly on available technologies and the customs of preindustrial England, dinner *à la Russe* was predicated on new technologies and the customs associated with industrial England, technologies that ironically raised the status of dinner *à la Russe* to the height of fashion and then ultimately diminished its importance in the early twentieth century.

## THE DEFINITION AND ORIGINS OF DINNER *À LA RUSSE*

At its most basic, service *à la Russe* meant that the servants carved the joints of meat at the dining-room sideboard and rather than putting the food on the table in two or three courses for diners to help themselves, servants plated and handed diners their meals in a series of courses, usually between six to ten for a dinner party. When not serving food or drinks, servants stood at a respectful distance behind diners to respond to any need or request that arose. This style was popular with Russian Tsars and nobility, and its adaptation throughout western Europe was indirectly the result of the Treaty of Paris and the Congress of Vienna, events that ended the Napoleonic Wars in 1814 and 1815 and that also resulted in some of the nineteenth century's most elaborate dinners.

During negotiations that determined the fate of France and the new political boundaries of Europe, nobility and politicians from France, Great Britain, Austria, Prussia, and Russia were constantly intermingling and food was used strategically as a means to smooth differences, create goodwill, and also celebrate the peace. Many culinary historians agree that dinner *à la Russe* was formally introduced to Parisians by the Russian Prince Kourakin. The Germans likewise had been serving their formal meals in a series of courses.[3]

During the early nineteenth century, dinner *à la Française* (the established and accepted style used in France and England) coexisted with dinner *à la Russe*. Which style was used depended on the chef's recommendations, the country, the city, the host, the purpose of the banquet, and also the logistics: how many guests and what service might best accommodate that number? As diplomats and royalty traveled from London to Berlin, Vienna to Paris, and Paris to St. Petersburg, these two services might also have been used in calculated ways to honor, celebrate, and of course flatter the various constituents who for those two years were working toward a peaceful resolution to war and conflict.

In regards to England specifically, the terms dinner *à la Française* and dinner *à la Russe* are confusing because what the labels suggest and what typically occurred during dinner did not always match. The English gentry, as we saw in the previous chapter, adapted dinner *à la Française* to fit its own needs, customs, and the variables of daylight and season; although the service itself originated in France, many squires, gentlemen farmers, and prosperous city professionals deliberately anglicized it, using English names such as "bill of fare" for "menu", and "side" or "made dish" for "entrée." This patriotic English spirit was still forceful among the gentry, even though the royalty and court under the Prince Regent, George, Prince of Wales (1762–1830) had become enamored with all things French. Indeed, the Prince Regent paid the astronomical sum of £20,000 (roughly equivalent to £120,000 in today's terms) to lure Marie-Antoine Carême to his Carlton House palace and Brighton Pavilion to become *chef de cuisine*.[4]

The term *à la Russe* can be equally confusing because although the service was Russian, the food was usually French, and more specifically, a kind of French food that came to be known as haute cuisine. Dinner *à la Russe* in England likewise meant French food, or French-inspired food, served in the Russian style. The names of the courses were French, not Russian, and the most coveted chefs who produced the food were French, not Russian. To understand why dinner *à la Russe* became increasingly popular in England, it is helpful to consider briefly the change in English attitudes toward the French, for without an appreciation of French cooking and chefs, this style probably would not have become as established in England as it did.

## THE FRENCH CONNECTION

One entertaining narrative of the French takeover of British cuisine comes from Edward Spencer's *Cakes and Ale: A Memory of Many Meals* (1897). The English might have won Waterloo, Spencer remarked, but

> from that period dates the "avenging of Waterloo" which we have suffered in silence for so long. The immigration of aliens commenced, and in the tight little island were deposited a large assortment of the poisonous seeds of alien cookery which had never exactly flourished before. The combat between the Roast Beef of old England and the bad fairy "*Ala*," with her attendant sprites Grease, Vinegar, and Garlic, commenced; a combat which at the end of the nineteenth century looked excessively like terminating in favour of the fairy.[5]

Likely, Spencer had read Jean-Anthelme Brillat-Savarin's masterpiece *Physiologie du Goût* (1826) where this famous gourmand had commented that in spite of France losing the war and being compelled to pay its allies seven hundred and fifty million francs, the nation's credit rose and its payments were made with ease. "What power came to our aid?" asked Brillat-Savarin. "What divinity worked this miracle? ... *Gourmandise*. When the Britons, Germans, Teutons, Cimmerians, and Scythians made their irruption into France, they brought with them a rare voracity and stomachs of no common capacity."[6]

The rise of French cuisine and its chefs came from the fallout of the French Revolution and the Napoleonic Wars. Prior to both of these upheavals, chefs were usually employed by aristocratic families, but as the aristocracy broke up, chefs cast about for new opportunities. Some moved to England and around the Continent where they were once again employed by aristocratic families; others began opening restaurants throughout Paris, turning that city into Europe's first restaurant capital, a place where wealthy people (as Brillat-Savarin suggested) traveled simply in order to eat the food. The rise of French cuisine coincided with the rise of gastronomy or the study of food as a serious topic of inquiry.[7] Along with Brillat-Savarin, Grimod de la Reynière (1758–1837) established French gastronomy and raised his nation's cultural currency, particularly in England. He established a "Jury Dégustateur" or Tasting Jury that met at his home, Hôtel de La Reynière. Along with a select group of gourmets, Grimod sampled the finest foods available in Paris. The Jury Dégustateur held 465 weekly sessions that lasted five hours each, and the group published its official judgments in the *Almanach des Gourmands*, published from 1803–1812. To ensure that the group focused exclusively on the quality of the food, Grimod ordered each dish to be served one at a time, a fashion that caught on in Parisian restaurants and that helped bring dining *à la Russe* out of rarified aristocratic circles and make it available to the bourgeoisie.[8]

Grimod had a profound effect on English food lovers. His *Almanach* inspired English imitations such as the 1815 *Epicure's Almanack, or Calendar of Good Living in London*, a book designed to introduce Londoners and visitors alike to the capital's finest inns, taverns, coffeehouses, and eating-houses. Significantly, England did not yet have restaurants; that kind of establishment where people sat at private tables, ordered their meals from a waiter, and chose from a selection of dishes was a later nineteenth-century development, one that we will explore in this chapter's conclusion. Other English gastronomes published their own guides and essays as well. Launcelot Sturgeon's *Essays, Moral, Philosophical, and Stomachical* (1822) was indebted to Grimod's *Almanach des gourmands*, as was Thomas Walker's weekly essay series, *The Original* (1835). William Blanchard Jerrold, author of *The Epicure's Year Book and Table Companion* (1868), continued the work of those before him. He searched out London's best cuisine and in the process acknowledged his debt to both Grimod and Walker.

Of course, French influence in London had been established centuries before. As early as the 1600s, London sported a tavern in Abchurch Lane, run by Arnaud III de Pontac's multilingual son François-Auguste. Arnaud clearly sensed that sophisticated Londoners would respond enthusiastically to French wines and foods, and so they did. The tavern was first known as Pontack's Head, or Pontak's, and the name became synonymous among the fashionable with French food and wine. Chatelain's, another French-run eating establishment, opened in Covent Garden in the reign of Charles II.[9] From the Restoration onward, French food and French cooks became increasingly admired; the period from the French Revolution to the end of the Napoleonic Wars when anti-French sentiment reached a pitch was more an aberration than a norm in England. French chefs, most notably Marie-Antoine Carême, Louis Eustache Ude, Charles Elmé Francatelli, Alexis Soyer, and Auguste Escoffier joined forces with gastronomic writers and published English-language cookbooks, while also working as chefs in London's exclusive clubs and later in the century, restaurants.

Thus far, we have focused on the most elite social circles: those fabulously wealthy and privileged people who had servant staffs of twenty to thirty, a French chef and sous chef, as well as the means to travel abroad, dine with nobility, and in general, develop a fine appreciation of haute cuisine and the art of eating. In the early nineteenth century, most people could not adopt a dinner *à la Russe* style or prepare the haute cuisine that accompanied it because both required a technological sophistication that was not yet widely available. In other words, neither *à la Russe* dining nor haute cuisine fit in with the restrictions with which most people lived: set hours of daylight, seasonal dependency on foodstuffs, primitive methods of food preservation, basic cooking techniques, and basic cooking equipment. Middle-class Victorians were financially limited, even if they were "genteel" or of "gentle" birth. The cities where they lived were limited as well. But all this began to change rapidly by the 1870s. As technology and industry began to make life easier for those already in the comfortable classes, dinner *à la Russe* became easier to manage. However, before we examine the middle class in relation to dinner *à la Russe* and French cuisine, it helps to detail how this style was supposed to work, and how initially, money, breeding, and privilege were at the heart of it. As with dinner *à la Française,* keep in mind that the English adapted this style to their own tastes, and because the host and hostess controlled the number of the courses served, the meal varied.

## THE FORMAT OF DINNER *À LA RUSSE*

In late-eighteenth- and early-nineteenth-century England, a dinner party was not by our current standards an informal or relaxed event, but it did lend itself to conviviality and interaction among participants. When food dishes sat on the table, people were engaged in serving themselves and their partners, and they also had some control over what they ate and how much they ate. Servants were usually less involved in the meal and their absence at key moments resulted in conversations that were probably less stilted than what they would have been otherwise. Invitations to dinner were not necessarily formal; sometimes, they might be as little as a casual but hearty request to "come and eat a leg of mutton with us," the popular early-Victorian dinner invitation, as one gentleman passed his friend on the street.

In many ways, the *à la Russe* style helped to impose, as Valarie Mars succinctly put it, "a formal etiquette that overtly divided those who knew how to dine from the rest. Formal etiquette became important as it became more necessary to maintain social distance."[10] Victorians, born in an age of extraordinary opportunity for creating and losing wealth, where more men gained suffrage, and where hundreds of new occupations no longer fit neatly within the socioeconomic framework of previous generations were not only more class-conscious, they were also more anxious to keep the *hoi polloi* "firmly outside the castle walls."[11] Dinner *à la Russe* was initially seen by the most elite Victorians as a means to do precisely that. As a result, by the 1850s and 1860s, those who wished to host a dinner party felt compelled to follow a strict protocol from the time of issuing invitations to the moment when they wished their guests a good night. While some families issued dinner invitations out of genuine friendship, many more believed that hosting a dinner party was the surest means of enhancing or cementing social significance among one's circle. In other words, if they passed the test and rose to the standards of those attending the affair, they might see ample reward for their effort. To breach etiquette at any stage of the process was to jeopardize a lot of hard work, and as a result of this anxious mood, the guidebook market flourished, particularly when the manuals pertained to dinner *à la Russe*. Among the more popular were Charles Pierce's *The Household Manager* (1857), *Manners and Tone of Good Society* by "A Member of the Aristocracy" (1890), and the tiny pocket-book, *How to Dine* (1879).

Dinner invitations for which *Cassell's Book of the Household* offered the standard format and language were to be issued twenty-one to fourteen days prior to the event. They were to convey to their recipients the level of formality so that they might know how to dress. Invitations in first-person indicated a smaller, intimate affair, likely dinner *à la Française*; third-person indicated dinner *à la Russe* and evening-dress:

> *Mr And Mrs Robinson*
> *request the pleasure of Mr And Mrs Johnson's*
> *company at Dinner, on Friday, February 16th,*
> *at half-past 7 o'clock.*
> *74, Park Road.—January 9th.*[12]

Invitations were embossed if the guest list exceeded ten people; for smaller affairs, an invitation could be elegantly handwritten. Whereas the 1830s Victorian dinner party began as early as three o'clock to take advantage of natural lighting, the 1880s dinner party began around eight o'clock. Gas lighting in all but the poorest city homes was standard, and streets were paved and lighted as well, so there was less concern about the logistics of traveling after dark.

As with early Victorian dinner parties, guests continued to gather in the drawing room, having been admitted by the butler. How one was to enter the drawing room was important. *Manners and Tone of Good Society* noted that it would be vulgar for a lady and gentleman to enter the drawing room arm-in-arm or side-by-side. Etiquette dictated that the lady enter first with the gentleman following in her wake.[13] Conversation topics were also important. To help ensure that no one said something unseemly or insulting, the hostess introduced the persons of highest rank to one another if the affair were small so that they might speak more freely. She was advised to desist doing so at larger parties, however, because those already acquainted would naturally acknowledge one another, leaving the lesser-known or less-high ranks to make their way as best they could. While women sat and made conversation on one side of the room, the men stood and, without a smoke or a drink to help ease the tension, made conversation at the other end—what Sarah Paston-Williams rightly labeled as the ordeal of "*mauvais quart d'heure*."[14] In advising the mistress on how to conduct the drawing-room conversation, Isabella Beeton was no less blunt: That half hour is the first "great ordeal" for the mistress. Her handling of it will either allow her to pass the entire affair "with flying colours, or, lose many of her laurels."[15]

The more leisurely pace, hospitality, and general sense of comfort and security among friends that characterized early Victorian dinner parties was replaced with rigid orchestration, not only in the requisite drawing-room mingling and order of seating, but also in regards to the meal itself. In the 1830s, a mistress turned to her seated guests and graciously informed them that they "saw their meal." Now, the guests were presented upon sitting down with a printed menu, listing the number of courses and what would be offered for each. Nothing was left to imagination. To save mishap or embarrassment, many mistresses combined the function of the menu with that of the name or place card, thus helping guests locate quickly and discreetly their place at the table. After being seated, all one could do was wait; servants saw to the meal.

*Cassell's Book of the Household* explained to readers that for dinner *à la Russe* "everything must be handed, and nothing placed on the table except decorations, cruets, &ct ... More waiting is required with this arrangement than when the dishes are carved at the table; but, on the other hand, the host and hostess are much more at liberty to attend to their guests."[16] For parties of eight to ten, *Cassell's* recommended that the mistress have at least two waiters in addition to her cook and kitchen maids. While one waiter carved meat and plated the food, the other gave diners their plates and poured their wine. Two waiters, however, would have been an uncomfortable minimum number for ten guests, because oftentimes, each course would have two to three options (for example, boiled turkey or roast pigeon), and guests would need to choose what they desired before a waiter made up their plates. In such cases, a third servant (perhaps a kitchen maid who had changed from her soiled uniform into her dress uniform) might carve the meats, putting each on a separate platter, and then the waiters took orders and carried the food to each diner. At all times the servants were present.

Choreography made the meal a success or failure: "If the pauses between each course are too long, if each guest is not supplied quietly and quickly with every want, if the waitress loses her presence of mind and allows the guests to become conscious of the fact that she is flurried; also if the pauses between the courses are too short, and the dinner is hurried through, then, however well cooked the dishes may be, however excellent the wine, and witty the company, the dinner will be a failure," warned *Cassell's*.[17] Done correctly, food arrived to the diners hot and appetizing, thus an improvement over the *à la Française* style, which depended largely on the competence of the master's carving skills, the number of meats he had to carve, and how fast he could hand round the plates. The butler was now the most important servant in regards to choreography. He stood behind the master's chair and watched his waiters to ensure that they attended to all the diners' needs. He rang the bell or discreetly pressed a button embedded in the wall to notify the kitchen staff that the diners were ready for the next course. The cook and the butler ideally had met earlier with the mistress and had worked out how to orchestrate the courses and when to serve each one.

If a family had grand pretensions but had been unsuccessful in securing a French chef on a full-time basis, it was considered essential that one should be engaged at least on the day of the party to prepare the sophisticated foods that were to be served. For an *à la Russe* dinner, guests naturally paid more attention to the food because each dish was presented separately—and dramatically—and thus must be eye-catching. Victorians placed a great deal of importance on visual appearance, usually more so than on the food's taste, a point to which I will return momentarily.

The most fashionable dinner parties now began with an *hors d'oeuvre*. Although tiny, it stimulated taste buds and whetted the appetite. Many served a fish-based *hors d'oeuvre*, such as anchovies on toast, along with a selection of Greek olives. Caviar was likewise popular. As in former times, the dinner proper commenced with soup, now ladled into bowls by a waiter. First, however, guests looked at their menu card to decide which soup to choose. It was proper to offer a clear consommé-based soup and a cream-based purée. In similar fashion, the fish was served with the plate set before the guest when his/her soup bowl was removed. If the mistress offered two fish dishes, guests once again looked at their menu card and told the waiter which one they preferred. It was not in good form to choose some of each for any course in the dinner, and as with *à la Française*, a guest was never pressured to take all the courses and women were expected to decline one or two. The joints often served during the *relevé* course were followed by *entrées*, what previously had been called the made or side dishes. Next came the *entremets*, or smaller, dainty dishes that usually included a number of sweets.

Dessert no longer demanded that servants remove the tablecloth. For dinner *à la Française*, food dishes had been placed symmetrically up and down the table; they were easy enough for the servants to remove, along with the tablecloth. For dinner *à la Russe*, all that white space was to be filled with spectacular arrangements, including flowers, silver candelabra, mirrors to mimic a stream running down the table (complete with fresh moss and ferns along the mirrors), and huge crystal or silver epergnes. Removing the tablecloth was impossible without fuss and disturbance, not to mention accidents. Instead, the servants would have placed cloth slips down the table sides, easily removing them and making it unnecessary to worry about brushing away crumbs before dessert. By 1900, families still giving formal dinners often rebelled against this earlier fashion by keeping the tablecloth as uncluttered as possible, leaving vast spaces of white instead.

In the early Victorian period, the wine glasses and tumblers were generally kept on the sideboard until the diner had requested a drink. For dinner *à la Russe* in England (the fashion was different in France), the glasses were placed at each individual setting. Three were provided along with a water tumbler. Previously, a diner choose whatever drink took his fancy; now the host controlled what one was to drink with what course, although he followed some general guidelines when it came to serving which wine when. A guest could, however, also choose to pass on alcohol and polite women were either to abstain from certain wines or to follow the French convention of diluting theirs with water. For the soup course, the host usually served a slightly chilled Spanish Amontillado. Fish went best with a crisp German white wine that the English called "Hock," or with

Artificial lake for a dinner table from *Cassell's Book of the Household* (1889–1891). This suggestion for a dinner *à la Russe* centerpiece suggests the importance of visual effects. The table is no longer crowded with food, but instead with a full-length mirror laid down its center and surrounded with fresh flowers and ferns. The bowls of fruit will remain on the table for dessert.

Chablis, a dry white French Burgundy. Often, Hock or Chablis were served for the *hors d'oeuvre* as well. Champagne was often served with the entrées, and as a favorite drink of the women, a considerate host offered it three or four more times during the course of the dinner. Roast mutton or beef lent themselves to claret, the most fashionable wine among men from the 1860s on. A sweet wine such as Sauternes was traditionally offered with the *entremets*, and for dessert, more champagne, more dessert wine, or vintage port were typical.

When dessert was on the table, the waiters placed the wine decanters by the host and for the first time they exited the room. For approximately ten minutes, women and men lingered at the table until the hostess rose to lead her women guests back to the drawing room for tea or coffee. Upon rising, they took a minute to put back on their gloves while the men likewise rose and remained standing until they had exited the room. Men no longer lingered for long at this point; fashion dictated that they follow to the drawing room after fifteen to twenty minutes. Thus, the goodwill and camaraderie that women and men had often experienced in the hours after the dessert were now curtailed; time was important to this meal, one that had been reduced to two and a half hours from start to finish. Etiquette dictated that the guests were to call on the host and hostess within a week's time to thank them for the affair.

## ADAPTING DINNER *À LA RUSSE* TO MEET THE DEMANDS OF THE MODEST MIDDLE CLASS

Considering its intricacy and formality, not to mention the challenges that so many courses would have presented a housewife with her small kitchen and maid-of-all-work, dinner *à la Russe* was slower to catch on with the majority of middle-class Victorians, although its upper rung, the "carriage-keeping class" of businessmen, financiers, bankers, and industrialists were likely to be using this service by the 1870s. For the more modest, why tamper with a dining style that worked and, for that matter, had worked for more than one hundred and fifty years? Such was the attitude well into the century. However, if guidebooks can be used as evidence, by the 1880s and 1890s, most middle-class people had also adapted the *à la Russe* service, at least for entertaining. Along with step-by-step instructions, guidebooks suggested shortcuts to make this service less expensive, but no less impressive. And so we arrive again at the roles that technology and industry played in dictating dinner fashions, for both technology and industry made it not only possible for people to cook what and how they wanted, but it also made the food products on which a dinner *à la Russe* depended more affordable. As increasing numbers adopted the *à la Russe* service and took advantage of a growing processed foods industry, haute cuisine itself became modified and turned into something that critics derided as bad English food served under the guise of French names.

## PSEUDO-FRENCH CUISINE

Edward Spencer faulted Victorians for their pretensions when it came to calling their food by French names and he likewise called attention to their willingness to pay extra money for plain English foods labeled as French. Cooks merely clothed "purely English food in French disguises," complained Spencer. A plain leg of mutton becomes a *gigot*; a curry becomes a *kari*. A pheasant, now called a *faisan*, is suddenly "charged for at special rates in the bill."[18] English people, Spencer continued, wanted their joints whole and their vegetables well boiled, but they liked the seeming sophistication that went along with the French names. Even some of the aristocracy and royalty who hired French chefs at outrageous prices still requested that they prepare more or less English food under French names—a habit that outraged French chefs who saw themselves as artists, not as servants.

In *The French Chef* (1813), a cookbook written specifically for an English audience, Ude offered his "Court Bouillon for Fish *au bleu*." Not only did the poaching liquid call for an abundance of spices and herbs (thyme, bay leaves, mace, cloves, parsley) and root vegetables, but also for "two bottles of white and a bottle of red wine with salt &ct." Ude continued: "This *marinade* being stewed properly, will serve several times for stewing the fish."[19] At this point in *The French Chef*'s early editions (up through 1822), Ude then proceeded without comment to his next fish recipes. However, by the 1828 edition of *The French Chef*, Ude began adding this revealing *nota bene*, probably based on negative feedback to his recipe: "This manner of boiling the fish is too expensive in England, where wine is so dear; but a very good *cour bouillon* can not be made with vinegar. Besides, fish *au cour bouillon* is always eaten with oil and vinegar, which is not customary in England."[20] Ude knew from his previous frustrations in trying to cater to English tastes that many would not take to the rich complexity inherent in his court bouillon or to eating a fish served in olive oil and vinegar. He understood that the Victorians—more so than their Georgian predecessors—preferred fish boiled in salt water, even if they could afford wine, and indeed, the majority of his fish recipes in the *French Chef* call for just that: salt and water.

As Ude warned in his preface "Advice to Cooks," the difficulty that a passionate (and likely transplanted) French chef will encounter in an English kitchen is "a national prejudice which exists against French, Cookery," and the French chef's stubborn persistence in practicing his calling as if he were still in France.[21] Ude, who had worked as chef to King George IV, the Duke of York, and *chef de cuisine* at the exclusive London gambling club, Crockford's, understood that what most English wanted was the status of a French chef—but not authentic French cuisine. While Ude might have been very critical of the limited English palate, he nonetheless established the cardinal rule of successful English restaurants: The cook "must remember that the customer comes first and that his wishes must be met without a murmur of complaint."[22] Initially, both a dinner *à la Russe* and haute cuisine were exclusive, but as chefs like Ude, Soyer, and Francatelli modified the French culinary repertoire to accommodate an even wider range of tastes, that exclusivity was bound to be compromised.

## THE SERVANT SHORTAGE AND ITS EFFECTS ON DINNER *À LA RUSSE*

Watering down the poaching broth (literally), simplifying French sauces, and substituting less complex cooking methods for elaborate ones did make haute cuisine less expensive, but even modified, the prospect of preparing so many courses of fancy food overwhelmed many housewives, given their own lack of cooking skill and their limited servant staffs. Even wealthy Victorians struggled to hire a full-time French chef and experienced English cooks (cooks were female, chefs were male) were almost as difficult to find. Between 1881 and 1901, the number of girls under age fifteen entering domestic service fell by 34 percent, in part because of compulsory elementary education, but also because working-class girls had more employment options than their mothers and grandmothers had encountered.[23] While middle-class Victorians found older, competent cooks desirable, most cooks learned the trade by starting young as scullery maids, advancing to kitchen maids, and ultimately becoming cooks. The number of accomplished cooks thus declined as the number of young girls entering service declined. Consequently, experienced cooks demanded competitive wages, and even inexperienced ones were more expensive than a typical kitchen or scullery maid. In 1857, it required a yearly income of £500 to employ a cook, housemaid, and parlor-maid; by 1873 that figure had jumped to £750 to hire the same number.[24] One's salary did not keep up with such inflation, and as a result, the number of servants per household began to shrink.

An advertisement in the 1913 edition of Nancy Lake's *Menus Made Easy* suggests that the servant shortage by that decade was severe. Mrs Hunt, Ltd, a London placing agency, "would charge the person seeking the cook the fees—not the cook herself." More importantly, Mrs Hunt, Ltd assured any prospective cooks that the agency had "some thousands of Places on our Black List. If you get suited through us you will not get into one of these." Over one hundred Clerks, the advertisement continued, work to suit "nearly three hundred Customers every day."[25] The terms might have been exaggerated to catch a reader's attention, but nonetheless, the advertisement's location—right after the title page instead of in the back of the book—suggested urgency. Regardless of a servant shortage, one's social status and chances of rising higher seemed to compel middle-class families to give a monthly, if not a weekly, dinner party, and dinner *à la Russe* was the fashion. For those occasions, the mistress had to make whatever arrangements necessary to ensure that she and her servants could create the dishes for at least six courses and also serve the courses with aplomb.

## THE RISE OF AGNES B. MARSHALL

Enter Mrs. Agnes B. Marshall, one of the era's shrewdest and most talented cookbook authors and cooking-school teachers. Remembered today for her ice cream creations (she is credited for having invented the "coronet" or ice cream cone before the Americans claimed that honor at the 1904 St. Louis fair), Marshall also produced the best-selling *Mrs. A.B. Marshall's Book of Cookery* (1885). In its numerous editions, the cookbook outlined the dinner *à la Russe* courses, suggested several menus, included hundreds of recipes, and perhaps most importantly, attached a comprehensive glossary of French cooking terms designed to help a modest housewife at least sound sophisticated and accomplished. Aside from making money, Marshall also helped average middle-class people pull off an *à la Russe* dinner with less staff, less money, and less skill.

As with Isabella Beeton twenty years before her, Marshall astutely assessed and capitalized from the psychological state of middle-class women in regards to their domestic challenges. Not only was Marshall right in surmising that many women felt anxious about fitting in and helping their husbands succeed professionally, she also knew that they felt helpless when it came to fancy cooking and that they were frustrated at not having competent servants, state-of-the-art equipment, and spacious kitchens. To meet these women's needs, Marshall took a multipronged approach. Not only did she write cookbooks that often doubled as etiquette guides, but she also ran the popular Marshall's School of Cookery, located at 30 & 32 Mortimer Street, London, where mistresses and servants could enroll in day classes or longer ones designed to teach them about the fine points of a dinner *à la Russe* and how to create the necessary dishes associated with French haute cuisine. With equal foresight, Marshall operated a domestic staff agency out of her cooking school, supplying desperate mistresses with staff cooks who could be "sent to any part of the country for special Dinners, Ball Suppers, Wedding Breakfasts, etc." She also would hire out all the requisite flatware, epergnes, and other important table decorations for such events should a mistress not have such supplies herself.[26]

But her most important contribution to ensuring that the dinner ran smoothly was to produce—in her name—an entire line of convenience foods that could take the strain out of preparing sauces, aspics, and flavor combinations on which haute cuisine was based. In this respect, Marshall was the precursor to today's television chef: one who combines hugely popular classes with a wealth of self-authored cookbooks while endorsing food products and cookware on the side. Included among Marshall's endorsed shortcut products were the following: Luxette, "the dainty purée" for *hors d'oeuvres* and savories; quick-dissolving leaf gelatin for producing the requisite jellies and aspics; preground almonds for marzipans, almond icing, nougat, cakes, and puddings; baking powder; food coloring in the era's most desirable shades, including carmine, sap green, saffron, and purvio (mauve); concentrated fruit essences from orange to banana; liqueur syrups; bottled pepper sauces; and even bottles of already-prepared consommé.

Some of these convenience foods were expensive, with the consommé selling for 1 shilling, 6 pence for a small bottle and 2 shillings, 9 pence for a large one. A small tin of Marshall's Luxette brand purée sold for 1 shilling. Nonetheless, many women considered these prices reasonable when compared to the time and cost it took to produce such items in their own kitchens. Jellies and aspics were traditionally made from boiling calve's hoofs for several hours; consommé from boiling beef bones with vegetables for hours, then reducing the broth, clarifying it with egg white, and finally proceeding with the recipe for which consommé was required. Even taking time to blanch and pound almonds to a paste was difficult work in a kitchen where six to ten courses were to be served that evening, and for those of us today who rely on food processors, it is difficult to imagine the amount of time it could take a kitchen servant or (in a worst-case scenario) the mistress to push through a hair sieve or a tammy cloth two gallons' worth of soup. Before cheap wire mesh sieves, Victorians used hair sieves that looked somewhat like a wooden bucket with a fine hair mesh at the bottom. The soup or sauce was poured into the sieve, and with a large pestle, the maid patiently pushed the contents through. A thick soup turned into velvety, silken purée by pushing it through such a sieve. Wealthy families with large servant staffs could afford to have their cooks do things the old-fashioned way, but thousands more genteel people simply could not maintain the staff or give them the time to continue such practices. Even with Marshall's shortcuts, executing a multicourse dinner party was a challenge with many dishes requiring multiple steps and sophisticated technologies to complete them.

Advertisement for Luxette, from *Mrs. A. B. Marshall's Cookery Book* (1885). "Luxette" was one of many Marshall products designed to help Victorian housewives manage the production of a multicourse dinner *à la Russe*. Illustration courtesy of the Morse Department of Special Collections, Hale Library, Kansas State University.

In the previous chapter, I discussed how dinner *à la Française* was based largely on the technologies available to early Victorians, and how during a transitional period in the mid-nineteenth century, new items and technologies were available but not yet economically feasible or they required a more sophisticated city infrastructure than what had been in place. By the time that Agnes Marshall became famous, new technologies and innovations were more available and there to be taken advantage of by most middle-class families. Although Marshall stamped her name on numerous shortcut food products, she was by no means the only one to market such necessaries as baking powder and vanilla extract. Other manufacturing firms were also supplying stores nationwide with products that today we do not give even a second's thought when it comes to cooking. To understand how dinner *à la Russe* became as much a product of late-nineteenth-century technology as dinner *à la Française* had been the product of its own time and place, let us examine some of innovations that made Marshall a household name and made dinner *à la Russe* possible for the middle classes.

## THE TECHNOLOGIES AND INNOVATIONS BEHIND A LATE-VICTORIAN DINNER *À LA RUSSE*

In England, dinner *à la Française* had traditionally celebrated seasonal bounty and emphasized both the economics and the pragmatics of eating foods in season, but late-century Victorians did not concern themselves as much about season because they did not have to. Industrial canning, refrigerated railcars, and steamships made the problem of preserving and transporting perishable goods less pressing.

### Canned Foods

While most people still desisted from serving fresh peas in February, they might well have served canned peas, and for that matter, asparagus and carrots as well. The quality of canned goods was mediocre, but when a soup called for peas, an enterprising cook could get away with the canned product because after she had seasoned and pureed it, its quality would have gone unnoticed by most guests. Canned (or bottled) foods had been available to consumers for much of the nineteenth century, but it took years to fine-tune the process by which all goods could be guaranteed safe from spoilage and it also took decades to ensure that canned goods were not adulterated. As the pure food laws took effect in the 1870s, adulteration ceased to be a concern and the food inside the cans or bottles arrived home less frequently spoiled. Specialty grocers stocked goods designed to appeal to middle-class women who did not have the equipment, help, or space to preserve their own food (assuming that they even knew how to do it). Some canned products, particularly mutton and beef, were marketed to poorer people who could seldom afford fresh meat, but many canned goods were affordable only by the prosperous classes: Alaskan salmon, Mediterranean apricots and peaches, cherries in maraschino syrup, and particularly pineapple, were regarded as luxuries. A small can of salmon, for example, cost 9 pence, and so while it was likely stored in a middle-class pantry along with canned fruits necessary to construct a quick and elegant sweet, it was not an everyday food.[27]

Customs and the values traditionally associated with food and cooking had altered radically from the early 1800s. For centuries women had been praised for the quality of their homemade preserves, cheeses, and baked goods. But by the 1880s, *Cassell's Book of the Household* advised women who might have a desire to do their own preserving to think again: "In a vast majority of cases it will be considered wiser to buy preserves ready made and use them sparingly, than to purchase the fruit and sugar and have the trouble of making them."[28] What had been considered extravagant—buying bottled preserves and factory-produced cakes—was now considered economical; growing, canning, and baking were often treated by domestic economists as useless indulgences for all but the wealthiest.

## Shipping Perishable Foods

More appealing than canned vegetables and fruits were fresh ones. The mid-1850s saw the beginning of what would become a twentieth-century norm: perishable foods available regardless of the growing season. While strawberries in York might not be ready until June or July, those imported by steamer from France might be available at the greengrocer by April, or they might be growing prolifically in Cornwall and Devonshire in May and shipped via rail to York the day after their harvest. Citrus fruits' thick rinds had always made them easier to transport fresh than any other fresh food, and thus the English taste for lemons, oranges, and citron had been long established. Prior to the 1850s, these fruits made their way to England via old-fashioned sailing ships that hailed from Spain, Portugal, and Sicily. By the 1850s, they were brought in via steamship from the Azores, Madeira, Malta, and Crete. Costermongers and greengrocers lined up below London Bridge during the winter and spring months to purchase oranges as they came off the barges. "One-fourth of our London supply of oranges, say 25 millions annually, is said to be sold in the streets and theatres; leaving 75 million to be sold by the shopkeepers," reported George Dodd in *The Food of London* (1856). As for lemons, London consumption was estimated around twenty million annually.[29]

Developments in refrigerated shipping as well as in canning resulted in lower food prices and the eventual introduction of exotic fruits and vegetables to English markets, particularly tomatoes, bananas, and pineapples. Tomatoes were highly perishable and did not grow well in most parts of England, although the Clyde Valley became famous for its "Scotch Tomatoes." Earlier in the century, their use had been limited to sauces and ketchups but even then the fruit remained unpopular when available. As fresh tomatoes became a more common item at greengrocers and city markets, Victorians began to overcome their prejudice against them, and because Italy could ship high-quality canned tomatoes to England in mass quantity, the fruit began to appear as a staple ingredient in a number of dinner *à la Russe* courses. Canned tomato imports increased tenfold from 1897 to 1908.[30]

Several of Marshall's dishes from her dinner party menu at the head of this chapter required either fresh or canned tomatoes. *Poulet à la Valencienne,* a classic chicken and rice dish fundamental to Spanish cuisine would have included canned tomatoes. For her version, Marshall recommended half a pint of tomato pulp and half a pint of stock.[31] Likewise, the sauce that accompanied *Côtelettes de Pigeon à l'Américaine* consisted of meat stock, white wine, sliced fresh mushroom, and one fresh, sliced tomato. Significantly, the classic version of this sauce would have been composed of more tomato than Marshall called for. To achieve a bright red color in both, she instead advised readers to add "a few drops of Marshall's carmine."[32]

Tomatoes were also appearing on the dinner table raw as well as cooked by the 1890s. Famous journalist and food critic George Augustus Sala wrote his own cookbook *A Thorough Good Cook* (1895) and included several tomato-based recipes, adding as a note that "fifty years ago tomatoes, or 'love-apples', were scarce and dear, and were usually sold, preserved in bottles, as sauce for hot meat. At present there is usually an ample supply, and sometimes a glut, of tomatoes, English or foreign, sold at very reasonable prices."[33] Just as they are popular today dressed with oil and vinegar, so too in the late nineteenth century.

Fresh bananas and pineapples were even more exotic than tomatoes, and they were real status foods among late-century Victorians. In her 1894 edition of *Menus Made Easy,* Lake included a recipe for *Bananas au rhum* to be served as a show-stopping entremet; she included four banana recipes, including one for banana ice cream, in her 1913 edition. Pineapples had long been grown in the aristocracy's greenhouses; now they were increasingly popular at middle-class dinner parties because their price had fallen and they were more available. Lake's *Pain d'ananas a la Royale* (a mould of pineapple purée set in jelly and garnished with whipped cream) appeared in various guises in 1890s cookbooks, as did recipes for pineapple ice cream, including those in Sala's *A Thorough Good Cook* and Marshall's *Fancy Ices.*

### Home Refrigeration and Ice

Marshall's suggested dinner menus took full advantage of the latest technology available to a middle-class family in 1895, and nowhere was the technology more noticeable than in the elaborate, molded ices that graced the dinner table. "A very wide choice is offered to those who take the trouble to look for it, extending from 'the ice pudding' *par excellence,* through a long list of soufflés, mousses, bombes, plombières, muscovites, &c., &c."[34] The Punch course, designed as a palate cleanser between the *Relevé* and *Rôt* courses, could now be a Sorbet course. Certainly, Marshall noted, a beautifully presented semifrozen sorbet served in a bowl that itself was made of ice is much more impressive and fashionable than a glass of cold punch. Plentiful amounts of cheap ice made such a sensual feast possible—and without a great deal of effort and fuss.

The scarcity and expense of ice and refrigeration in the earlier decades limited iced desserts to the wealthy. As the century progressed, England imported vast quantities of ice from North America and Scandinavia, and methods of both preserving and utilizing it became more efficient. Ice companies in the 1880s and 1890s maintained huge "ice depots" in cities and at ports, and from these, they delivered cheap ice via rail to any part of the country, be it rural, urban, or suburban, within twenty-four hours (previously, this process had been done by barges traveling slowly along canals). Ice was then stored in smaller ice-houses and it was delivered to people's doorsteps where it was then stored in the family refrigerator (or what in the United States was called an ice box).

Refrigerators were expensive, however. They ranged in price from £6 to £16, and they were tiny in regards to storage capacity, given that most of the bulk of it was filled with ice and insulation. Most Victorians did not have such a refrigerator. They relied on marble-slab counters in the scullery (and as far away from the range as possible) to store perishable foods. Regardless of her rather shameless self-promotion, Marshall's patented ice cave did make it easier for people of moderate means to create at least one or two fancy ices for a dinner party. The outer shell of the cave was filled with a mixture of crushed ice and salt, creating an intense cold. A one- to four-quart mold filled with custard or fruit syrup was then placed inside the cave. By the end of the century, ice cream for the dessert had become commonplace, affordable by almost all middle-class people because of Marshall's ice cave and other imitations, and also because many ice-cream shops and restaurants installed electric freezers at the turn of the century.

## Gas Cookers

Abundant ice, canned goods, imported fresh ones, lower tariffs, and lower prices were all essential to helping Victorian middle-class mistresses and their servants construct a dinner *à la Russe* menu, but so too was the ease that a gas cooker brought to middle-class kitchens by the 1880s and 1890s. Taking advantage of an 1847 Act of Parliament that regulated gas supply to the public, James Sharp's Southampton firm began selling gas ranges to the public by 1850, although chef Alexis Soyer had been using them in the Reform Club kitchen since 1841.[35] Soyer was one of the first to promote the technology, touting the ease and efficiency of gas-range cooking. Victorians tolerated, even admired, Soyer's eccentricity and theatrics, but they were reluctant to use gas for cooking with some legitimate reasons. For one, gas (which in the Victorian era was a byproduct of coal) was an unreliable and expensive form of heat in the early

32 *Advertisements.*

BY ROYAL LETTERS PATENT.

# MARSHALL'S PATENT ICE CAVE.

Charged ready for use.

USES.

FOR SETTING ICE PUDDINGS without the use of grease or chance of brine entering, and without the expense of special moulds. Ice puddings when moulded can be turned out and kept ready for use at any minute, so that the ice can be made and held ready before commencing to serve the dinner if necessary.

FOR FREEZING SOUFFLÉS it offers great advantages, as the progress of freezing can be examined from time to time The soufflés can always be kept ready for use.

FOR INVALIDS to have always at hand a supply of ice or iced food or drink, or for food or drink to be kept hot for any length of time. It is especially useful in nurseries, in the latter respect.

FOR CONFECTIONERS to send out iced puddings, etc., quite ready for serving; for keeping ice creams, etc., ready for selling.

FOR KEEPING ICES during Balls, Evening and Garden Parties, and for taking ice creams, etc., to Races, Picnics. etc.

*AND FOR REFRIGERATORS GENERALLY.*

SIZE No. 1 will hold one quart mould. Size 2, two quart moulds. Size 3, four quart moulds. Size 4 will hold six large champagne bottles. Sizes No. 2 and upwards can be used for icing mineral waters, etc., and kept in dining, smoking, and billiard rooms.

**PRICES.**

No. 1, £1. 11*s*. 6*d*. No. 2, £2. 2*s*. No. 3, £3. 3*s*. No. 4, £4. 4*s*.
Special No. 3, £3. 3*s*.

LARGER AND SPECIAL SIZES TO ORDER.

**SPECIMEN PAGE FROM 'BOOK OF MOULDS.'**

Advertisement for Mrs. Marshall's Patented Ice Cave, from *Mrs. A. B. Marshall's Cookery Book* (1885). Marshall's Ice Cave often served as a refrigerator as well as an ice-cream freezer. They came in four sizes, selling from £1, 11 shillings, 6 pence for the smallest, up to £4, 4 shillings for the largest. Illustration courtesy of the Morse Department of Special Collections, Hale Library, Kansas State University.

1850s. Gas could also be extremely dangerous if a leak occurred and it made the air uncomfortably dry, sucking up large amounts of oxygen. Whereas the coal range had a large hot water receptacle, early gas cookers did not come with one, and this made them unattractive to consumers. Other complaints had a less legitimate basis. Many believed, for example, that a joint baked in a gas cooker would be penetrated by noxious fumes, making the meat not just unpalatable, but poisonous.

Rumford had attempted to rectify this complaint with coal-fired ranges and the Shrewsbury Portable Gas Oven Company tried to rectify it with their gas ranges as well by putting the jets underneath the oven rather than inside it, and creating a vent to force fumes out of the oven. On top of the oven sat a convenient hotplate, thus allowing the cook to bake, fry, and boil simultaneously—one of the key advantages touted by coal-fired range producers.[36] As more people became comfortable with the idea of using gas ranges for cooking and as they had opportunities to taste food that had been made with them, prejudices disappeared; point-by-point, they offered tremendous advantages over the coal-fired range. Many people were obviously persuaded by the cost. By the 1880s, gas had dropped to 3 shillings, 6 pence per 1000 feet, meaning that a middle-class family need not expend more than 2½ pence a day for fuel. The same amount of cooking on a coal range raised the price to between 7 pence and 1 shilling a day.[37] Some switched to gas cookers because they produced less heat. For those wanting the warmth of a kitchen coal fire in the winter, hybrid coal/gas models were available. Many women must have been persuaded by the gas cooker's ease, particularly those who employed only a general maid. If the range were enameled, one simply wiped out the interior oven; if not enameled, one lime-washed it occasionally. Gone were the days of blackleading the cast-iron ranges, fussing in the cold and dark to get the coal fire going, cleaning out the flues, and being so filthy that one had to bathe before breakfast. Indeed, the gas cooker was probably one of the main reasons why many middle-class people found themselves able to deal with a servant shortage, and eventually, to decide that servants were redundant anyway. Using gas for cooking cut down on not only kitchen work but all housework. A substantial portion of a parlor maid's job was the daily and even hourly dusting, polishing, and sweeping that resulted from coal smoke residue settling on all surfaces, tarnishing the brass, silver, and glass, smudging the tablecloths and curtains, and embedding itself in the carpets.

## THE SOCIAL AND CULTURAL IMPLICATIONS OF THE DINNER *À LA RUSSE*

In the last decades of the nineteenth century, food and dining became a vehicle by which one showed off social status and raised it—or in some cases, compromised it. In recalling those decades, Arnold Palmer wrote that his generation (those born shortly after the end of the Victorian era) recognized the age for

2 *Advertisements.*

THE

# 'HOUSEWIFE'

SERIES OF

# GAS COOKERS

ALL the latest improvements in Cooker Construction are embodied, and all fads and unnecessary complications are avoided. The Cookers are made in graduated sizes to suit families from three to fifteen in number.

**SIZES OVERALL.**

23″ wide,
33″ high.
20″ deep.

**SIZES INSIDE.**

15½″ wide.
24″ high.
13½″ deep.
Door opening 14½″.

**'Housewife,' No. 3**

PRICES FROM £3 10s. to £7 10s.

All particulars to be obtained from—

**FLETCHER, RUSSELL & Co. Ltd.**

**15 Fisher Street, Southampton Row, W.C.**

*Works :—Palatine Works, Warrington.*

Advertisement for a gas cooker from *Mrs. A. B. Marshall's Cookery Book* (1885). This brand-name gas cooker resembled many rival firms' products. By the 1890s, the prices were on average cheaper than coal-fired range models with similar features. Illustration courtesy of the Morse Department of Special Collections, Hale Library, Kansas State University.

what it was: "competitive, snobbish, parvenu, purse-proud, vulgar, earnest, and indefatigable." Many of the rising middle- and upper-middle-class Londoners were "also the first, or nearly the first, arrivals in a new enclosure in the social order, created and fenced by their wealth. They had had a job to get in, they were having a job to get out, and they meant to make it as difficult as they could for others to get in and out."[38] The dinner table, Palmer contended, became the place where these pecking-order games were carried on at their most intense.

However, technology and an industrialized foods industry made the game increasingly difficult for those who used dinner parties as a means to flush out and expose social interlopers. A dinner *à la Russe* now meant that food became a tool in the wife's arsenal. She could manipulate the courses so that they appeared exquisite in taste and presentation at the same time that she could secretly economize by serving tiny portions for each course, manipulating the number of courses, and using lower-quality cuts of meat because the entire joint did not have to be brought in for all to admire before the host carved it. A Marshall menu, such as the one that opens this chapter, allowed a mistress to scrimp on some courses and save her pennies for a couple of real stunners. If she had read Marshall's cookbook carefully, she would have known that a discriminating guest expected that a *Saumon bouilli* was to be topped with *Sauce Ecrevisses.* Just as a mistress in the 1830s understood that the classic accompaniment to boiled mutton was caper sauce, a mistress in the 1890s knew that in haute cuisine, poached salmon was often topped with a crayfish sauce. Here was her first chance to impress. Crayfish had been so heavily harvested in Europe that finding the delicacy was difficult, and when it was found, its expense was exorbitant. A distinct message was being conveyed via that salmon course about sophistication and money both. However, without too much worry of being detected, the cook following Marshall's recipe could have eliminated the lobster spawn that such a sauce traditionally called for to add depth, and instead she would have substituted "a teaspoonful of Luxette and a few drops of carmine."[39]

She could execute the same cunning with her *Bécassines sur Croûtes,* prosaically known as "Snipes on Toast." Snipes were migratory game birds similar to woodcocks but smaller. These birds were rare even in the autumn when they were in season, and thus, they were regarded as a delicacy. However, the portions that the mistress had her waiters dole out to admiring guests would have been small or "dainty," and so she could expend some money on snipes but make up for it elsewhere in her menu by using leftover vegetables and stock for her soup, *Croûte au Pot. Abricots à la Condé* could be done up more cheaply with canned apricots and (once more) a drop of Mrs. Marshall's food coloring to revitalize their color. Her *Caviar sur Croûtes* relied on croutons of stale bread fried golden in butter, and topped with a lower-grade caviar than the sturgeon caviar that would have been de rigueur in earlier decades.

Furthermore, the guests' expectations and attention were not necessarily focused on the fine flavor of the foods, but rather, on the appearance of each

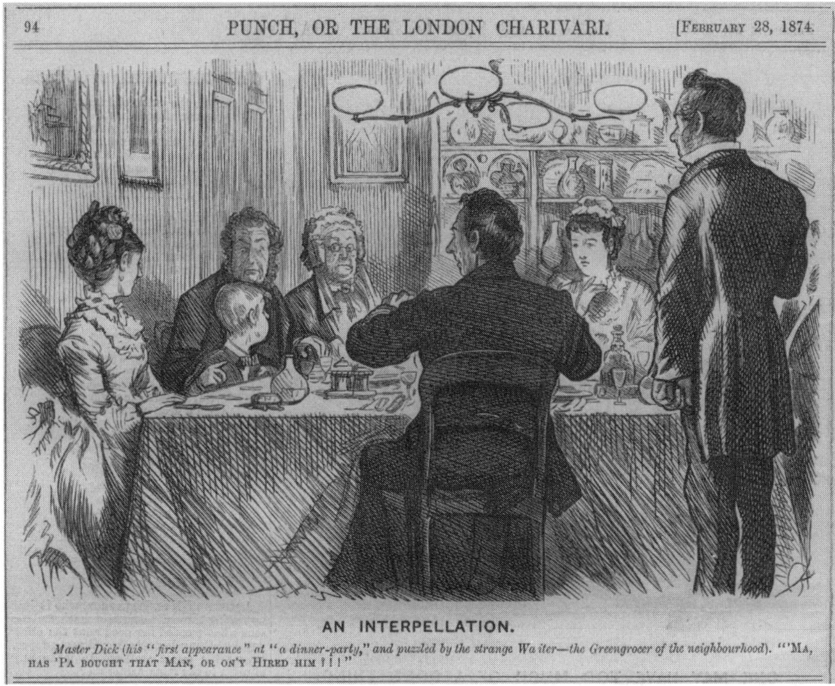

94 PUNCH, OR THE LONDON CHARIVARI. [FEBRUARY 28, 1874.

AN INTERPELLATION.

*Master Dick (his "first appearance" at "a dinner-party," and puzzled by the strange Waiter—the Greengrocer of the neighbourhood).* "'MA, HAS 'PA BOUGHT THAT MAN, OR ON'Y HIRED HIM ! ! !"

"An Interpellation." This February 28, 1874 cartoon from *Punch* magazine conveys the length to which some socially conscious Victorians went to impress their dinner-party company. Because the *à la Russe* service required many servants, a desperate mistress often hired local tradespeople to play the part of domestic, live-in servants. Here young Master Dick questions his parents as to why the family greengrocer is suddenly their waiter. Illustration courtesy of the Morse Department of Special Collections, Hale Library, Kansas State University.

dish as it was served to them by gloved greengrocers-disguised-as-waiters. As plates were handed, the guests focused also on the elaborate centerpiece that now took the place of symmetrically arranged dishes of food on the dinner table. Factory-produced china and silver electroplate replaced expensive tableware luxuries. Given the 1845 removal of glass tax, glass became the rage, and the more of it on the table, the better the table presumably looked. With candles placed strategically up and down the table, the effect was just as striking as it would have been if the crystal were hand-cut, the lace handmade, and the china hand-painted.

## THE RISE OF THE RESTAURANT

But by the close of the nineteenth century, many Victorians had simply tired of all this effort, be it to impress, to fit in, to keep others from fitting in, or to deceive. If we return to the introduction of this chapter, *Cassell's Book of the*

*Household's* stern "can-do" tone might make more sense, now that we have examined the numerous complexities and anxieties that arose for many families trying to host such a dinner party, and trying to work up their courage if they were invited to attend one. The linking of railroad terminals with restaurants and luxury hotels in the 1870s and 1880s, a rise in Continental travel, and women's increased freedoms outside the home, particularly in regards to employment and ability to go about their business unencumbered by male chaperones, all resulted in Victorians' greater interest in eating at restaurants for reasons of pleasure and expedience. By 1890, restaurant dining became fashionable and for prosperous people it presented a solution to the escalating stress of a dinner party.

The Great Exhibition in 1851 was the impetus to a developing restaurant culture. Luxury hotels, including the Grand Hotel on Trafalgar Square and the Langham at Portland Place, served meals to hotel patrons, but these meals were utilitarian affairs and patrons chose from an extremely limited menu. As train stations became attached to large hotels and it was feasible to offer wealthy clients more appealing food choices, entrepreneurs built restaurants attached to the hotel and station both. By the 1880s, hotels began opening their dining rooms to anyone who desired to eat at the establishment rather than to hotel guests alone. These restaurants served six-course meals in the *à la Russe* style.

London nightlife also began thriving as people traveled more cheaply and easily, street lighting became commonplace, and restaurants along with cafés and taverns added to the enjoyment of spending time away from home. To accommodate theatergoers, many hotel restaurants such as Evans Hotel and Supper Rooms, as well as a plethora of Soho restaurants such as Romano's and Café de l'Europe served dinners between five thirty and eight o'clock, and again from ten o'clock to midnight. Understanding the changing cultural climate, small restaurant owners felt encouraged to market "ethnic" foods to a wider customer base than just the Bohemians who crowded Soho on a weekend night. With the help of Nathaniel Newnham-Davis's guidebook, *Dinners and Diners* (1899), more adventurous middle-class Victorians could find Italian pasta at Gatti's in the Strand, French "peasant" food at Les Restaurant des Gourmets in Lisle Street near the Empire Theater, and vegetarian food—an increasingly popular option toward the end of the century—at the woman-friendly St. George's Café in St. Martin's Lane.

Clearly the social gesture of the at-home dinner party was more the woman's burden than the man's, and women rebelled. Many accounts from the late nineteenth century attest to women's determination to become a part of a culture that had heretofore been largely denied to them: the right to eat in public. In earlier decades, genteel women had suffered from limited eating options when they shopped, traveled, or worked. Men might assume that a lone woman in a public dining room was a prostitute. Many establishments, such as the American Bar at the Criterion, did not allow women on the premises even if they had a male escort; others had "Ladies Only" dining quarters where those who were traveling could eat in as private a space as possible. However, by the 1890s, women became a part of the restaurant scene not only because they began boldly to go into restaurants with other women or with men, but also because (as Nathanial Newnham-Davis implied in *Dinners and Diners*) many chefs and restaurant managers understood that a woman in a beautiful evening gown enhanced the overall image of the restaurant, drawing in more diners, and thus increasing their reputation and profit margins.

Offering menus with a wide variety of foods from which to choose, restaurants took away much of the need for people to open their own homes to guests for dinner. Private rooms could be secured in the capital's leading restaurants and for prices as low as half-a-crown or as high as five pounds, a person could eat a meal accompanied with wine and spirits. Formality, stiff rules of etiquette, and obsession with the material accoutrements that had obscured the guests' focus on food were often relaxed at even the fanciest restaurants. Live music, brilliant electric lighting (from the 1890s onward), and the energy of people talking and eating, ushered in a new age and new attitude toward food and also toward one's friends, business colleagues, and acquaintances.

The demise of the formal at-home dinner party with its elaborate *à la Russe* style was also the result of employment shifts and trends. Larger numbers of middle-class women worked outside the home in a wide array of jobs. Working-class women likewise had many more options, seldom opting for a life of domestic servitude. Finally, professional men continued to put in longer and longer hours at their offices. While restaurants were popular, what became in some ways even more so were the inexpensive teashop chains. With no ceremony and with all the courses placed on the table at once, these meals, which might be summed up as "meat and two veg," were not "dinner" so much as they were "tea." Except for formal occasions, "tea" replaced "dinner" in thousands of middle-class homes by the turn of the century, and convenience and ease slowly began to win out over rigid rules. In a manner that reflects today's eating patterns, dinner *à la Russe* became largely confined to restaurants and special dinner occasions at home.

# 8

# The Holidays, Celebrations, and Other Festivities

**Roast Goose with Sage and Onions.** After it has been picked and singed with care, put into the body of the goose two parboiled onions of moderate size, finely chopped, and mixed with half an ounce of minced sage-leaves, a saltspoonful of salt, and half as much black pepper, or a proportionate quantity of cayenne; to these add a small slice of fresh butter. Truss the goose, and after it is on the spit, tie it firmly at both ends that it may turn steadily, and that the seasoning may not escape; roast it at a brisk fire, and keep it constantly basted. Serve it with brown gravy, and apple or tomata[sic] sauce. When the taste is in favour of a stronger seasoning than the above, which occurs, we apprehend, but seldom, use raw onions for it, and increase the quantity; but should one still milder be preferred, mix a handful of fine bread-crumbs with the other ingredients, or two or three minced apples.

—Eliza Acton, *Modern Cookery, in All its Branches*, 1849 edition

In one of the most memorable scenes from Charles Dickens' *A Christmas Carol* (1843), Mrs. Cratchit approaches the dining table, "flushed, but smiling proudly: with the pudding, like a speckled cannon-ball, so hard and firm, blazing in half of half a quartern of ignited brandy, and bedight with Christmas holly stuck into the top. Oh, a wonderful pudding! Bob Cratchit said, and calmly too, that he regarded it as the greatest success achieved by Mrs Cratchit since their marriage."[1] Charles Dickens's description of this unique English food is one reason why people today often associate the Victorians with Christmas. The holiday seems quintessentially Victorian, and with good reason: The Victorians revived this languishing holiday, making it into the nation's most important. More than any of the era's leading authors, Dickens championed and promoted the spirit of Christmas constantly in his weekly magazine *Household Words*, in his novels and short stories, and in his private life. The celebration was also helped along by young Queen Victoria's husband, Prince Albert, who in 1840 brought from his native Germany the tradition of putting up a Christmas tree, complete with ornaments and lighted candles. The nationally distributed press as well as cookbooks encouraged Victorians to celebrate Christmas in the same spirit as the Crachits and a reformed Ebenezer Scrooge, and by the 1860s, more efficient distribution of name-brand food products encouraged Victorians to indulge in the same holiday treats. However, Christmas also evoked many people's nostalgia and longing for old ways and customs. For these reasons, Christmas in Victorian England became a simultaneous celebration of national unity as well as a celebration of regional loyalty; a simultaneous celebration of modernity and a celebration of traditions, most of which stretched far back in the nation's history predating the Puritans' attempt to ban or minimize Christmas festivities in 1642.

Christmas might be the holiday we most readily associate with Victorian England, but other important celebrations, including fairs, harvest festivals, Account Day feasts, Easter and Lent, weddings and christenings, also encouraged Victorians to take stock of their status as the world's most powerful empire; at the same time they allowed more modern modes to recede as regional customs and foodways reasserted themselves. I end this history of food and cooking with holidays because they suggest to what degree regionalism and preindustrial customs survived in spite of industrialization and even today remain largely responsible for England's reconnection to its rich food past.

## THE TWELVE DAYS OF CHRISTMAS

As Tara Moore appropriately asked in "Victorian Christmas Books: A Seasonal Reading Phenomenon," "What would Christmas be without its food?" The feasting scenes in countless Victorian Christmas books and annuals that Moore has studied attest to the power of food, particularly in an era when thousands often went to bed hungry. English people's association of certain foods with the holiday, and their sense that the holiday would be incomplete without a Christmas pudding or a roast goose led many to join Christmas clubs with the intent to put aside a few pennies a month in order to purchase these necessities at Christmas.[2] Below is a description of some of the foods and traditions that Victorians indulged in.

## THE IMPORTANCE OF THE CHRISTMAS PUDDING

The plum pudding's association with Christmas takes us back to medieval England and the Roman Catholic Church's decree that the "pudding should be made on the twenty-fifth Sunday after Trinity, that it be prepared with thirteen ingredients to represent Christ and the twelve apostles, and that every family member stir it in turn from east to west to honor the Magi and their supposed journey in that direction."[3] Continuing that tradition, the Collect in the *Book of Common Prayer* for the fifth Sunday before Christmas read: "Stir up, we beseech thee, O Lord, the wills of thy faithful people; that they, plenteously bringing forth the fruit of good works, may by thee be plenteously rewarded; through Jesus Christ our Lord. Amen." "Stir-up Sunday," as the Victorians called this important day of preparation for Advent, was a perfect time to make the pudding and allow it to season properly in anticipation of the Christmas Day feast. Banned by the Puritans in the 1660s for its rich ingredients, the pudding and its customs came back into popularity during the reign of George I. Known sometimes as the Pudding King, George I requested that plum pudding be served as part of his royal feast when he celebrated his first Christmas in England after arriving from Hanover to take the throne in 1714. By 1740, a recipe for "plum porridge" appeared in *Christmas Entertainments*.[4] In the Victorian era, Christmas annuals, magazines, and cookbooks celebrated the sanctity of family as much as the sanctity of Jesus' birth, and the tradition of all family members stirring the pudding was often referenced. As with the Christmas Clootie pudding in Scotland, the English Christmas pudding usually included small trinkets that told one's fortune. After the family had all participated in stirring the batter, the mother would secretly drop in a thimble (for spinsterhood), a ring (for marriage), a coin (for wealth), a miniature horseshoe (for good luck), and various other items to be found by the diners during the Christmas feast itself.

This steamed or boiled fruit pudding usually weighed about a pound. If the family could afford to do so, they made their plum puddings even heavier and richer at Christmastime by adding more dried fruit (currants, raisins, and prunes), more eggs, more spice, and probably more brandy than what the more typical "plum pudding" called for. The mother put the stiff batter into a pudding cloth, wrapped it up into a ball, and boiled or steamed it for three hours. Or, she followed the new Victorian-era fashion of putting the batter into a basin and then steaming it. To serve, she unwrapped or unmolded the pudding, placed it on a platter, and decorated its top with a sprig of holly that represented the thorns of Christ's crown and the blood from his wounds. She then poured brandy around the pudding, ignited it, and carried it flaming to the table. In spite of the Christian association of holly with Jesus, this tradition of flaming the pudding, along with the traditional English Christmas game of "snap dragons" (where children try to draw raisins out of flaming brandy) links Christmas to the Celtic Druids, who during winter held ceremonies where great fires were built to give power to the declining sun and to hold back the cold and dark that signified death.[5]

Poorer families made the richest version of plum pudding that they could afford. Some joined Christmas clubs, as I note above, and others simply did their best to store away the dried fruits and spices fundamental to the pudding's success. Even workhouse inmates anticipated a plum pudding on Christmas

Day. Growing up in the Union Workhouse in Tring, Hertfordshire, Lucy Luck recalled in her unpublished autobiography that "weeks before Christmas," the children would "cut pieces of paper in fancy shapes to put" the Christmas pudding on when it arrived.[6] In remembering Christmas in Oxfordshire in the 1880s, Flora Thompson wrote that farm laborers had "very few holidays," and that Christmas, the most important, was an understated affair because most people were very poor. Nonetheless, children and adults alike looked forward to a "joint of beef, which duly appeared on the Christmas dinner-table together with plum pudding ... A bottle of homemade wine was uncorked, a good fire was made up." Families then "settled down by their own firesides for a kind of supper."[7]

## BEEF, GOOSE, AND TURKEY: THE TRADITIONAL CHRISTMAS MEATS

Thompson's mention of a "joint of beef" brings us to the other crucial component of the Christmas meal: the meats that rich and poor alike indulged in. The rural poor in many parts of England ate roast beef for Christmas because farmers up through the nineteenth century maintained the tradition of slaughtering an ox and distributing beef to their laborers as a gift. Tom Mullins, a young farm laborer in Staffordshire during the 1870s, remembered that his employer, Michael Bass, was particularly generous toward his workers. Not only did he distribute beef at Christmas, but he also handed out ample portions of food to his workers and the parish poor whenever they came to his door hungry.[8] Beef was a requisite dish on wealthy Victorians' Christmas tables as well, given that their feast was composed of several meats, and later in the century, several courses. Writing in the Christmas Eve edition of Dickens' *Household Words* (1853), Henry Morely contended: The "hottest fire in the house is made, of course, in order to do proper justice to [the Englishman's] beef. Even the churl who would shut a house-door in the face of his brother, upon Christmas Day opens it gladly to his beef." Should the man really hate his brother, Morely continued in an aside, perhaps the beef gravy along with the roast might help to drown all his animosities forever.[9]

Victorians who could afford it favored Scottish cattle breeds over English for their Christmas roast. Prior to the railroad, cattle were herded by drovers (the English equivalent of the cowboy) from Scotland down to outlying counties of London, particularly East Anglia. They were then fattened before being taken to London for slaughter and sale at the Smithfield Market. Two of the most popular breeds developed in the nineteenth century were the Aberdeen-Angus, now the most widely recognized Scottish breed, and the Scotch Shorthorn, established shortly after the Aberdeen-Angus in the 1830s. Not only were Scottish breeds improved in the nineteenth century to produce the most flavorful beef, so too were English ones, in particular the Red Devon cattle of Exmoor. These smallish cattle produced both excellent milk and beef and they were able to fatten themselves on the sparse moorland pasture.[10]

From the reign of Elizabeth I up until World War II, many English people also celebrated Christmas with a roast goose stuffed with onions and sage. Because of its large size, the goose was the perfect bird for festivities, including not only Christmas, but also Michaelmas, a holiday that is discussed below. Many rural Victorians enjoyed the flavor of roast goose and rabbit combined. While the goose fattened itself on field stubble left after harvest, the rabbit fattened on stolen grains. Meanwhile the first windfall apples were ready for applesauce and scallions grew well in the cool weather. In her succinct and practical way, Dorothy Hartley explained in *Food in England* that "it is not accident, but design, that arranges such things as goose-and-rabbit pudding, sage-and-onion stuffing, applesauce and dumplings." To extend the goose, a Victorian countrywoman might pack into it a couple of rabbits along with the sage-and-onion stuffing and slices of fat bacon: "The rather dry rabbit meat absorbed the flavour of the goose and stuffing, and smaller children got these 'inside pieces' for their serving, as it was not so rich, and left more goose for the hungry men."[11]

Unlike geese, turkeys were not indigenous to Europe. They were introduced by the conquistadors on their way back from the Americas (primarily Mexico) in the sixteenth century. Turkeys were raised in Norfolk, Suffolk, and Cambridge, giving rise to some of England's distinct breeds, including the Norfolk Black that most closely resembles a wild turkey, and the Cambridge Bronze. When a Norfolk was bred with another breed called the Virginian, the resulting breed reached fifteen pounds—a perfect size for a large Christmas feast.[12] By the end of the Victorian era, the Christmas turkey had replaced the Christmas goose for many families. However, in spite of its size and flavor, those in the North staunchly continued to prefer a goose for Christmas well into the twentieth century, if not up to today.

Victorians enjoyed both roast and boiled turkey. Remembering the "old-fashioned" Christmas dinner bills of fare from the 1850s, Edward Spencer recalled a "noble Sirloin of Scotch Beef" and a "Boiled Turkey with celery sauce." Spencer explained: "The French stuff him in his roasted state, with truffles, fat forcemeat, or chestnuts, and invariably 'bard' the bird . . . with fat bacon . . . It is only we English who boil the 'gobbler,' and stuff him (or her, for it is the hen who usually goes into the pot) with oysters, or forcemeat, with celery sauce."[13] Spencer's memories echoed Isabella Beeton's 1860s advice: "hen turkeys are preferable for boiling, on account of their whiteness and tenderness." After simmering "very gently for about 1½ to 1¾ hour, according to the size," Beeton suggested that the turkey be accompanied with "either white, celery, oyster, or mushroom sauce, or parsley-and-butter, a little of which should be poured over the turkey."[14]

## A WIDE VARIETY OF CHRISTMAS CAKES AND PIES

While Victorians everywhere celebrated Christmas with plum pudding, beef, turkey, and goose, they showed their regional affiliation and heritage in the numerous baked goods that also appeared during the holiday. In the Lake District, for example, many Victorians celebrated Christmas morning by eating hakin or hackin, which had been popular since medieval times. This particular holiday treat resembled the earliest Christmas plum frumenty or porridge (precursors to the plum pudding) in that they were very moist concoctions based on meat broth, shredded beef or mutton, raisins, currants, prunes, sugar, spices, wine, and lemon. For centuries, this mixture had been prepared in the same manner as a Scottish haggis, in other words, by boiling it in sheep or pig intestines or stomach until cooked.[15] By the Victorian era, hackin was prepared in a pudding basin or cloth like the plum pudding or it was used as pie filling, essentially making it the precursor of the standard mincemeat pie. Relying on botanist Richard Bradley's 1763 account, Laura Mason and Catherine Brown described the following Lake District tradition, one that lasted until the final years of Queen Victoria's reign: If the maid of the house failed to have the family's hackin cooked by daybreak on Christmas morning, then she was "led through the Town, between two Men, as fast as they can run with her, up Hill and down Hill, which she accounts a great shame."[16]

Some regional Christmas foods were not accompanied by such drama but were nonetheless treasured by the communities who made them every Christmas. Pepper cake, another Lake District specialty, was distributed when carolers or visitors came calling. A type of gingerbread, pepper cake was made with large amounts of black treacle and Jamaican allspice, or what the Victorians called Jamaican pepper. Lincolnshire Victorians celebrated the season with plum bread, a low rounded cake-like loaf full of sultanas, currants, citrus peel, and enriched with eggs. ("Plum" is a generic term used by the English to describe dried fruits that go into breads and puddings.) Unlike other similar fruit breads that rely on butter or clarified beef dripping as shortening, Lincolnshire plum bread relied on lard due to the area's traditional pork specialties.[17] Victorians in North Yorkshire celebrated Christmas with Yule spice cakes, also sometimes called Yorkshire Spice Cakes. As with the Yorkshire teacake, these were so popular that the recipe and tradition of making them spread south and became known throughout England, partly as a result of cookbooks such as *Cassell's Dictionary of Cookery* (1896). Like the Lincolnshire plum bread, Yorkshire spice cakes were baked in a loaf shape and loaded with dried fruit and only lightly sweetened with sugar. Slices accompanied by cheese were traditionally given out to visitors and carolers during the Christmas season.[18]

The association of spice and fruit with Christmas had to do with cost. Ginger, nutmeg, mace, cinnamon, pepper, allspice, and cloves were expensive imports. Most people could not afford them except for special occasions, if even then. Although cheaper by the nineteenth century because they were imported from England's colonies, these spices were still beyond the reach of many people, except for holidays when small indulgences could be more easily justified by all but the most impoverished.

## WASSAIL AND SMOKING BISHOP TO BRING HOLIDAY CHEER

Wassail! Wassail! all over the town,
Our toast it is white and our ale it is brown,
Our bowl is made of maplin tree:
We be good fellows all—I drink to thee.

This popular Gloucestershire carol greeted many Victorian families when they opened their doors to caroling groups. After the carol was finished, the family invited the singers inside to warm themselves and drink from the communal wassail bowl (traditionally made of maple wood). Wassailing, or carol singing, was revived in the Victorian era, as was the tradition of drinking from the wassail bowl. The Victorians borrowed from the Elizabethan custom of inviting singers inside so that they could distribute alms and thus ward off evil spirits that might later visit the house.[19]

The recipes for wassail punch varied from family to family; the important thing was that the punch be piping hot. Those who retained old-fashioned tastes such as Charles Dickens and Benjamin Disraeli (the Prime Minister in 1868 and from 1874 to 1880) enjoyed a wassail punch based on ale or cider that was heated until it formed a foamy, creamy head. Sometimes, the foam was called "lamb's wool." While the ale and/or cider were heating, fresh grated nutmeg, ground cinnamon, whole cloves, lemon slices, and finally, hot roasted crabapples were added to the punch. Wassail was particularly appreciated in apple-growing regions such as Kent. As late as Dickens' time, some Kentish farmers continued the ancient tradition of saluting their apple trees on Christmas Eve by drinking a "libation of cider and sops of toast." This event recalled an ancient fertility rite; the Anglo-Saxon *waes hael* meant "be thou hale."[20] In a similar version of the ancient ceremony, farmers would surround a tree at dusk and shoot bullets through branches and bang pots and pans to make a huge din in order to scare off evil spirits. Then the tree would be "wassailed": the punch poured around its roots. The participants bowed to the tree and sung a wassail song to ensure a good crop next harvest.[21] Most Victorians elsewhere did not celebrate the season in such an elaborate way, but wassailing was treated as an ancient custom worth reviving because it created a continuity with the past.

Given the chill and damp nature of the weather at Christmas, Victorians also indulged in a variety of other hot-mulled wines and alcoholic punches. When Scrooge heartily suggests to Cratchit that they must sit down and discuss the clerk's future in the firm, he insists that they do so over a Christmas bowl of Smoking Bishop. This favorite holiday drink of wealthy Victorians consisted of red wine, port, roasted Seville oranges (which were appreciated for their thick, bitter rinds), sugar, and spices. Its whimsical name recalled its medieval origins when it was sometimes served at guildhalls and university banquets in bowls that resembled a bishop's miter. In keeping with the clerical theme, Victorians also enjoyed Smoking Pope made with burgundy; Smoking Cardinal made with Champaign or Rhine wine; Smoking Archbishop fortified with claret; and Smoking Beadle that called for raisins and ginger wine.[22] Working-class Victorians, as Thompson recalled, could not afford such fancy drinks, but they often enjoyed a bottle of homemade wine with their Christmas dinner, particularly elderberry. Regarded as a curative for many ailments, elderberry wine had a beautiful dark purple/black color and a fine, rich flavor. Hot Gin punches were also popular with the poor. The Cratchits, in Scrooge's vision of Christmas Present, treated themselves to a holiday hot gin punch, served out of a jug and poured into the family's "display of glass, two tumblers, and a custard cup without a handle."[23]

## THE LENTEN SEASON AND EASTER

Given that holidays of all sorts called for special foods, particularly those that were more expensive and usually richer than most people consumed everyday, it makes sense that many of the same foods that people ate at Christmas showed up again at Easter and for special occasions throughout Lent. Again, we see by the nineteenth century how regional traditions remained intact, holding together many local communities, at the same time that national food traditions and customs were being solidified.

### Lent

Although Lent continued throughout the Victorian era to be regarded as a traditional period of fasting and sober reflection, this forty-day season afforded some breaks in rigor, and the day before Lent, known in England as Shrove Tuesday, was one of feasting. "Pancake Day," as it was often called, was a half holiday. After a church service during which parishioners were to be shriven of their sins, they returned home to eat pancakes made out of foods forbidden during Lent: eggs, fat, sugar, and/or meat. Oftentimes, pancake eating was a communal affair followed by ball games and various larks that were designed to take maximum advantage of this final day of pleasure before Lent officially began on Ash Wednesday. The town of Olney, in Buckinghamshire continued its annual pancake race throughout the Victorian era; it began in the 1400s and is still taking place today.

On the fourth Sunday of Lent, English people traditionally celebrated Mothering Sunday. This holiday had its origins in sixteenth-century England when people were to make a pilgrimage to their mother church, or the cathedral in the diocese where they lived, to honor the church's patron saint. By the Victorian era, Mothering Sunday was traditionally a holiday for servants who were allowed to return home and visit their families. Fasting requirements were relaxed so that people could indulge for a day in rich foods and celebration. In some parts of the country, particularly in Shrewsbury and the surrounding countryside, girls were encouraged to bake their mothers a Simnel Cake as a gift and thus the holiday was sometimes known in that region as Simnel Sunday. Simnel Cake, which derives from the Latin word *simila* for fine, white flour, was by the nineteenth century an enriched yeast cake, full of currants and almonds. Although the cake today is known for its balls of marzipan that represent the apostles, that custom was not thought to be practiced widely in Victorian England; instead, the cake was decorated with preserved fruits and flowers. In Bristol, Mothering Sunday was commemorated with Mothering Buns as well as cakes. These small, fairly plain yeast rolls were topped with the much-appreciated caraway or aniseed comfits (candies) that also flavored Bath buns and seed cake.[24] Mothering Sunday in current times is treated as the United Kingdom's version of Mother's Day and the simnel cake continues to play a part in the festivity as well as for Easter Sunday.

The fifth Sunday in Lent, known as "Care" or "Carling" Sunday, is virtually forgotten in England today and it went unnoticed by many Victorians as well. However, those in Northumberland and Northern Lancashire traditionally recognized the day by eating pigeon peas. Technically called black peas or *Cajanus cajan*, these "Carling peas" as they came to be known, were often soaked Saturday night, boiled, and then fried in lard or butter and served with vinegar for Sunday dinner. Reasons for eating peas on Carling Sunday are lost in obscurity, although the folk legend has it that a shipwreck off the coast of Newcastle during a particularly bad famine resulted in bags of pigeon peas washed onto the shore for the starving people to gather. Other historians equate the eating of peas with the Romans who ate beans to commemorate the dead. In the North, ready-cooked peas were treated as a festive food throughout the Victorian era, consumed at local fairs along with other special foods, particularly gingerbread or fairings (more on these below).[25] Another localized food tradition came on Palm Sunday when people in Oxfordshire and likely other neighboring counties ate figs, thus nicknaming Palm Sunday "Fig Sunday." Flora Thompson, in *Lark Rise to Candleford*, remembered that the "original significance of eating figs on that day had long been forgotten; but it was regarded as an important duty, and the children ordinarily selfish would give one of their figs, or at least a bit out of one, to the few unfortunates who had been given no penny."[26]

### Good Friday and Easter Sunday

Many Easter foods that the Victorians ate are still with us along with their foods' folklore. The most notable would be the hot-cross bun, which rose to nationwide prominence by the early nineteenth century when the London Chelsea Bun House began producing them en masse for Good Friday breakfasts.[27] However, as with some Christmas foods, including the flaming plum pudding, the hot-cross bun predates Christianity. The symbol of the cross on buns was used by the Greeks and Romans to represent the sun, with the sun symbol being a circle bisected by two right-angled lines to create four quadrants, one for each season of the year. Bread with such marks was excavated from volcanic ash in the ruins of Herculaneum in Rome.[28] In England, one popular folk legend about the bun originated in the nineteenth century and was known to sailors and Londoners alike. In 1824, a London widow was supposed to have told her young son that when he returned from his first sea voyage, she would have waiting for him hot-cross buns as he was to return on Good Friday. Presumably lost in a shipwreck, the son never returned, and yet every Good Friday, the widow baked a hot cross bun and added it to her collection so that by the time of her death, several were strung across the cottage's rafters. The house became known as the "Bun House," and when it was eventually turned into a pub, the buns were still saved to hang on the wall. To this day, Royal Navy sailors visit the pub (now called the Widow's Son) at Easter and add a new hot-cross bun to the string. Traditionally, hot-cross buns were given to sailors to keep them safe from shipwreck.[29] Other Victorians maintained that any bread baked on Good Friday would never go stale or moldy, and in many small countryside cottages, housewives hung hot-cross buns as good luck charms in their kitchen corners.

Less well-known and more localized Easter treats included Easter biscuits and wigs. The Easter cake, also called a biscuit, was common throughout the Southwest, from Bristol to Shrewsbury. Flavored with oil of cassia (very similar to cinnamon), lemon peel and/or orange peel, these short-crust treats were round and currant-flecked. Those from Somerset, called Sedgemoor Easter cakes, were also flavored with brandy. In Cumbria, part of England's North-West, the small town of Hawkshead and other neighboring villages and towns were known for their Lenten wigs, traditionally eaten for tea or supper during the fasting period. In the early Victorian period, many older people still used the term "wig" to designate a small bun made from fine white flour and raised with yeast. The term fell out of favor by the 1840s, although to this day Hawkshead retains the term to refer to its traditional Lenten (and Easter) buns.[30]

Finally, the chocolate Easter egg. Before they were made of chocolate, actual hard-boiled eggs were painted in celebration of Easter and rolled down hills by village children to symbolize the stone that was rolled away from Christ's tomb. The Victorian era is more associated with the chocolate Easter eggs that children today still of course enjoy. Hand-crafted first in France, English chocolate makers were intrigued and Frys was the first English firm to make and sell them in 1837, followed by Cadbury's in 1875, and finally Rowntree in 1904.[31]

## BOXING DAY AND OTHER BANK HOLIDAYS

Throughout much of the Victorian era, the nation recognized only two common-law holidays: Good Friday and Christmas Day. After the passage of the Bank Holidays Act in 1871, four more days were added on which banks were required to close: Boxing Day (the first weekday after Christmas), Easter Monday, Whitmonday (the day after Pentecost or Whitsunday), and the first Monday in August. Of the four, Boxing Day was perhaps the most important, at least in terms of food traditions. Many families distributed gifts on Boxing Day rather than on Christmas Eve or Christmas Day as they do now and this particular holiday had to do largely with charity toward the poor and gifts for house servants. As far back as Renaissance times, merchants, lords, and large landowners would give their servants and tradespeople boxes of food, money, and other gifts on the day after Christmas and this tradition continued into the Victorian era. Many families gave servants only money, but others distributed small delicacies and treats along with money, perhaps tea, cakes, bottles of homemade wine (for a particularly trusted and well-established housekeeper or butler), and fancy biscuits. The 1872 edition of *Mrs. Beeton's Everyday Cookery* instructed mistresses to ensure that on the last quarterly payday for servants, December 25, a nice Christmas-box "be added to encourage good service and promote kindly feelings."[32] Because most servants were extremely busy on Christmas Day seeing to the family's celebration, they traditionally were given their holiday the day after Christmas. One of the best accounts of Boxing Day and how it related to tradespeople and laborers associated with the family's household came from the unpublished diaries of William Tayler, a footman who wrote for his December 26, 1837, entry:

> This is what is called about here Boxing Day. It's the day the people goe from house to house gathering their Christmas boxes. We have had numbers here today—sweeps, beadles, lamplighters, waterman, dustmen, scavengers (that is the men who clean the mud out of the streets), newspaper boy, general postmen, twopenny postmen and waits. These are a set of men that goe about the streets playing musick in the night after people are in bed and a sleepe . . . All these people expect to have a shilling or half a crown each.[33]

For prosperous families, Boxing Day was a perfect time for a celebratory high tea—the more informal late-afternoon meal that wealthy people enjoyed on the servants' day off. The leftover goose, beef, Yorkshire pudding, and potatoes were taken out of the larder, another bowl of wassail or smoking bishop was made up by the fire, and all gathered round to eat as much of the leftover food as they wanted. Most would have completed the Boxing Day feast with what was traditionally known as Monday's pudding, for which Isabella Beeton offered the following recipe:

> Cut the remains of a *good* cold plum-pudding into fingerpieces, soak them in a little brandy, and lay them cross-barred in a mould until full. Make a custard with . . . milk and eggs, flavouring it with nutmeg or lemon-rind; fill up the mould with it; tie it down with a cloth, and boil or steam it for an hour. Serve with a little of the custard poured over, to which has been added a tablespoonful of brandy.[34]

## "HARVEST HOME" AND MICHAELMAS

Although of solemn significance, Easter and Christmas made less impression on rural laborers than did fall harvest celebrations or "natural holidays" as Flora Thompson called them. While the farmers traditionally gave their laborers beef and money during the Christmas season, most families were nonetheless too poor to expend a great deal of money on ample food and spirits. "Harvest home," as the harvest celebration was known colloquially, was another matter. For this banquet and its subsequent festivities, all expenses were paid by the farmer, and in good years, he spared no expense.

For three weeks or more, the men worked gruelingly hard hours to get the harvest in, but according to Thompson they "enjoyed the stir and excitement of getting in the crops and their own importance as skilled and trusted workers, with extra beer at the farmer's expense and extra harvest money to follow." Thompson witnessed in the 1880s some of the last vestiges of age-old harvesting traditions. The men might have looked upon the "mechanical reaper with long, red, revolving arms like windmill sails" as a mere auxiliary, "a farmers' toy," she recollected, but they had "no idea that they were at the end of a long tradition" that within a matter of years would be entirely gone.[35] With the bailiff supervising, the men mowed, reaped, and bound the corn, which in the South and Midlands would have been primarily wheat, while in the North, it would have been oats, barley, and some wheat. Then came the busiest time of all: "Every man and boy put his best foot forward then, for when the corn was cut and dried it was imperative to get it stacked and thatched before the weather broke. All day and far into the twilight the yellow-and-blue painted farm wagons passed and repassed along the roads between the field and the stock-yard." By the end of harvest, the men and boys were exhausted, but at that point the festivities began and "in the cool dusk of an August evening, the last load was brought in," and as the men and boys walked along with their pitchforks on shoulders, they shouted the age-old chants of the autumn:

Harvest home! Harvest home!
Merry, merry, merry harvest home!

When they neared the farmer's house, the chant changed to:

Harvest home! Harvest home!
Merry, merry, merry harvest home!
Our bottles are empty, our barrels won't run,
And we think it's a very dry harvest home.

At this point, the farmer, his wife, daughters, and servants came out with jugs and bottles of beer. Ceremoniously, the farmer "invited the men to his harvest home dinner, to be held in a few days' time, and the adult workers dispersed to add up their harvest money and to rest their weary bones."[36]

Such harvest dinners were really Christmas in August (or September, depending on the area), and once more Thompson offered readers some of the most descriptive and important details that we have of a nationwide time of feasting: "And what a feast it was! Such a bustling in the farmhouse kitchen for days beforehand; such boiling of hams and roasting of sirloins; such a stacking of plum puddings, made by the Christmas recipe; such tapping of eighteen-gallon casks and baking of plum loaves." Seated at long tables laid out of doors in the shade of the barn, all gathered at noon for a meal that included along with the meats and plum pudding, huge bowls of vegetables, cottage loaves of bread, cheese, butter, jams and preserves, and pickles. The farmer carved the meats at the head table while his wife served tea from an urn at hers. No one begrudged anyone on that day, although for the rest of the year, Thompson reminded readers, the farmer was accused of paying his men starvation wages—and most likely did.[37]

Michaelmas, celebrated on September 29 and in the Anglican Church known as the Feast of St. Michael and All Angels, was also a harvest festival. Whereas on Boxing Day employers made gifts to their employees, on Michaelmas the gift-giving went two ways. Up into the Victorian era, a farmer often hosted a banquet for his laborers, but laborers came to the banquet not only with their quarterly rent for their cottage allotments (Michaelmas being a nationwide rent day), but also with the gift of a "stubble" goose, one that had fed on pasture all year. The thinking went that such a gift would soften the landlord's heart and keep him from raising the rent, but clearly the tradition grew out of feudal times when peasants were obligated to give portions of their harvests to the overlords.[38] For rural laborers in Staffordshire and elsewhere in the nation, Michaelmas commenced a weeklong holiday so that laborers could attend a hiring fair to find work for the next farming season.

## THE DISTINCT CULTURE OF CORNWALL AND ITS CELEBRATIONS

Before I turn to such fairs and the vital role they played in Victorian community life, I would first like to explore Cornwall, a region that like Yorkshire, retained many of its customs and foodways in spite of heavy industrialization and poverty. Made up of small mining and fishing communities far removed from London's sphere of influence, Cornish people continued to observe their own ancient holiday rituals that came with a variety of distinct foods.

Up to the eighteenth century, many English foods were flavored and colored with saffron, a rare spice that comes from the stamen of the Crocus flower. Although some Northumberland recipes still occasionally called for it, by the Victorian era, saffron's use was mainly limited to Cornwall. The region still produced the spice in the nineteenth century based on evidence in wills and documents that specify saffron meadows. In ancient times, the area had alliances with Phoenician traders and saffron was routinely traded for tin. Likely Cornwall had been growing saffron for centuries.[39] Given saffron's expense, most Cornish Victorians limited their use of the spice to festivals and celebrations, and once more Easter figures prominently, given that Cornish saffron cake served with clotted (scalded) cream was a traditional Good Friday food. Saffron's beautiful golden color made the cakes eye-catching and the cake's dried fruits contrasted pleasingly with the mild, astringent flavor of saffron.[40] Along with Easter, no Cornish celebration, be it a wedding, christening, or community fair, was considered complete without saffron cakes.

A better-recognized Cornish food would be the pasty or hoggan. While many today think of this hand-held food as rather greasy, something to be consumed casually and with little thought, the pasty played as important role in Cornish holidays as did saffron cakes. A typical Sunday dinner for a miner's family often included a pasty loaded with meat or fish, turnips, and onion. Teachers who ran "dame schools" where mining children paid a penny a week for instruction often accepted a corner of the family's Sunday pasty on Monday morning in lieu of fees. On baking day, a Cornish housewife created a pasty for each family member. She rolled out a short crust pastry, which when baked would be of a brittle, flaky texture. She topped each circle of crust with the family member's preferred filling (meat going to men if it were available), and then enclosed the filling in the crust. The person's initials were marked on the corners for easy identification. Traditionally, a pasty contained meat, turnip, and onion and was joined at the side to resemble a half moon. A hoggan was made without the potato and was joined at the top.[41] Mackerel or pilchard-stuffed pasties were also popular at the large weekly Truro fair. Rather than being made up individually, the pasties were baked in a long strip with the fish's head and tail protruding and thus helping the stallholder figure out how many fish were required by a hungry customer. St. Austell, north-east of Truro, made its market-day and fair pasties the same way, although they were stuffed with a local skinless sausage instead of fish.

Many of Cornwall's other celebratory foods were also based on a short crust. While the pasty was more common in mining families, fishing families often enjoyed "fuggan," or heavy cake. Like the pasty, fuggan consisted of a rolled short crust or rough puff pastry. The housewife then topped it with potatoes or slices of pork before pressing them down into the dough. Sweet fuggan was full of currants. Marked with a distinctive criss-cross pattern thought to resemble the fishing nets, this specialty was indeed associated with the returning home of fishermen. When women saw the boats coming into harbor, they quickly made up batches of fuggan to welcome home their husbands, fathers, and sons.[42]

Cornish laborers recognized holidays that were not associated with the Church, State, or rest of the country and they often risked their jobs and livelihood to keep those days free from work, in spite of mine owners' and captains' protest.[43] Many Cornish people recognized May 1 as the start of the new year and they celebrated Christmas twice: on December 25 and eleven days later on January 5. Other important Cornish holidays that involved food, drink, and revelry were Paul's Tide on January 14, the first Friday in March, Midsummer Day, and Picrous Day, which fell on the second Thursday before Christmas. Rather than fight the tin miners, who if fired from work could just walk a mile or so down the road to another mine and find work there—more mines than workers was the Victorian-era norm—the mine owners would contribute a shilling per man for each of the holidays, and the miners engaged in copious feasting, drinking, and the ancient violent games that typified Cornish culture.

Along with these Cornish holidays were Accounting Days that involved feasts for the mining owners, clerks, captains, and shareholders. When a mine was "cutting rich" (extracting great amounts of ore to sell at competitive prices), the count house desks were put away and replaced with long trestle tables covered with white linen. The officials sat down to a distinctly Cornish feast that involved a good deal of seafood and fish, such as crab and lobster pies and conger eel pies, along with boiled fowl, roast beef, and mutton. As the miners came up from their shifts, they, too, were treated outside the count house to roast ox, bread, and much beer.

Finally, Cornwall became famous with Victorian tourists because of its fairings, an edible souvenir common at fairs all over England up through the end of the nineteenth century, but which had their own distinctive flavor and shape, depending on the locale. Cornish fairings were rough, circular-shaped ginger biscuits heavily spiced with cinnamon and ginger. They were first sold at area fairs but became popular when in 1886, John Cooper Furniss began selling them along with his distinctive macaroons from his Truro bakery. The bakery eventually boxed them up and sent them via mail-order around the country. Along with a ginger biscuit, a "proper and complete" Cornish fairing included caraway comfits (lambs' tails), candied sticks of Angelica, almond comfits, and Macaroons."[44]

## MARKETS AND FAIRS

Fairs and annual market days were the most ancient opportunities for festivities and holidays and carried significant meaning in English literature from the folk tale "Jack and the Beanstalk" to Thomas Hardy's *Jude the Obscure*. As a break in the laborer's often weary, back-breaking routine, a fair or market day offered potential excitement: time and space to court a lover, an opportunity to make some money (or lose some), or a chance to secure better employment. Many fairs in the early Victorian era still centered around the trading and buying of livestock. York's most important fairs, which were held annually from medieval times on Whitmonday, St. Peter's Day, and Lammas Day (August 1), centered on cattle selling. Nottingham was the center of the nation's largest goose fair, where geese brought in from Norfolk and the East Midlands were sold. But fairgoers had more on their minds than cattle and geese. They wondered through the stalls and booths, listened to charlatans hawking miracle cures, observed penny shows that paraded out the odd and the weird, and of course bought all manner of typical snacks. Just as Cornwall had its own distinctive gingerbread fairing, so too did all regions of England. In Barnstaple, vendors sold gingerbread "wives." George Mercer, a confectioner in Grantham in the East Midlands resembled John Cooper Furniss; he created a gingerbread fairing in the early nineteenth century that became famous beyond its borders. Grasmere in the Lake District had its distinctive gingerbread as well. It was sold not only for fairings, but also became popular year-round with tourists and locals alike. Dorothy Wordsworth, sister of the famous Romantic poet William Wordsworth, mentioned in one of her 1803 Grasmere journal entries that she and her brother had a craving for it. Market Drayton, a town in Shropshire, became known for its oblong, finger-shaped gingerbread fairings and four gingerbread bakers flourished there as late as 1900.[45] Finally, Bath fairs were famous for their gingerbread valentines.

* * * *

As I noted in the teatime chapter of this history, Victorian England had the technology in place to facilitate rapid travel of people, material goods, food, and ideas. A Victorian tourist back from Truro who fancied a box of Furniss's biscuits at her home in Oxford could obtain them via mail. A father in Manchester who read about the Queen's Christmas Tree in the *Illustrated London News* could be entranced enough by the novelty to buy a Christmas tree next year for his family. A reader who loved Yorkshire teacakes might send in her recipe to Isabella Beeton's *Englishwoman's Domestic Magazine* where it could be published, and shortly thereafter, become a part of Beeton's *Book of Household Management* (which was what happened in this case). Within a matter of months, Yorkshire teacakes were no longer Yorkshire's alone, and soon enough, the product—not just the recipe—was available from bakers and eventually stores all over the country. At no time in England's earlier history could ideas, people, and food travel so quickly and the effect on the culture was nothing short of profound. In many histories of the nineteenth century, scholars have convincingly argued that as a result of industry and technology, Victorians were the first people to see themselves as English first, often at the expense of any lingering sense of a regional identity.

Certainly this view influences English culinary history as well where researchers inevitably define the Victorian era against the "country house or manor cooking" of the eighteenth-century Georgians. And as I hope this history has made clear, the Victorians were not like the Georgians. They were less dependent on season and geography when it came to procuring their food and they worked with an array of cooking technologies unavailable to the Georgians. Nationwide distribution of food by the 1850s, not to mention the regular importing of meat, vegetables, and grains from elsewhere by the 1860s, inevitably resulted in a national diet, or, in the view of more critical historians, in a homogonous diet. However, holidays and celebrations encouraged Victorians to rediscover and celebrate their own family's roots, particularly via foods and customs directly associated with them. A Yorkshire housewife might have been inclined for much of the year to rely on Soyer's *Modern Housewife* or Beeton's *Book of Household Management* for menu inspiration, but at Christmas, out came her grandmother's recipes for parkin, a distinctive oaten gingerbread, and Christmas pie, a standing pie unique to Yorkshire and filled with spiced poultry and game birds that were literally tucked one inside the other, starting with the pigeon and ending with the turkey. Her only "modern" (Victorian) alteration was to add pork, either bacon or sausage, to the recipe.[46]

Today, globalization and European Union regulations, the founding of the Slow Food movement, and a heightened awareness among many people that culinary customs and regional recipes are as befitting of protection as a creative or scientific production has resulted in current English cookbook authors and chefs emphasizing repeatedly the importance of region to the nation's food history. As they seek back in time for these regional English foodways, it helps to remember that many Victorians appreciated those regional traditions as well, and perhaps a lot more than we imagine. Victorians eagerly took advantage of technology and industry to save them money and time, and they eagerly tried out recipes that came from far away and learned to regard them as English, but not always at the expense of their own sense of family and ancestral identity, no matter if they were miners in Cornwall or gentry residing in Hampshire.

# APPENDIX: VICTORIAN RECIPES

These recipes have been modified to take into account modern cooking equipment and measurements, as well as standard serving portions and widely available ingredients. The original recipes that introduce most chapters in this book can of course be used instead of these adapted versions. A conversion chart follows the recipes.

## JANE READE'S ALMOND CHEESECAKE

Makes one 10-inch, deep-dish pie, 8–10 servings
This "cake" is really a pie.

### Crust

1 1/3 cups unbleached white flour
1 tablespoon granulated white sugar
Pinch of salt
1/2 cup chilled lard or unsalted butter, cut into small pieces
4–5 tablespoons ice water

### Directions

Heat oven to 425°F. Sift flour, sugar, and salt together in a mixing bowl. Cut fat into flour until mixture resembles small peas. Add ice water, one tablespoon at a time, gently stirring the dough with a fork until it is moistened and easily gathered into a ball. Wrap in plastic wrap and refrigerate for approximately half an hour. When chilled, put dough on a floured surface and roll into circle that will fit easily in the pie pan. Transfer to a pie pan, crimp edges, and prick the bottom a couple of times with a fork. Bake for approximately 5 minutes, or until the pastry looks half done. Cool the crust while making the filling.

### Filling

½ cup granulated, white sugar
¼ pound (one cup) blanched almonds, ground fine in food processor
¾ cup melted, unsalted butter, cooled
1 tablespoon orange-flower water
4 eggs, 2 separated with their whites beaten until stiff
Scant ¼ cup sack, or a good-quality cream sherry
⅛ teaspoon pure almond extract (optional)

### Directions

In a large bowl, mix the melted butter, sack, almond extract, ground almonds, sugar, and orange-flower water. Add the whole eggs, one at a time, mixing each until well incorporated. Add the two egg yolks one at a time, mixing each until well incorporated. Gently fold in the beaten egg whites. Pour filling into the pie shell and return to the oven. Bake for approximately 45 minutes or until set and light brown at 300°F. If pie-crust edges brown too quickly, cover them with foil strips.

## AGNES BEAUFOY'S LEMON CHEESECAKE

Makes one 10-inch, deep-dish pie, 8–10 servings

### Crust

Use the same crust recipe as the one given for Reade's Almond Cheesecake, once again baking it at 425°F for approximately 5 minutes until half done. Do not bake completely.

### Filling

2 lemons, the zest and the juice of both (approximately 6 tablespoons juice and 2 tablespoons zest)
½ cup (1 stick) of unsalted butter
3 tablespoons heavy whipping cream
4 well-beaten eggs, minus two whites. Beat the two egg whites in until stiff. Put the egg whites aside.
½ cup of granulated sugar

#### Directions

In a double boiler, cook together the butter, cream, and the eggs (minus the two egg whites), lemon zest, and juice till the mixture thickens. Stir constantly and be careful not to overcook or your eggs will scramble. Cool mixture for approximately 15 minutes. Gently fold the mixture into the two beaten egg whites until well incorporated. Pour into the half-baked pie shell and bake at 350°F until set and the top has attractive spots of light brown (approximately 20–25 minutes). Cool and refrigerate for best taste.

### TREACLE PUDDING

Makes one large pudding, approximately 15 servings

#### Ingredients

1 ¾ cups self-rising flour
2 tablespoons demerara or dark brown sugar
1 teaspoon cinnamon
1 teaspoon ginger
½ cup shredded suet, or vegetable shortening, or unsalted butter cut into tiny pieces
1 cup black treacle or unsulfered molasses
Juice and zest of medium to large lemon (3 tablespoons juice and 1 tablespoon zest)
1 cup whole milk

#### Directions

Mix flour, spices, and sugar in a large bowl. Cut the fat into the flour until the mixture resembles tiny peas. Add treacle, lemon juice, and milk. Stir until well mixed. The batter should resemble a cake batter—not overly thick, not overly thin. For a North American audience without access to a pudding basin or cloth, try this method: Grease a 12-cup (10 in. by 4 in.) bundt or tube pan. Pour batter into pan, cover tightly with greased heavy-duty aluminum foil. Place a metal vegetable strainer or a small metal rack inside a large, heavy-bottomed stockpot. Fill the pot one-third with water and lower the bundt pan onto the strainer or rack so that the pan is not resting on the bottom of the pot. (Water must not come more than half-way up the sides of the bundt pan.) Cover the stockpot with a tight-fitting lid. Steam the pudding for approximately 2 ½ hours until it is completely cooked. You will need to replenish the water in the pot once or twice.

*Note:* Suet can be difficult to obtain. If you find it from an old-fashioned butcher, freeze it, and then grate it so that it resembles crayon shavings. Proceed with recipe. Cold butter or vegetable shortening make fine substitutes.

## SEED CAKE

Makes one large cake, approximately 12–15 servings

### Ingredients

1 cup white granulated sugar
3 ½–4 cups flour
1 cup milk plus (approximately) ½ cup more for cake batter
1 tablespoon yeast
1 cup unsalted butter (two sticks)
½ cup of currants or 1 ounce caraway seeds
½ teaspoon allspice
1 teaspoon cinnamon
1 teaspoon ginger
½ teaspoon nutmeg
⅓ cup brown sugar

### Directions

Preheat oven to 350°F. Grease and Flour a 10-inch by 3-inch cake tin.

Heat 1 cup of milk with butter to 105–110°F and dissolve in it one tablespoon of yeast. When yeast is foamy, pour it into a mixing bowl and add white sugar, flour, and spices. Add up to ½ cup more room-temperature milk until the batter is fairly stiff but not pulling away from the sides of the bowl. Add in currants or seeds. Spoon batter into pan, top with brown sugar, cover, and allow it to rise for ½ hour. Bake cake for approximately 40 minutes or until the brown sugar begins to melt and form a crust. Cake is complete when an inserted toothpick comes out clean. This cake is best served with tea or coffee.

## MRS. BEETON'S CURRIED FOWL AND BOILED RICE

Serves 4 as a main dish

### Ingredients

1 3–4 pound chicken
4 tablespoons butter
1 small tart cooking apple, peeled and diced
2 large yellow onions, diced
2 cups veal or chicken stock
1 tablespoon of curry powder*
1 tablespoon white, unbleached flour
4 tablespoons heavy whipping cream
1 tablespoon lemon juice
Prepared white rice

### Directions

Dice onions and fry gently in butter in a large frying pan until they turn light brown and become fragrant. Meanwhile, cut chicken into serving-size pieces: legs, thighs, two breast portions, and wings. (Use back and neck to make soup stock at a later time.) Add the chicken pieces to the frying onions and brown the chicken on both sides. Add the diced apples and cook until they begin to soften. Add the curry powder along with salt to taste. Stir well. Add two cups of stock, cover, and simmer for approximately 20–30 minutes until meat is very tender. Mix the lemon juice with ¼ cup of the chicken stock taken from the pan. Stir 1 tablespoon of flour into the lemon juice and stock until no lumps remain. When the chicken is cooked, add the flour mixture to the pan and cook until slightly thickened. Finish off with cream. Test for seasoning and add more salt if necessary. Serve over hot, fluffy rice.

**Note:* Using Dr. Kitchener's recipe, Beeton offered the following for a homemade curry powder: " ¼ lb. coriander seed, ¼ lb of turmeric, 2 oz. of cinnamon, ½ oz. cayenne, 1 oz. mustard seed, 1 oz. ground ginger, ½ ounce allspice, 2 oz. fenugreek seed. Gently roast the seeds (the bottom of a hot iron skillet works best). Pound them in a mortar until fine, or grind them in a spice or coffee grinder. Bottle and use accordingly." Beeton follows the curry powder recipe with this note: "We have given this recipe for curry-powder, as some persons prefer to make it at home; but that purchased at any respectable shop is, generally speaking, far superior, and, taking all things into consideration, very frequently more economical." Such still holds true today.

## MRS. MARSHALL'S *POULARDE À LA VALENCIENNE*

Serves 4 as a main dish or 6–8 an entrée

This complicated dish will impress on readers the difficulty that came from attempting to create six other courses of equal difficulty for a dinner party. Marshall suggested using food coloring to help enhance the color of the rice. I have omitted that step.

### Ingredients for the Chicken

1 3–4 pound chicken
2 tablespoons butter
2 cups homemade chicken stock or canned stock, low sodium
1 large Spanish onion, diced (approximately 2 ½ cups)
1 large carrot, peeled and diced
¼ cup finely minced fresh parsley (plus 2 tablespoons for garnish)
2 tablespoons fresh thyme leaves
½ teaspoon dried sage or 2–3 teaspoons fresh, minced
½ teaspoon dried basil, or 6–7 leaves, minced
4 whole cloves

½ teaspoon cracked pepper
1 teaspoon salt (or to taste)

**Ingredients for the Rice**

1 cup of Patna or Basmati rice
1 tablespoon of olive oil
⅛ teaspoon of cayenne pepper
1 cup of chicken stock
1 cup of tomato puree
½ cup sliced mushrooms (button mushrooms work fine)
¼ lb Serrano or Parma ham, julienned
1 fresh white truffle, large enough to grate over the rice (optional)

**Directions**

*Step One*: In a large, oven-proof stockpot, melt two tablespoons of butter and sauté gently the diced onion and carrot until onion turns translucent. Add fresh herbs and spices and cook for a couple minutes more, until aromatic. Place chicken on top of the vegetables. Salt and pepper generously. Pour stock around the chicken. Place the stockpot in the oven, covered, at 350°F. Bake for approximately 1hour, turning the chicken one time in the process.

*Step Two*: Remove chicken from stockpot and strain the gravy. Keep in a bain marie or pour into a gravy boat and reheat in a microwave when it comes time to serve the completed dish. Brush some of the gravy over the chicken and transfer to a baking dish. Return to the oven to brown the bird at 350°F. This will take approximately 30 minutes. Watch carefully and if it becomes too brown, remove from oven and tint with foil to keep warm.

*Step Three*: Rinse and drain rice. Sauté ham in a two-quart saucepan in a little olive oil until it begins to crisp. Remove and set aside. Add mushrooms to the pan and sauté until they begin to release their juices. Add tomato puree and stock along with rice. Season with cayenne pepper and salt. Bring to a boil, turn heat to very low, cover the pan, and cook until done (approximately 10 to 15 minutes). When done, stir in the ham.

*Step Four*: Put rice on a platter and top with the browned chicken. Sprinkle more fresh parsley and/or grated white truffle over the chicken and rice as a garnish. Pass the gravy at the table.

## CHRISTMAS PLUM PUDDING (**Author's family heirloom recipe**)

Makes one large pudding, approximately 15 servings

**Ingredients**

¾ cup flour
1 teaspoon salt

1 teaspoon cinnamon
¾ teaspoon baking soda
½ teaspoon mace
½ teaspoon ground cloves
¼ teaspoon grated nutmeg
½ cup fine bread crumbs, softened in ¾ cups hot milk
1 cup soft brown sugar
1 cup grated suet (or vegetable shortening or butter cut into small pieces)
1 cup raisins
1 cup currants
1 cup candied fruit
½ cup chopped almonds
½ cup brandy

**Directions**

Mix flour, spices, and sugar in a large bowl. Cut the fat into the flour until the mixture resembles tiny peas. Add milk and breadcrumbs. Add 2 tablespoons of brandy. Stir until well mixed. If batter is too stiff to spoon into the mold easily, add more hot milk. Coat nuts, candied peel, and dried fruit with a bit of flour. Add in nuts, candied peel, and dried fruit to the batter. Mix again. Use the same technique for steaming this pudding as suggested for treacle, or use a pudding mold that can be tightly covered. Steam the pudding for approximately 2 ½ hours until it is completely cooked. You will need to replenish the water in the pot once or twice. Unmold the pudding on platter, cool, and cover until ready to serve. (Most Victorians stored the plum pudding for several days to allow it to season.) When ready to serve, pour the brandy over the pudding and around it. Ignite and carry to the table while it is still flaming. Plum pudding is best served with a hard sauce ("hard" meaning alcohol-based, such as brandy or whiskey). Whipped cream or warm caramel sauce are also good accompaniments.

## CONVERSION CHART

The following chart for metric measurements is to serve as a guide, not as exact conversions.

**Liquids (cups and teaspoons)**

2 U.S. cups = 480 ml
1 U.S. cup = 240 ml
½ U.S. cup = 120 ml
¼ U.S. cup = 60 ml
1 tablespoon = 1.5 ml
1 teaspoon = 5 ml

### Dry Goods (in cups)

1 U.S. cup = 350 g for treacle
1 U.S. cup = 200 g for brown or white sugars and rice
1 U.S. cup = 175 g for candied peel, and raisins
1 U.S. cup = 150 g for whole wheat flour
1 U.S. cup = 125 g for white flour, self-rising flour, currants, ground almonds
1 U.S. cup = 100 g for suet, butter or shortening, and chopped nuts
1 U.S. cup = 50 g for breadcrumbs

### Butter

1 U.S. stick of butter = 100 g (8 tablespoons)
¼ U.S. stick of butter = 25 g (2 tablespoons)

### Oven Temperatures

475°F = 240°C = gas mark 9
350°F = 180°C = gas mark 4
300°F = 150°C = gas mark 2

# NOTES

## CHAPTER 1

1. Reade and Ensham, *Mss. Cookbook,* England.

2. Spurling, *Elinor Fettiplace's Receipt Book,* 10.

3. Grieve, *A Modern Herbal,* 2: 790.

4. Colin Spencer, *British Food,* 340; Hartley, *Food in England,* 460–461; Redon et al., *Medieval Kitchen,* 153.

5. Adamson, *Food in Medieval Times,* 67.

6. Adamson, *Food in Medieval Times,* 16; Turner, *Spice,* 101.

7. Mason, *Sugar-Plums and Sherbet,* 31–33; Drummond and Wilbraham, *Englishman's Food,* 35.

8. Flanders, *Victorian House,* xxxvi; Colin Spencer, *British Food,* 276.

9. Davies, *The Isles,* 756–757; Morgan, ed., *Oxford Illustrated History of Britain,* 428.

10. Burnett, *Plenty and Want,* 1; Cooper, "Technology, Tradition and the Dilemmas of Design," 204.

11. Coffin, "Riots in South Eastern Counties."

12. Engels, *Condition of the Working Class in England,* 10.

13. Tannahill, *Food in History,* 288.

14. *Cassell's Book of the Household,* 4: 9.

15. Black, *Victorian Cookery,* 16.

16. Wilcox-Rossi, *Dinner for Dickens,* 128.

17. Colin Spencer, *British Food,* 245; Burnet, *England Eats Out,* 54.

18. Anne C. Wilson, "Meal Patterns and Food Supply in Victorian Britain," xvii; Tames, *Feeding London,* 29.

19. Colin Spencer, *British Food,* 213.

20. *Cassell's Book of the Household,* 4: 165.

## CHAPTER 2

1. Boorde, *A Compendyous Regyment, or A Dyetary of Helth*, 251.
2. White,"First Things First," 3.
3. de la Rochefoucauld, *A Frenchman in England*, 28–29.
4. Colin Spencer, *British Food*, 212; Moritz, *Journeys of a German in England*, 35.
5. Mayhew, *London Labour and the London Poor*, edited and abridged ed 86.
6. Burnett, *Plenty and Want*, 54.
7. Throughout this section and the next, I am indebted to Judith Flanders' *Victorian House* and the extensive research she has done on the inner workings of a Victorian home. See in particular chapters 3 and 4 from *Victorian House* for more information on the kitchen and scullery in middle-class terraced houses.
8. Davies, *Victorian Kitchen*, 55.
9. Buckmaster, *Buckmaster's Cookery*, 12–13.
10. Ibid., 14.
11. Burnett, *Useful Toil*, 217.
12. *Cassell's Book of the Household*, 1: 79.
13. Ibid., 1: 336.
14. Southgate, *Things a Lady Would Like to Know*, 425.
15. *Cassell's Book of the Household*, 1: 39.
16. Soyer, *Modern Housewife*, American ed., 6. Citations are to the American edition.
17. Ibid., 8.
18. Ibid., 7, 9
19. "Wyvern" [A. Kenny Herbert]. *Fifty Breakfasts*. London: Edward Arnold, 1894. Quoted in Davies, *Victorian Kitchen*, 121.
20. Burnett, *Useful Toil*, 217.
21. Eliot, *Middlemarch*, 98–100.
22. Palmer, *Movable Feasts*, 72–73.
23. *Cassell's Book of the Household*, 1: 37.
24. *Mrs Beeton's, Every Day Cookery*, ii.
25. Cobbe, "Little Health of Ladies," 289.

## CHAPTER 3

1. Nesbit, *Five Children and It*, 175, 180–182.
2. *Cassell's Book of the Household*, 3: 209.
3. The most salient and helpful explanation of the evolution of the words "lunch" and "luncheon," as well as "bever" come from C. Anne Wilson's, "Luncheon, Nuncheon and Related Meals" in *Eating with the Victorians*. See pp. 34–37, from which the information in this and the next paragraph has been taken.
4. Thompson, *Lark Rise to Candleford*, 50.
5. Latham, ed. *The Shorter Pepys*, 224.
6. Ibid., 594.
7. Gaskell, *North and South*, 24.
8. Palmer, *Movable Feasts*, 55.
9. Hare, Augustus, ed. *Life and Letters of Maria Edgeworth*, 2: 455–456.
10. Nesbit, *Five Children and It*, 166.

11. Beeton, *Book of Household Management*, 1864 reprinted ed., 811. Citations are to the 1864 reprinted edition.
12. Buckmaster, *Buckmaster's Cookery*, 87.
13. Bloom, *Victorian Vinaigrette*, 36, 39.
14. Flanders, *Victorian House*, 45.
15. Mrs. Frederick Pedley, *Infant Nursing and the Management of Young Children*, London: George Routledge and Sons, 1866, 99ff. Quoted in Flanders, *Victorian House*, 46.
16. Burnett, *Useful Toil*, 176.
17. Flanders, *Victorian House*, 112.
18. Bloom, *Victorian Vinaigrette*, 5.
19. Burnett, *Useful Toil*, 216.
20. Soyer, *Modern Housewife*, 28.
21. Ibid., 28.
22. Rossi-Wilcox, *Dinner for Dickens*, 171.
23. *Cassell's Book of the Household*, 4: 254.
24. Thompson, *Lark Rise to Candleford*, 22.
25. Sala, *Twice Around the Clock*, 146.
26. Palmer, *Movable Feasts*, 58–59.
27. Sala, *Twice Around the Clock*, 146.
28. Colin Spencer, *British Food*, 285.
29. Sala, *Twice Around the Clock*, 138.
30. Dickens, *Dictionary of London*, 51.
31. Burnett, *England Eats Out*, 92.
32. Hewett and Axton, *Convivial Dickens*, 7–8; Burnett, *England Eats Out*, 93.
33. Burnett, *England Eats Out*, 41.
34. Colin Spencer, *British Food*, 267.
35. Thompson, *Lark Rise to Candleford*, 51.
36. Burnett, *England Eats Out*, 118.
37. Colin Spencer, *British Food*, 299
38. Ibid., 300
39. Burnett, *England Eats Out*, 108.

## CHAPTER 4

1. Nesbit, *Phoenix and the Carpet*, 167.
2. Ukers, *All About Tea*, 2: 404–405.
3. Ayrton, *English Provincial Cooking*, 21.
4. Laura Mason, e-mail message to author, March 4, 2006.
5. "Tea," *Cambridge World History of Food*, 1: 716–717.
6. Paston-Williams, *Art of Dining*, 159.
7. Sharon Britton of R. Twinings & Co. Ltd, e-mail message to author, March 8, 2006; Pettigrew, *Social History of Tea*, 38–39.
8. Pettigrew, *Social History of Tea*, 44.
9. *Dictionary of Daily Wants*, 3: 987.
10. Ibid., 3: 986.
11. Moxham, *Tea*, 41.

12. Moritz, *Journeys of a German in England in 1783*, 47.
13. Moxham, *Tea*, 98–99.
14. Burnett, *Plenty and Want*, 8.
15. Ibid., 65.
16. Ibid., 98.
17. *Times*, January 1, 1845, 3.
18. Drummond and Wilbraham, *Englishman's Food*, 243.
19. Burnett, *Plenty and Want*, 194.
20. Ibid., 194, 78–79.
21. Freeman, *Mutton and Oysters*, 87.
22. Pettigrew, *Social History of Tea*, 102.
23. Kemble, *Records of Later Life*, 304.
24. The story of afternoon tea's origins is confusing, because it has many elements of folklore. I have relied primarily on the versions offered in Ukers' *All About Tea* (1935), Pettigrew's *A Social History of Tea* (2001), Ellis's *Fish, Flesh and Good Red Herring* (2004), and Laura Mason's "Everything Stops for Tea" (2004).
25. Pettigrew, *Social History of Tea*, 104.
26. Palmer, *Movable Feasts*, 55; Mrs. Eliot James, *Our Servants, Their Duties to Us and Ours to Them*. London: Ward Lock and Co., 1883, 139–142. Quoted in Flanders, *Victorian House*, 231.
27. "Tea and Chatter," *Beauty & Fashion*. December 6, 1890. Quoted in Pettigrew, *Social History of Tea*, 120–121.
28. Toulmin, *Landmarks of a Literary Life*, 149.
29. *Cassell's Book of the Household*, 2: 95.
30. Ibid., 2: 95.
31. *Dictionary of Daily Wants*, 3: 987.
32. Ellis, *Fish, Flesh and Good Red Herring*, 95.
33. *Dictionary of Daily Wants*, 3: 988.
34. *Cassell's Book of the Household*, 2: 95.
35. *Cassell's Book of the Household*, 2: 95.
36. "Tea and Chatter," *Beauty & Fashion*. December 6, 1890. Quoted in Pettigrew, *Social History of Tea*, 107.
37. Pettigrew, *Social History of Tea*, 107; *Cassell's Book of the Household*, 2: 96.
38. Burnett, *Useful Toil*, 101.
39. Thompson, *Lark Rise to Candleford*, 100–101.
40. Scholars and culinary enthusiasts alike owe a debt of gratitude to Laura Mason and Catherine Brown for their painstaking research into the traditional, distinctive foods of Great Britain. Information on all of the above-listed cakes and bread can be found in their *Traditional Foods of Britain: An Inventory* (1999 and 2004 editions).
41. *Cooking, or, Practical and Economical Training for Those Who Are to Be Servants, Wives, and Mothers*. London: J Masters, 1851. Quoted in Hartley, *Food in England*, 509.
42. Tusser, "The Plough mans feasting days," 123.
43. Ayrton, *English Provincial Cooking*, 40–41.
44. I am indebted to the information on regional cooking and customs found in Elisabeth Ayrton's *English Provincial Cooking*. See pp. 34–42 for information on seed cake and the foods of East Anglia.
45. Gaskell, *Cranford*, 57.

## CHAPTER 5

1. Thompson, *Lark Rise to Candleford,* 26–27.
2. Ibid., 27.
3. Burnett, *Useful Toil,* 38.
4. Ibid., 46.
5. Ibid., 29.
6. Ibid., 38.
7. Hartley, *Food in England,* 101.
8. Burnett, *Useful Toil,* 66–67.
9. Thompson, *Lark Rise to Candleford,* 26.
10. Mason and Brown, *Traditional Foods of Britain,* 55.
11. Ibid., 59.
12. Thompson, *Lark Rise to Candleford,* 27.
13. Mason and Brown, *Traditional Foods of Britain,* 76–77.
14. Ibid., 65.
15. Thompson, *Lark Rise to Candleford,* 26.
16. Ibid., 106. Thompson is jokingly discussing use of Pennyroyal as an abortifacient.
17. Mayhew, *London Labour,* edited and abridged ed., 82–83.
18. Mayhew, "Education of the Costerlads," *London Labour, Victorian London* Web site, electronic text.
19. Sala, *Twice Around the Clock,* 138.
20. Ibid., 144.
21. Reeves, *Round about a Pound,* 102.
22. Rowntree, *Poverty,* 66, 134–135.
23. Reeves, *Round About a Pound,* 68.
24. Mason and Brown, *Traditional Foods of Britain,* 82.
25. Ibid., 92.
26. Mayhew, *London Labour,* edited and abridged ed., 13.
27. Perren, "Markets and Marketing," 191.
28. Caird, *Landed Interest and the Supply of Food,* 57–62.
29. Morgan, ed., *Oxford Illustrated History of Britain,* 224–226, 380–381.
30. Perren, "Markets and Marketing," 194.
31. Burnett, *Plenty and Want,* 1–2.
32. Tannahill, *Food in History,* 285–286.
33. Perren, "Markets and Marketing," 210.
34. Burnett, *Plenty and Want,* 7.
35. Burnett, *Plenty and Want,* 6–7. Research into how much wheat England imported between 1801 and 1850 is made difficult by the lack of consistent records and statistics. The topic is covered in great detail, however, in Vol. VI of *The Agrarian History of England and Wales* edited by G.E. Mingay. Of particular importance is Perren's chapter "Markets and Marketing," 190–274.
36. Burnett, *Plenty and Want,* 8.
37. Ibid., 26.
38. Davies, *Case of Labourers,* 28–29.
39. Burnett, *Plenty and Want,* 41.

40. Reports of Special Assistant Poor Law Commissioners on the Employment of Women and Children in Agriculture (1843), 69–70. Quoted in Burnett, *Plenty and Want*, 25–26.
41. Francatelli, *Plain Cookery Book for the Working Classes*, 11.
42. Ibid., 9.
43. Reeves, *Round About a Pound a Week*, 59.
44. Colin Spencer, *British Food*, 160.
45. Ibid., 228.
46. Ibid., 228.
47. Cobbett, *Cottage Economy*, 52.
48. Martineau, "New School for Wives," 85.
49. Willis Family Recipe Book. Szathmary Culinary Archives. University of Iowa.
50. Smith Culinary Manuscript. Szathmary Culinary Archives. University of Iowa.
51. Colin Spencer, *British Food*, 294.
52. Mason, "Poverty and Policy," 208; Rowntree, *Poverty*, xix.
53. Mason, "Poverty and Policy," 208; Rowntree, *Poverty*, xix.
54. Rowntree, *Poverty*, 275.
55. Reeves, *Round About a Pound a Week*, 97.
56. Tannahill, *Food in History*, 334.
57. Colin Spencer, *British Food*, 301.

## CHAPTER 6

1. Beeton, *Book of Household Management*, 905.
2. Dods, *Cook and Housewife's Manual*, 60.
3. Beeton, *Book of Household Management*, 13.
4. Trusler, *Honours of the Table*, 5.
5. de la Rochefoucauld, *Frenchman in England*, 29.
6. Trusler, *Honours of the Table*, 4
7. Dods, *Cook and Housewife's Manual*, 47.
8. Boswell, *Life of Johnson*, 263–264.
9. Dodd, *Food of London*, 482–483.
10. Trusler, *Honours of the Table*, 5–6.
11. Brears, "*À la Française*," 98–99.
12. de la Rochefoucauld, *Frenchman in England*, 30.
13. Mason and Brown, *Traditional Foods of Britain*, 31, 35, 39.
14. de la Rochefoucauld, *Frenchman in England*, 30–31.
15. Ibid., 32.
16. Trusler, *Honours of the Table*, 2.
17. Buckmaster, *Buckmaster's Cookery*, 19.
18. Davies, *Victorian Kitchen*, 52.
19. Ibid., 54.
20. Ibid., 52.
21. Rossi-Wilcox, *Dinner for Dickens*, 132.
22. *Cassell's Book of the Household*, 1: 208–209.
23. Dods, *Cook and Housewife's Manual*, 128.
24. *Cassell's Book of the Household*, 1: 209.

25. Beeton, *Book of Household Management*, 27.
26. Rossi-Wilcox, *Dinner for Dickens*, 169.
27. Paston-Williams, *Art of Dining*, 275.
28. Berriedale-Johnson, *Victorian Cookbook*, 60.
29. Ibid., 60.
30. Burnett, *Plenty and Want*, 79–80. See Burnett for a fuller analysis of *Lancet* findings.
31. Hughes, *Short Life and Long Times*, 96.
32. Hassan, John, *History of Water*, 16.
33. 1 Timothy ch 5, verse 23. NIV
34. Hassan, *History of Water*, 15.
35. Ibid., 11, 17.
36. Ibid., 22.
37. Mitchell, *Daily Life*, 119
38. Sheppard, *London*, 284; flauders, 91.
39. Hassan, *History of Water*, 11.
40. Flanders, *Victorian House*, 91; Hassan, *History of Water*, 11.
41. Sheppard, *London*, 281.
42. Hassan, *History of Water*, 21–22.
43. Beeton, *Book of Household Management*, 954–955.
44. Palmer, *Movable Feasts*, 84–85.

CHAPTER 7

1. *Cassell's Book of the Household*, 1: 102.
2. Ibid., 1: 102.
3. Visser, *The Rituals of Dinner*, 202.
4. Kelly, *Cooking for Kings*, 123.
5. Edward Spencer, *Cakes and Ale*, 68–69.
6. Brillat-Savarin, *Physiologie du Goût*, 163.
7. Ehrman, *London Eats Out*, 69.
8. Gigante, *Gusto*, 3–4.
9. Tames, *Feeding London*, 124–126.
10. Mars, "À la Russe," 114.
11. Colin Spencer, *British Food*, 279; Mars, "À la Russe," 114.
12. *Cassell's Book of the Household*, 2: 97.
13. Paston-Williams, *Art of Dining*, 321.
14. Literally, a time of annoyance or temporary discomfort. Paston-Williams, *Art of Dining*, 321.
15. Beeton, *Book of Household Management*, 12.
16. *Cassell's Book of the Household*, 1: 106.
17. Ibid., 1: 108.
18. Edward Spencer, *Cakes and Ale*, 70.
19. Ude, *The French Chef*, 1822 ed., 89.
20. Ude, *The French Chef*, 1828 ed., 96.
21. Ude, *The French Chef*, 1828 ed., xxiii. Acknowledgement goes to Colin Spencer for his initial analysis of Ude's court bouillon recipe. See Colin Spencer, *British Food*, 273.

22. Ehrman, *London Eats Out*, 71.
23. Burnett, *Useful Toil*, 139.
24. Ibid., 144.
25. Lake, *Menus Made Easy*, "Advertisement," 1913 ed.
26. Marshall, "Advertisements, Price List and Description" in *Mrs. A. B. Marshall's Cookery Book*, 4.
27. Colin Spencer, *British Food*, 282; Mason, "Everything Stops for Tea," 74.
28. *Cassell's Book of the Household*, 1: 13.
29. Dodd, *Food of London*, 391–392.
30. Capatti, "The Taste for Canned and Preserved Foods," 497.
31. Marshall, *Mrs. A. B. Marshall's Cookery Book*, 239.
32. Ibid., 6.
33. Sala, *Thorough Good Cook*, 24–25.
34. Marshall, *Mrs. A. B. Marshall's Cookery Book*, 495.
35. Davies, *Victorian Kitchen*, 57.
36. Ibid., 57.
37. Ibid., 58.
38. Palmer, *Movable Feasts*, 88.
39. Marshall, *Mrs. A. B. Marshall's Cookery Book*, 11.

## CHAPTER 8

1. Dickens, *A Christmas Carol*, 88.
2. Moore, "Victorian Christmas Books," 123.
3. Simon Callow, *Dickens' Christmas*, 121–122.
4. Mason and Brown, *Traditional Foods of Britain*, 251.
5. Bailey, *Cooking of the British Isles*, 188.
6. Burnett, *Useful Toil*, 69.
7. Thompson, *Lark Rise to Candlford*, 217.
8. Burnett, *Useful Toil*, 65.
9. [Morely], "Beef," 196.
10. Mason and Brown, *Traditional Foods of Britain*, 145; 147.
11. Hartley, *Food in England*, 194.
12. Mason and Brown, *Traditional Foods of Britain*, 173-174; Rossi-Wilcox, *Dinner for Dickens*, 262.
13. Edward Spencer, *Cakes and Ale*, 94.
14. Beeton, *Book of Household Management*, 493–494.
15. Rhodes, *New Classics*, 333.
16. Mason and Brown, *Traditional Foods of Britain*, 307.
17. Ayrton, *English Provincial Cooking*, 81; Mason and Brown, *Traditional Foods of Britain*, 237, 284–285.
18. Mason and Brown, *Traditional Foods of Britain*, 239.
19. Callow, Dickens' *Christmas*, 127.
20. Hewett and Axton, *Convivial Dickens*, 25.
21. Callow, *Dickens' Christmas*, 128.
22. Hewett and Axton, *Convivial Dickens*, 32; 38.
23. Dickens, *A Christmas Carol*, 89.

24. Mason and Brown, *Traditional Foods of Britain*, 237–238; 289; 53–54; Bailey, *Cooking of the British Isles*, 188.

25. "Customs and Traditions of Bishop Auckland"; Mason and Brown, *Traditional Foods of Britain*, 54.

26. Thompson, *Lark Rise to Candleford*, 220.

27. Mason and Brown, *Traditional Foods of Britain*, 235

28. Bailey, *Cooking of the British Isles*, 188.

29. "Widow's Son," *Traditional and Historic London Pubs*; Burrell, *In the Royal Manner*, 40, 49.

30. Mason and Brown, *Traditional Foods of Britain*, 235, 254.

31. Burrell, *In the Royal Manner*, 42.

32. *Mrs Beeton's Every Day Cookery*, xv.

33. Burnett, *Useful Toil*, 184.

34. Beeton, *Book of Household Management*, 658.

35. Thompson, *Lark Rise to Candleford*, 221–222.

36. Ibid., 224–225.

37. Ibid., 225–226.

38. Ayrton, *English Provincial Cooking*, 60.

39. Wetherall, "Mackerel Punts and Pilchards," 82.

40. Mason and Brown, *Traditional Foods of Britain*, 231.

41. White, *Good Things in England*, 320.

42. Mason and Brown, *Traditional Foods of Britain*, 279.

43. For her research into Cornish celebrations and foodways, I acknowledge Elisabeth Ayrton whose *English Provincial Cooking* contains a treasure-trove of traditional Cornish recipes. The information in the following two paragraphs comes primarily from her work. See 113–115 and 129–130.

44. White, *Good Things in England*, 320.

45. Mason and Brown, *Traditional Foods of Britain*, 257.

46. Ibid., 196.

# Glossary of Cooking Terms

**Amontillado:** A dry, pale sherry that comes from the region of Montilla, Spain. As it ages, it assumes a slightly darker color and rich flavor.

**Angelica:** A licorice-flavored plant much favored by the English for use as a candy or as a cake garnish.

**Aspic:** A clear jelly that is often poured in a fancy mold and used to bind together other foods such as meats, vegetables, or fruits. Aspic can also be used as a glaze for roasted meat.

**Biscuit:** A sweet cookie or a savory cracker.

**Claret:** A common English word used to describe red wines from the Bordeaux region of France.

**Corn:** The British word for grains of all kind, including wheat, barley, oats, rye, and maize.

**Cottage Loaf:** A typical English country bread created by forming one large round and placing a slightly smaller round on top before baking.

**Curd Tart:** A tart made with soft new cheese (curds), sweetened with sugar and enriched with eggs.

**Dripping:** The fat that comes from roasted meat. The best dripping comes from beef and after the dripping is cooled and solidified, it can be used for a number of dishes, including pastry and pies. Dripping often replaced butter as a bread spread.

**Faggots:** Homemade sausages made of pig offal (often minced heart and/or liver), oatmeal, and seasonings. Faggots were often used for sandwich filling or reheated and eaten with potatoes and gravy. They were particularly popular in Wales and West Central England.

**Flummery:** Traditionally, a thick jelly or pudding made from soaking oatmeal in water for a lengthy period of time. The water is drained off and boiled to a near-solid mass.

Called *Llymru* in Wales where the dish likely originated, flummery could be made with almonds during Lent and by the Victorian era was often the generic name used for cream puddings that had been set with calf's foot, isinglass, or hartshorn—all jelling agents.

**Forcemeat** (forstmeat, forstballs, forcedmeat, etc.): A stuffing mixture often composed of meat pounded together with vegetables such as onion, and sometimes thickened with egg or breadcrumbs.

**Fricassée** (fricassee, frigasee, etc): Traditionally, a fricassée was usually made of chicken simmered in a rich white sauce. Other meats that were cooked in such a fashion included veal, calves' liver, and pigeon.

**Frumenty:** Boiled wheat grains often flavored with sugar or honey and mixed with milk and/or beaten egg yolks.

**Haute Cuisine:** Literally, "high cooking." French term used to describe the cuisine created in large part by Marie-Antoine Carême during the Napoleonic War era and perfected by chef Georges Auguste Escoffier.

**Hock:** A common English word for a German white wine, one originally from Hochheim am Main.

**Joint:** A piece of meat (beef, mutton, or pork) that is then carved into individual portions after it has been roasted, baked, or boiled.

**Ketchup** (Katchup): A generic English word for sauce. Early ketchups were usually made of mushrooms, or anchovies, or green (unripe) walnuts.

**Madeira:** A fortified wine that comes from the Portuguese archipelago of that name.

**Mince** (or Minced): ground meat, such as hamburger meat.

**Negus:** A hot drink, typically made with hot water, port, sugar, and spice.

**Nettle:** A plant whose leaves have stinging hairs. Nettles are a highly nutritious food with added therapeutic value. The young leaves can be used in stews and soups or eaten raw in salads.

**Offal:** Trimmings off the butchered animal, including the intestinal organs such as heart, liver, kidney, and lights (lungs).

**Orange-Blossom Flower Water** (or orange-flower water): The essence distilled from the flowers of Seville orange trees and used as a flavoring for numerous pastries, confectionaries, and puddings.

**Plum Duff:** Typically a less rich version of the plum pudding, flavored with a small number of currents and raisins.

**Podovies:** Beef patties.

**Pottage:** A thick soup based on the combination of meat, vegetables, legumes, and/or grains such as barley or oats cooked for a long period in one pot. Pottages composed entirely of grains are called porridge, including oatmeal porridge and farina, a wheaten porridge.

**Pudding:** In current British usage, the generic name for the dessert course. In the Victorian era, a pudding could be savory (such as Yorkshire) or sweet (such as plum). Traditionally, the term referred to a dish that was steamed, boiled, or baked. Puddings are composed of several ingredients that are bound together upon cooking to form a solid mass. Sweet puddings often resemble cakes; savory puddings are often batters, such as Yorkshire pudding; they can also refer to boiled sausages, such as black puddings.

**Radish Pods:** The seed pod of the radish. Early Europeans and Americans often favored radish pods over the more common radish roots. They were often pickled for winter use.

**Roly-Poly Pudding:** A pudding that is made by rolling the dough into a flat rectangle, covering it with jam, rolling it up, and then steaming or boiling it. Often served with warm custard sauce.

**Sack:** A fortified wine from the regions around Jerez, Spain. Some times the word was used in England to mean sherry.

**Salamander:** A kitchen implement used to brown the tops of food. Made of iron, the salamander worked like a modern-day broiler.

**Saveloy:** A spicy, cheap sausage; common street food in Victorian England.

**Small Beer:** Weak, low-alcohol beer.

**Smelts:** The British were familiar with the European variety of these small silvery salmonoid fishes. They spawn in rivers and streams, and spend the remainder of life in cold northern seas.

**Souse:** A verb that means to pickle. Typically, pork was pickled for winter use.

**Spotted Dick:** Another suet pudding that is the same as or very similar to plum duff. The spots refer to the currants.

**Sprats:** The British were familiar with the European variety of these small herring-like fish.

**Tammy Cloth:** A stiff cloth that acted in the same way as a fine-meshed sieve. Used to create smooth soups and turn sauces into a velvety consistency.

**Tansy:** A curative and highly nutritious herb used to create teas and the Eastertime tansy cake.

**Treacle:** A thick product of sugar syrup and molasses with a near-black color and strong, slightly bitter flavor. Treacle is a key ingredient in many English gingerbreads, most notably, the Yorkshire specialty, parkin.

**Trotters:** Pig's feet; often pickled or stewed in the Victorian era.

**Whey:** The liquid that separates from curds when one makes cheese.

**Wig:** A light-textured yeast bun.

# BIBLIOGRAPHY


## MANUSCRIPTS CONSULTED

Beaufoy, Agnes. *Mss. Cookbook*. Manhattan, KS: Morse Department of Special Collections, Hale Library, Kansas State University, 1819–1869.

Reade, Jane and Mrs Symonds Ensham. *Mss.Cookbook*. Manhattan, KS: Morse Department of Special Collections, Hale Library, Kansas State University, 1728–1822.

Smith, J. Family. *Smith Culinary Manuscript*. Iowa City, IA: The Chef Louis Szathmáry II Collection of Culinary Arts, Special Collections Department, University of Iowa Libraries, 1840–1860.

Willis Family Recipe Book. *Willis family of Brace-boro'*. Lincolnshire, England: The Chef Louis Szathmáry II Collection of Culinary Arts, Special Collections Department, 1833–1861.

## OTHER RARE BOOKS COLLECTIONS CONSULTED

Division of Rare and Manuscript Collections. Ithaca, NY: Cornell University Library, Cornell University.

Margaret Husted Culinary Collection. Denver, CO: University of Denver Special Collections, University of Denver.

Spencer Research Library. Lawrence, KS: University of Kansas.

## COOKBOOKS AND OTHER PRIMARY SOURCES CONSULTED

Acton, Eliza. *Modern Cookery, in All Its Branches*. 2nd London ed. Philadelphia, PA: Lea and Blanchard, 1849.

Beeton, Isabella. *Book of Household Management*. London: S.O. Beeton, 1861. Reprinted by S.O. Beeton, 1864.

Bloom, Ursula. *Victorian Vinaigrette*. Bath, England: Chivers Press, 1982 [1956].

Boorde, Andrew. *A Compendyous Regyment, or A Dyetary of Helth*. Edited by F.J. Furnivall. Early English Text Society. London: Trubner, 1870 [1542].

Boswell, James. *The Life of Samuel Johnson*. Edited and abridged by Christopher Hibbert. Abridged Penguin edition. London: Penguin, 1979 [1791].

Brillat-Savarin, Jean-Anthelme. *Physiologie du Goût*. Translated by Fayette Robinson and M.F.K. Fisher. In *Gusto: Essential Writings in Nineteenth-Century Gastronomy*. Edited by Denise Gigante. New York: Routledge, 2005 [1826], 144–174.

Buckmaster, John Charles. *Buckmaster's Cookery: Being an Abridgment of Some of the Lectures Delivered in the Cookery School at the International Exhibition for 1873 and 1874*. London: Routledge, 1874.

Caird, James. *Landed Interest and the Supply of Food*. London: Cassell, Petter & Galpin, 1878.

*Cassell's Book of the Household: A Work of Reference on Domestic Economy*. 4 vols. London: Cassell & Co, 1889–1891.

Cobbe, Frances Power. "The Little Health of Ladies." *Contemporary Review* 31 (1878): 276–296.

Cobbett, William. *Cottage Economy*. New ed. London: William Cobbett, 1835.

Davies, David. *The Case of Labourers in Husbandry, Stated and Considered*. London: G.G. and J. Robinson, 1795.

Dickens, Charles. *Dickens's Dictionary of London, 1879: An Unconventional Handbook*. Reprint, London: Howard Baker, 1972 [1879].

———. *A Christmas Carol*. Edited by Richard Kelly, Broadview Press Edition. Petersborough, Ontario Canada: Broadview Press, 2003 [1843].

*Dictionary of Daily Wants*. 3 vols. London: Houlston & Wright, 1858–1861.

Dodd, George. *Food of London: A Sketch*. London: Longman, Brown, Green, and Longmans, 1856.

Dods, Meg [Christian Isabel Johnstone]. *Cook and Housewife's Manual*. 10th ed. Edinburgh: Oliver & Boyd; London: Simpkin, Marshall, and Co., 1856.

Edgeworth, Maria. *Life and Letters of Maria Edgeworth*. 2 vols. Edited by Augustus J. C. Hare. Boston, CA: Houghton Mifflin, 1895.

Eliot, George. *Middlemarch*. Edited by Rosemary Ashton, Penguin Classics Edition. Harmondsworth, Middlesex: Penguin, 1994 [1871–1872].

Engels, Frederick. *Condition of the Working Class in England*. New York: Macmillan, 1958 [1845].

Francatelli, Charles Elme. *A Plain Cookery Book for the Working Classes*. New ed. London: Routledge, Warne, and Routledge, 1852.

Gaskell, Elizabeth. *Cranford*. Dover Thrift Edition, Mineola, NY: Dover, 2003 [1853].

———. *North and South*. Edited by Alan Shelston. Norton Critical Edition, New York: Norton, 2005 [1854–1855].

Kemble, Frances Ann. *Records of Later Life*. New York: Henry Holt, 1884.

Lake, Nancy. *Menus Made Easy; or How to Order Dinner and Give the Dishes Their French Names*. 8th ed. London and New York: Frederick Warne and Co., 1894.

Latham, Robert, Editor. *The Shorter Pepys*. Berkeley, CA: University of California Press, 1985.

Marshall, Agnes B. *Mrs. A. B. Marshall's Cookery Book*. Rev. ed. London: Marshall's School of Cookery, 1885.

Martineau, Harriet. "The New School for Wives." *Household Words* 5 (April 10, 1852): 84–89.

Mayhew, Henry. *London Labour and the London Poor*. Edited and abridged by Victor Neuburg. Harmondsworth, Middlesex, England: Penguin, 1985 [1851].

———. *London Labour and the London Poor*. The *Victorian London* Web site. http://www.victorianlondon.org/(accessed September 22, 2006).

[Morely, Henry.] "Beef." *Household Words* 8 (December 24, 1853): 385–388.

Moritz, Carl Philip. *Journeys of a German in England in 1782*. Translated by Reginald Nettel. New York: Holt, Rinehart and Winston, 1965 [1872].

*Mrs Beeton's Every Day Cookery and Housekeeping Book*. London: Ward Lock, 1872.

Nesbit, Edith. *Five Children and It*. Yearling Classic Edition, New York: Dell, 1986 [1902].

———. *The Phoenix and the Carpet*. Puffin Classics Edition, London: Penguin, 1994 [1904].

*New Female Instructor; or, Young Woman's Guide to Domestic Happiness*. London: Thomas Kelly, 1824.

Reeves, Maud Pemberton. *Round about a Pound a Week*. A facsimile of the 1913 edition. Edited by Standish Meacham. New York: Garland, 1980 [1913].

De la Rochefoucauld, Francois. *A Frenchman in England*. Translated by S.C. Roberts. London: Caliban, 1995 [1784].

Rowntree, B. Seebohm. *Poverty: A Study of Town Life*. A reprint of the 1922 edition, New York: Howard Fertig, 1971 [1901].

Sala, George Augustus. *The Thorough Good Cook: A Series of Chats on the Culinary Art and Nine Hundred Recipes*. London: Cassell & Company, 1895.

———. *Twice Around the Clock; or the Hours of the Day and Night in London*. London: W Kent, 1861.

Southgate, Henry. *Things A Lady Would Like to Know, Concerning Domestic Management and Expenditure*. 2nd ed. London: William P. Nimmo, 1875.

Soyer, Alexis. *The Modern Housewife, or Ménagère*. London: Simpkin, Marshall, 1849. American ed. New York: D. Appleton and Co., 1850.

Spencer, Edward. *Cakes and Ale: A Memory of Many Meals*. London: Grant Richards, 1897.

Thompson, Flora. *Lark Rise to Candleford: A Trilogy*. Reprint Society Edition. Oxford: Oxford University Press, 1948 [1845].

Toulmin, Camilla [Mrs. Newton Crossland]. *Landmarks of a Literary Life*. New York: Charles Scribner's Sons, 1893.

Trusler, John. *The Honours of the Table, or Rules for Behaviour during a Meal*. 3rd ed. Bath: G. Robbins, 1803.

Tusser, Thomas. "The Plough mans feasting days." In *Five Hundred Points of Good Husbandry*. London: Printed by T.R. and M.D. for the Company of Stationers, 1672.

Ude, Louis Eustache. *The French Chef*. Philadelphia: Carey, Lea and Carey, 1828; London: John Ebers, 1833.

## SECONDARY SOURCES

Adamson, Melitta Weiss. *Food in Medieval Times (Food through History)*. Westport, CT: Greenwood Press, 2004.

Ayrton, Elisabeth. *English Provincial Cooking*. New York: Harper & Row, 1980.

Bailey, Adrian. *Cooking of the British Isles*. New York: Time Life Books, 1969.

Berriedale-Johnson, Michelle. *Victorian Cookbook*. New York: Interlink Books, 1989.

Black, Maggie. *Victorian Cookery: Recipes & History*. Rev. ed. London: English Heritage, 2004.

Brears, Peter. "*À la Française*: the Waning of a Long Dining Tradition." In *Eating with the Victorians*. Edited by C. Anne Wilson, 2004, 86–111.

Burnett, John. *England Eats Out: A Social History of Eating Out in England from 1830 to the Present*. Harlow, Essex: Pearson Longman, 2004.

———. *Plenty and Want: A Social History of Diet in England from 1815 to the Present Day*. London: Nelson, 1966.

———. *Useful Toil: Autobiographies of Working People from the 1820s to the 1920s*. London: Allen Lane, 1974.

Burrell, Paul. *In the Royal Manner: Expert Advice on Etiquette and Entertaining from the Former Butler to Diana, Princess of Wales*. New York: Warner Books, 1999.

Callow, Simon. *Dickens' Christmas: A Victorian Celebration*. New York: Harry Abrams, 2003.

Capatti, Alberto. "The Taste for Canned and Preserved Food." In *Food: A Culinary History from Antiquity to the Present*. Edited by Albert Sonnenfeld. New York: Columbia University Press, 1999, 492–499.

Coffin, Cyril. "Riots in South Eastern Counties." *Agricultural Riots in Dorset* Web site. 1999. www.thedorsetpage.com/history/Captain_Swing/Captain_Swing.htm (accessed June 29, 2006).

Cooper, Suzanne Fagence. "Technology, Tradition and the Dilemmas of Design." In *Victorian Vision: Inventing New Visions*. Edited by John M. MacKenzie. London: V&A Publications, 2001, 187–213.

"Customs and Traditions of Bishop Auckland." *North-East Communigate* Web site. Northumbria University. http://www.communigate.co.uk/ne/thediscoverycentre/page8.phtml (accessed September 24, 2006).

Davies, Jennifer. *Victorian Kitchen*. London: BBC Books, 1989.

Davies, Norman. *The Isles: A History*. Oxford: Oxford University Press, 1999.

Drummond, J. C., and Anne Wilbraham. *The Englishman's Food: A History of Five Centuries of English Diet*. London: Jonathan Cape, 1939.

Ehrman, Edwina, Hazel Forsyth, Lucy Peltz, and Cathy Ross. *London Eats Out: 500 Years of Capital Dining*. London: Philip Wilson Publishers, 1999.

Ellis, Alice Thomas. *Fish, Flesh and Good Red Herring: A Gallimaufry*. London: Virago, 2004.

Flanders, Judith. *Victorian House: Domestic Life from Childbirth to Deathbed*. London: Harper Perennial, 2004.

Freeman, Sarah. *Mutton and Oysters: The Victorians and Their Food*. London: Gollancz, 1989.

Gigante, Denise, Editor. *Gusto: Essential Writings in Nineteenth-Century Gastronomy*. London: Routledge, 2005.

Grieve, Maud. *A Modern Herbal*. 2 vols. New York: Harcourt, Brace and Co., 1931.

Hartley, Dorothy. *Food in England*. London: Futura, 1985 [1954].

Hassan, John. *A History of Water in Modern England and Wales*. Manchester: Manchester University Press, 1998.

Hewett, Edward and W. F. Axton. *Convivial Dickens: The Drinks of Dickens and His Times*. Athens, OH: Ohio University Press, 1983.

Hughes, Kathryn. *The Short Life and Long Times of Mrs. Beeton*. New York: Knopf, 2006.

Kelly, Ian. *Cooking for Kings: Antonin Carême, The Life of the First Celebrity Chef.* London: Short Books, 2003; New York: Walker Publishing, 2004.

Mars, Valerie. "*À la Russe*: The New Way of Dining." In *Eating with the Victorians.* Edited by C. Anne Wilson, 112–138.

Mason, Laura. "Everything Stops for Tea." In *Eating with the Victorians.* Edited by C. Anne Wilson, 2004, 68–85.

———. "Poverty and Policy: The Rowntree Study of 1899." In *Feeding a City: York.* Edited by Eileen White. Blackawton, Totnes, Devon: Prospect Books, 2000, 203–212.

———. *Sugar-Plums and Sherbet: The Prehistory of Sweets.* Blackawton, Totnes, Devon: Prospect, 1998.

Mason, Laura with Catherine Brown. *Traditional Foods of Britain: An Inventory.* Blackawton, Totnes, Devon: Prospect, 2004.

Mitchell, Sally. *Daily Life in Victorian England.* Westport, CT: Greenwood Press, 1996.

Moore, Tara. "Victorian Christmas Books: A Seasonal Reading Phenomenon." PhD diss., University of Delaware, 2006.

Morgan, Kenneth O., ed. *Oxford Illustrated History of Britain.* Oxford: Oxford University Press, 1984.

Moxham, Roy. *Tea: Addiction, Exploitation, and Empire.* New York: Carroll and Graf, 2003.

Palmer, Arnold. *Movable Feasts: A Reconnaissance of the Origins and Consequences of Fluctuations in Meal-Times with Special Attention to the Introduction of Luncheon and Afternoon Tea.* Oxford: Oxford University Press, 1952.

Paston-Williams, Sara. *Art of Dining: A History of Cooking & Eating.* London: National Trust, 1993; New York: Henry Abrams, 1999.

Perren, Richard. "Markets and Marketing." In *The Agrarian History of England and Wales,* Vol. 7. Edited by G. E. Mingay. Cambridge: Cambridge University Press, 1989, 190–274.

Pettigrew, Jane. *Social History of Tea.* London: National Trust, 2001.

Redon, Odile, Françoise Sabban, and Silvano Serventi. *Medieval Kitchen: Recipes from France and Italy.* Translated by Edward Schneider. Chicago: University of Chicago Press, 1998.

Rhodes, Gary. *New Classics.* 1st U.S. ed. New York: Dorling Kindersley, 2001.

Rossi-Wilcox, Susan M. *Dinner for Dickens: The Culinary History of Mrs Charles Dickens's Menu Books.* Blackawton, Totnes, Devon: Prospect Books, 2005.

Sheppard, Francis. *London: A History.* Oxford: Oxford University Press, 1998.

Sonnenfeld, Albert. ed. *Food: A Culinary History from Antiquity to the Present.* New York: Columbia University Press, 1999.

Spencer, Colin. *British Food: An Extraordinary Thousand Years of History.* Columbia: Columbia University Press, 2002.

Spurling, Hilary. *Elinor Fettiplace's Receipt Book.* New York: Viking Penguin, 1986.

Tames, Richard. *Feeding London: A Taste of History.* London: Historical Publications, 2003.

Tannahill, Reay. *Food in History.* New ed. London: Review, 2002.

"Tea." In *Cambridge World History of Food.* Edited by Kenneth F. Kiple and Conee Ornelas Kriemhild. 2 vols. Cambridge: Cambridge University Press, 716–717.

Turner, Jack. *Spice: The History of a Temptation.* New York: Knopf, 2004.

Ukers, William H. *All About Tea.* 2 vols. New York: Kingsport Press, 1935.

Visser, Margaret. *The Rituals of Dinner: Their Origins, Evolution, Eccentricities, and Meaning of Table Manners*. New York: Grove Press, 1991.

Wetherall, Megan. "Mackerel Punts and Pilchards." *Saveur* (May, 2006): 74–84.

White, Eileen. "First Things First: The Great British Breakfast." In *Eating with the Victorians*, 2004, 1–31.

White, Florence. *Good Things in England*. London: J. Cape, 1932.

"Widow's Son." *Traditional and Historic London Pubs*. http://www.pubs.com/pub_details.cfm?ID=253(accessed September 24, 2006).

Wilson, Anne C., Editors. *Eating with the Victorians*. Phoenix Mill, Gloucestershire: Sutton, 2004.

———. "Luncheon, Nuncheon and Related Meals." In *Eating with the Victorians*, 32–40.

———. "Meal Patterns and Food Supply in Victorian Britain." In *Eating with the Victorians*, xiii–xviii.

# INDEX


Accum, Frederick, *Treatise on Adulterations of Food and Culinary and Culinary Poisons*, 117–18

Acton, Eliza, *Modern Cookery for Private Families*, 109, 148

Agriculture: employment in, 5, 11; laborers, 4–5, 14–15, 78–84, 88–91, 151–52, 159–60, 162; reform of, 15–16, 90–91; unrest and riots, 15–16, 93

Alcohol, 44, 107, 154–55. *See also specific types*

Alcoholism, 80. *See also* Temperance

Ale, 10, 26, 43, 49–50, 53, 56, 64, 89, 93–94, 107, 154, 159

Almonds, 1, 8–9, 135, 156

Apples, 83, 108, 148, 152, 154

Argentina, 19

Aristocracy. *See* Upper classes

Asparagus, 108, 137

Austen, Jane, 43; *Sense and Sensibility*, 65

Australia, 19, 26, 87

Avocado, 108

Bacon. *See* Pork

Bakers, 16, 50, 53, 55, 83, 87, 74, 115, 118, 156–57, 162

Baking, 83, 94–96, 112, 118

Bananas, 12, 138–39

Barley, 51, 83, 84, 91, 159

Bathhamption, 97

Beeton, Isabella, 101, 108, 118, 120, 128, 152; *Book of Household Management*, 28, 31, 40, 50, 76, 101, 104, 110, 116, 152; *Mrs. Beeton's Every Day Cookery*, 39–40, 158

Beaufoy, Agnes, 3, 11–12, 15, 17–18, 21, 97, 109

Bedford, Duchess of (Anna Maria Stanhope), 65–66

Beef, 6, 42, 53, 57, 86–87, 92, 106, 131, 137, 151–52, 159–60

Beer. *See* Ale

Berries, 4, 10, 107, 109, 155

Bever, 43

Birmingham, 14, 89, 96, 120

Biscuits, 52, 66, 76, 118, 157, 162

Black-lead, 30, 142

Bloom, Ursula, 47, 49

Boer War (South African), 57, 98–99

Boorde, Andrew, 24

Booth, Charles, 98

Bread, 9–10, 25–26, 37, 42, 46–47, 91–92, 117–18, 144; flours used in, 83, 157; importance in working-class diet, 2, 55–56, 8, 83–85, 88, 91–96, 162; as toast, 24–27, 35–37

Breakfast, 23–40, 42–43, 46–47, 69, 81, 84

Brillat-Savarin, Jean-Anthelme, 125
Bristol, 89, 119, 156–57
Brooke Bond, 63
Buckmaster, John Charles, 31, 41, 47, 111
Buns, muffins, and wigs, 75, 156–57
Burnett, John, 90
Butchers and butchering, 50–51, 53, 81
Butter, 12, 19, 25, 35, 49, 82, 83, 85, 88, 117, 152–53

Cabbages and kale, 5, 82, 88
Cadbury, 21. *See also* Chocolate, eggs
Cakes, 43, 66, 68, 71, 73, 138; Banbury, 74; currant, 26; Easter, 157; fruit, 76; fuggan (*or* heavy), 161; lardy, 74; pan, 42, 155; pepper, 153; plum, 153; saffron, 161; seed, 72, 75–76, 156; Shrewsbury, 74; simnel, 155–56; spice, 153; Staffordshire oat, 74; Suffolk, 74; teacake, 75, 153
Calling cards, 66, 68
Cambridge, 43, 76, 152
Candy. *See* Confectionary
Can opener, 18
Canteens, 54
Caraway seeds, 58, 75–76, 156, 162
Carême, Marie-Antoine, 124, 126
Caribbean colonies, 61, 149; Barbados, 10; Jamaica, 10
*Cassell's Book of the Household*, 18, 21, 32–33, 38, 42, 51, 68, 71, 115–16, 123, 128–29, 138, 145–46
Catherine of Braganza, 61
Catholicism, Roman, 8–9, 86, 149
Cavier, 122, 130, 144
Cheadle, Eliza, 66
Cheese, 5, 8–9, 49, 53, 76, 102, 107; as dietary staple, 82, 85, 88; making, 10, 17–18
Cheesecake, 3; almond, 1, 8–10; curd, 10, 17–18; lemon, 17–18. *See also* Recipes
Chef, 124–26, 129, 132–33, 147
Children, 14, 32, 37–39, 74, 80, 92, 97; diet of, 41–42, 46–48, 56–57, 79, 82, 99, 120, 152
China, 61, 63–64
Chocolate: drinking, 25, 44–45, 47, 56; eggs, 157
Chophouse, 45, 53–54
Cider, 107, 117, 154
Cities: conditions in, 50–51, 116; housing in, 16, 29, 55, 90, 111; infrastructure, 110–11, 119–20, 137; migration to, 15–16, 84, 89–90, 111. *See also specific cities*
Citrus fruits, 2, 9, 12, 17–18, 138, 153–54
Clubs, 45, 53, 56
Coal. *See* Fuel; Industry
Cobbe, Frances Power, 39–40
Cobbett, William, 94–96
Cockles and mussels, 82
Cocoa, 117. *See also* Chocolate, drinking
Cod, 20, 57
Coffee, 25, 44–45, 56, 64, 91, 117–18, 131
Coffee houses, 44–45, 53, 61–62
Coffee palaces, 56. *See also* Temperance
Cold meat cookery, 42, 50
Confectionary, 7, 117–18, 156, 162
Cookery books: manuscript, 1, 97; published, 18, 59, 66, 68, 149. *See also individual authors*
Cooking equipment, 20, 82, 87, 94–95, 134–35, 137; hair sieve, 135; hastener, 112, 114; ice caves, 140–41; pots, 82; toasting fork, 25, 36
Cooking school, 50, 134
Corn. *See* Grain
Corn Laws, 15, 19, 88, 91–93, 97–98
Cornwall, 74, 160–62
Cottage industries, 4, 14, 16
Count Rumford (Benjamin Thompson), 113, 142
Crayfish, 144
Cromwell, Oliver, 24
Cumbria, 157
Curry, 47, 116, 132
Custard, 47, 108, 140; custard powder, 19, 74

Davies, Jennifer, 112
Dessert, 47–48, 73, 108, 130–31, 139–41, 139. *See also* Puddings, iced
Devonshire, 74, 151, 163
Dickens, Charles, 113, 115, 117, 154; *A Christmas Carol*, 148–49, 154–55; *Dictionary of London*, 53; *Household Words*, 96, 149, 151; *Oliver Twist*, 84

*Dictionary of Daily Wants*, 58, 62, 69–70
Digestion, 46–48
Dining room, 33, 36–37
Dining-room table, 33–34, 60, 107–8, 130, 144–45
Dinner, 24, 42; children's nursery, 46–48; middle- and upper-class, 38, 60–61, 65, 102–3, 115, 120–21, 131–37; servants', 48–49; Sunday, 55–56, 87, 156, 161; working-class (dinner or tea), 16–17, 54–56, 78–79, 82
Dinner invitations, 127–28
Dinner menus (bills of fare), 100–103, 110, 116–17, 120, 122, 129, 130, 134, 139, 146–47
Dinner party, 67, 71, 127; dinner *à la française*, 101–10, 116, 120–21, 123, 127, 129; dinner *à la Russe*, 106, 109–10, 116, 120–45
Diseases, 88, 98; cholera, 119–20; rickets and scurvy, 8; typhoid, 119
Disraeli, Benjamin, 154
Dodd, George, 107, 138
Dods, Meg [Christian Isabel Johnstone], 102, 106, 115
Donkey tea. *See* Recipes
Dripping (beef), 49, 84, 106, 153
Drovers, 151. *See also* Livestock

East Anglia, 75–76, 151
East India Company, 63
Eating houses, 54
Economics, free-market, 19, 118
Economy, domestic, 50–51, 103, 138, 144
Edgeworth, Maria, 45–46
Education (Provision of Meals) Act, 57
Eels, 54, 86
Eggs, 9, 35, 47, 76, 82, 150, 155, 157
Eighteenth century, 2–3, 7, 14–15, 23–25, 35, 37, 51, 59–62, 88, 102, 133
Eliot, George, 37–38
Elizabethan period, 2, 7, 24, 42–43, 86, 152, 154–55, 158
Ellis, Alice, 69
Empire, British, 9–10, 12, 101, 149, 153. *See also specific colonies*
Engels, Frederick, 16
England: Midlands, 14, 82, 89, 159, 162–63; North, 14, 26, 51, 60, 82–83, 87, 89, 98, 152, 156, 159; South, 14–15, 26, 80, 89, 159. *See also specific cities, towns, and counties*
Epergne, 33, 130, 135
*Epicure's Almanack, or Calendar of Good Living in London*, 126
Escoffier, Auguste, 126
Essex, 75–76
Etiquette, 46–48, 92, 106–9, 127–31
Etiquette and conduct manuals, 66–68, 74, 127–31, 132. *See also individual titles*
European Union, 164

Factories, 14, 80, 90, 96, 97
Factory Acts, 56, 80, 97
Fairs and fairings, 160–63
Famine and starvation, 19, 88, 93
Farmers, 4, 18, 22, 24, 81, 88–89, 91, 102, 116, 151, 154, 159–60
Farms. *See* Agriculture
Fireside. *See* Hearthside cooking
Fish, 35, 55, 84–87, 104, 116, 130, 132, 135–36, 161–62; availability of, 4, 20. *See also individual types*
Fish and chips shops, 57
Fishing, 80, 82, 86, 160, 161
Flummery and Frumenty, 5, 8, 16, 75, 153
Food: adulteration of, 21, 63–64, 92, 94–95, 110, 116–18, 137; canned and processed, 17–19, 21–22, 57, 74, 85, 87, 110, 117–18, 132, 135–39, 144, 149; imports, 4, 9–10, 138–39, 153, 163; national identity and, 101–2, 124–26, 149; preservation, 2–3, 5, 10, 82; prices, 9–10, 20, 53–54, 56–57, 86–88, 91, 93–97, 135–39, 146–47, 153; procurement and shortages of, 2, 4, 6–7, 11, 21, 82–84, 88, 91, 93; symbolism or taste of, 6, 9, 21, 24–26, 35, 37, 44–46, 48, 52, 83, 107, 130, 144–45; waste and leftovers of, 27, 35, 42, 49–52, 103
Food stalls and vendors (costermongers), 16, 25–26, 50, 54, 80–81, 84, 138
Francatelli, Charles, 94, 126, 133; *A Plain Cookery Book for the Working Classes*, 53, 78, 94

France and French cuisine, 9, 101, 106–7, 124, 126, 132–34, 152; Paris, 94, 124–26
Fray Bentos' corned beef, 87
French Revolution, 125–26
Fruit, dried, 47, 76, 150, 153, 156
Fruit, fresh and/or canned, 42, 47, 55, 73, 83, 108, 138, 140, 144. *See also individual types*
Fuel, 30–31, 55, 82, 87–88, 94, 111, 112, 140, 142
Furniss, John Cooper, 162–63

Gardens and allotments, 4, 10, 12, 16, 79, 82, 88, 93, 95
Garlic, 9, 82
Gaskell, Elizabeth: *Cranford*, 65, 76; *Mary Barton*, 84; *North and South*, 45
Gastronomy, 125
Gelatin, 135. *See also* Jams, jellies, preserves
Gentry. *See* Upper classes
George I, "Pudding King," 150
George, Prince of Wales, 124
Georgian. *See* Eighteenth century
Germany, 9, 124, 149–50
Gin, 64, 155
Ginger, 76, 153, 162
Gingerbread, 74, 164. *See also* Fairs and fairings
Gladstone, William, 107
Glass, 145, 155
Gloucestershire, 154
Good King Henry ("poor man's" asparagus), 82
Grain, 19, 83, 152. *See also individual types*
Great Exhibition, 146
Greens, 50, 8–83, 88
Griddle, 83
Grimod de la Reynière, Alexandre Balthazar Laurent, 125–26
Grocers and merchants, 4–5, 18, 64, 74, 77, 109, 117–18, 138–39, 145, 158

Haddock, 35
Hampshire, 12, 15
Hardy, Thomas, 162
Hartley, Dorothy, 81, 152
Hassall, Arthur Hill, 118
Hearthside cooking, 16, 20, 82, 111–13, 115
Herbert, Col. A. Kenny [Wyvern], 36
Herbs and spices, 2, 4, 7, 83, 87, 117, 132, 148, 153. *See also individual names*
Herring (including bloaters and red), 35, 78, 84–86
Holidays: accounting days, 162; bank, 56, 157–58; Boxing Day, 157–58; Christmas, 76, 89, 148–55, 158, 161–62; Easter, 8, 156–57, 161; harvest, 75, 89, 159–60; Lent, 8, 75, 155–57, 161; Martinmas, 3, 81; Michaelmas, 159–60; Whitmonday, 162
Honey, 9, 83. *See also* Mead
Hotels and inns, 53, 146
Hunger, 12, 79, 149, 151
Husbandry, 6, 108, 151

Ice, 116–17, 140
Icebox, 117, 140
Ices and ice cream, 12, 73, 108, 134, 139–40
India, 63–64
Industrialism and Industrial Revolution, 11–21, 38–40, 42, 57, 59–60, 74–81, 85, 89–94, 96–98, 101, 119–20, 123, 149
Industry: coal, 20, 80; metal, 20, 161; textiles, 80
Ireland, 90, 95–98
Irish Potato Famine, 12, 97–98
Iron. *See* Industry, metal
Italy, 9, 139

Jack, bottle or spring, 112, 114
James, Mrs. Eliot, 48–49
Jams, jellies, preserves, 18–19, 25, 47, 74, 85, 135, 138–39
Jerrold, William Blanchard, 126
Johnson, Samuel, 106–7

Kent, 154
Kitchens, including larder and pantry, 20, 29, 32, 37, 48, 50, 74, 111–12, 116, 134, 140

Laboring classes. *See* Working classes; Agriculture, laborers
Lake District, 74, 82, 153, 163
Lake, Nancy, 134, 139
Lancashire, 16, 57, 156; hotpot, 16
Land: common, 4–5, 10, 88; ownership of and control over, 5–6, 81, 88–89, 159–60; enclosure of, 15–16, 88–91
Lard, 55, 81, 85, 88, 153
Leavening agents: baking powder, 19, 76, 135; yeast, 19, 94, 76, 157
Leazing, 83
Leeds, 89–90
Leeks, 83
Lighting: electric, 140, 147; gas, 19, 44, 52, 128
Lincolnshire, 97, 153
Lipton's Tea Company, 21, 63
Liverpool, 14, 89, 119–20
Livestock, 5; cattle, 151, 162; geese, 162; pigs, 51, 81–82, 88; sheep, 89. *See also* Drovers
Lobster, 87, 144
London, 4, 19, 25–26, 51–54, 60–64, 84, 86–87, 90, 117, 119–20, 126, 146–47, 156
Lunch and luncheon, 40–57, 59

Macaroni, 47, 107
Macaulay, Thomas Babington, 52
Mackerel, 86, 161
Manchester, 14, 19, 89, 120
*Manners and Tone of Good Society*, 128
Margarine, 12, 19, 26, 49, 85
Markets, 4, 10, 26, 55, 87, 109, 139; Billingsgate, 86; Lambeth New Cut, 86; Smithfield, 151
Marmalade, 9, 25, 37, 49
Mars, Valarie, 127
Marshall, Agnes B., 134–35, 137, 140–41; *Fancy Ices*, 139; *Mrs. A.B. Marshall's Cookery Book*, 122, 144
Martineau, Harriet, 96
Mason, Laura, 60, 153
Matches, 31
Mayhew, Henry, 25, 54–55, 84, 86
Mead, 9. *See also* Honey
Meal arks, 81
Meat: and one's class, 5, 7, 16–17, 85–88, 99, 137; availability and cost of, 26, 55, 92; carving; 106, 129, 144; preparing (roasting, baking, boiling, etc.), 46–47, 111–16, 129, 142; source of protein, 85, 91. *See also individual types*
Medicine, 2, 10, 83
Medieval Period. *See* Middle Ages
Melville, Herman, 52
Men: as masters of the house, 29, 32, 35, 37–40, 68; attitudes toward wives, 35, 38–40; duties during dinner, 104–9, 128–31; workday routines and food options, 44–45, 51–56, 121, 147
Mercer, George, 163
Mexico, 152
Middle Ages, 8, 24, 42, 89, 149–50, 153–54, 162
Middle classes: definition of, 5–6, 88; diet, 9–10, 19, 65, 91, 93, 101; income range, 27–28, 50–51, 53–54, 79–80, 116–17, 127, 134; occupations, 5–6, 44; size of, 12; values, 26–29, 37–40, 42, 46–50, 56, 66–68, 101–2, 120–21, 138, 142, 145
Military, 18, 45
Milk and cream, 5, 8–10, 20, 26, 33, 42, 46–47, 74, 82, 85, 117, 151, 161
Miller, 83
Mines and Miners, 14, 80, 160–62. *See also* Cornwall
Morely, Henry, 151
Moritz, Carl Philip, 25, 62
Morning calls, 39, 65–66, 72
Mushrooms, 4, 10, 83, 108, 139, 152
Mutton, 6, 42, 49–51, 86–87, 92, 101, 106, 115, 131, 132, 137, 144, 162

Napoleonic Wars, 15, 88, 90–91, 101–2, 125–26
Nash, Thomas, 86
Negus, 103
Nesbit, Edith: *Five Children and It*, 41–42, 57; *Phoenix and the Carpet*, 58–59
Nettles, 7, 10
Newcastle, 156
Newnham-Davis, Nathaniel, *Dinners and Diners*, 146–47

Nonshench, nuncheon, and nonsenchis, 43
Norfolk, 152, 162
Norman influences, 9–10
Northumberland, 86, 160
Nottingham, 162
Nutrition, 46, 88, 96; malnutrition, 16–17, 57, 79, 88, 93–98, 118. *See also* Vitamins and minerals
Nuts, 4, 83. *See also individual types*

Oatmeal, 26, 81–82, 87, 91, 159
Offal, 50, 81
Oleo. *See* Margarine
Olney, 155
Onion, 83, 87, 148, 151, 161
Orange-flower water, 9
Oranges. *See* Citrus fruits
Oven, brick, and beehive, 6, 83, 111–12. *See also* Ranges
Owen, Robert, 54
Oxfordshire, 43, 73, 78–79, 89, 151, 156
Oysters, 84, 86–87, 108, 152

Palmer, Arnold, 38, 121, 142, 144
Paston-Williams, Sarah, 128
Pasty, 161
Peak District, 74
Peas, 109, 156
Pedley, Mrs. Frederick, 47
Peel, Sir Robert, 98
Pepper: black, 9, 92, 117; cayenne, 117, 148; Jamaican allspice, 153
Pepys, Samuel, 44–45, 52
Persian influences in English cookery, 9
Pheasant. *See* Poultry and game
Pickles, 47, 117
Pies and tarts: berry, 82; Christmas, 164; crab and lobster, 162; eel, 162; meat, 54, 101–2; mincemeat, 153
Pigs. *See* Livestock; Pork
Pineapple, 108, 138–39
Plaice, 84, 86
Plate warmer, 104–5, 112
Pomegranate, 9
Poor laws, 91, 93
Pork: bacon, 4, 35, 55, 78, 81–82, 84, 87, 99, 152; faggots, 87; ham, 26, 35, 81; sausage, 4, 26, 81, 87, 161
Porridge, 35, 37
Portugal, 61, 106, 138
Potato, 16–17, 42, 49, 53, 55–56, 81, 84–85, 87, 93–96
Pottages, soups, and stews, 82, 87, 93, 96–97, 104, 130, 135
Poultry and game, 4, 42, 47–48, 107, 109, 116–17, 132, 139, 144, 148, 152, 160, 162
Poverty, 12–17, 51, 85–86, 92, 96–99, 150–51, 160
Pre-industrial cooking and foodways, 1–10, 16, 20–22, 42–44, 82, 88–89, 101–10, 149–50
Prussia, 124
Pubs and publicans, 64, 95, 118, 156–57
Puddings, 16, 42, 49, 103, 108; black, 11, 81; Christmas and plum, 54, 148–51, 153, 159–60; Clootie, 150; dock, 82; haggis, 153; iced, 108; Pease, 16; Roly-Poly, 55, 82; spotted dick, 55; Steak, 87; Treacle, 55; Yorkshire, 75, 103
Pure Food Laws, 118, 137

Rabbit, 116, 152
Radish pods, 7, 10
Ranges: cast iron, 20, 29–32, 37, 82, 92, 94, 110–16, 142; gas, 21, 98, 121, 140, 142; open, 111–13
Reade, Jane, and Mrs. Symonds Ensham, 1–3, 5, 7–11, 20–21
Recipes: almond cheesecake, 1; bubble and squeak, 41; conserve of rose hips, 8; curd cheesecake, 10; donkey tea, 26; fish *au bleu*, 132; goose with sage and onion, 148; hakin (or hakin), 153; lemon cheesecake, 17; Monday's pudding, 158; Mrs. Barton's Recipe for Soup, sold to the poor, 12; nest of minced lamb, 42; red herring: seed cake, 58; smoking bishop, 154–55, 158; tansy cake, 8; toad in a hole, 42; toast, 23, 35–36; treacle pudding, 41; wassail, 154, 158
Reeves, Maud Pemberton, 84–86, 94, 99

Regionalism, 59, 74–76, 149, 152–53, 155–57, 163–64
Renaissance. *See* Elizabethan period
Rennet, 10
Restaurants, 12, 125–26, 140, 145–47; Albion, 52; Bay Tree, 52; Café de l'Europe, 146; Chatelain's, 126; Cheshire Cheese, 53; Criterion, 146; Crockford's (gambling club), 133; Gatti's, 146; Lyon's Corner Houses, 56–57; Pontack's Head, 126; Les Restaurant des Gourmets, 146; Romano's, 146; Simpsons-in-the-Strand, 52–53; St. George's Café, 146; Trocadero, 57; Wellington, 52
Rhubarb, 47
Rice, 139
Robinson, Henry Crabb, 52
Robinson, Thomas, 112
de la Rochefoucauld, Francois, 24–25, 104, 108–9
Rose-flower water, 9, 76
Rose hips, 8
Rosemary, 81, 83
Rowntree, Benjamin Seebohm, 98–99

Saffron, 9, 160–61
Sage, 148, 152
Sala, George Augustus: *Thorough Good Cook*, 139; *Twice Around the Clock*, 52, 84
Salad, 104, 139
Salmon, 87, 138, 144
Salt, 85–86, 92, 96, 133–34, 140
Samphire, Marsh, 82
Sandwich, 44, 52, 54–55, 68, 71, 87, 103
Scandinavia, 117, 140
Scotland, 4, 12, 26, 45, 81–82, 86, 89, 98, 138, 150–51, 153
Scullery, 29, 119, 140
Seafood, 4, 53–54, 82–84, 162
Seaweed, 4, 82–83
Servants, 6–7, 24, 51, 54, 68, 71, 103–4, 107–9, 123–24, 133–35, 155–56, 158; butler, 128–29, 158; cook, 18, 49, 60–61, 111–13, 116, 129, 133–35, 158; footman, 48, 61, 71, 104, 158; general maid, or maid-of-all-work, 28–37, 131, 142; kitchen maid, 18–19, 30, 110–11, 117, 129, 133; scullery maid, 133; waiters, 129–31, 144–45
Seventeenth century, 10, 24, 44, 61, 149–50
Sharp, James, 140
Sheffield, 90
Shrewsbury, 155, 157
Slow Food movement, 164
Smith, Adam, 96
Smith Family manuscript cookery book, 97
Snow, John, 120
Sole, 35
Somerset, 157
Soup. *See* Pottages, soups, and stews
Soup kitchens, 97
South America, 26
Southgate, Henry, 33
Soyer, Alexis, 12, 27, 31, 51, 53, 133, 140, 164; *Modern Housewife*, 23, 27, 35–36, 40, 49–50, 69, 121
Spain, 138–39
Spanish Armada, 95
Spencer, Edward, 125, 132, 152
Spit and Spit-roast, 112, 148
Sprats, 35
Staffordshire, 81, 74, 151, 160
Steam. *See* Technology
Steel. *See* Industry
Sturgeon, Launcelot, 126
Suet, 87
Suffolk, 74, 152
Sugar, 7, 9–10, 19, 33, 85, 91, 153
Supper, 24, 42–43, 47, 67, 99, 103, 151
Sussex, 87

Tansy, 8, 83
Tarts. *See* Pies and tarts
Taverns, 45, 146
Tea: afternoon tea, 59–71, 73–76; as a beverage, 25, 33, 44, 59–65, 68–71, 82, 99, 103, 117, 131, 160; as a meal (*see also* working-class dinner), 46, 48–49, 78–79, 58–60, 67, 147, 158; history of in England, 59–66; popularity of, 62–64; receptions, 72–73; taxes on and price of, 16–17, 19, 91, 61–64

Tea-bag, 77
Tea dress fashions, 66–67
Tea gardens, 62–63
Teakettle, 33, 68–69, 71
Teapot, 33, 68–69
Teashops, 147; Aerated Bread Company (ABC), 57; British Tea Table Company, 56; Fuller Tearooms, 57; Lyons, 56–57; Pearce and Plenty, 56
Tea Urn, 70–71
Technology: innovations in, 11, 40, 57, 98, 110–16, 126–27, 163; refrigeration, 20, 87, 117, 137–41; steam, 14, 138
Temperance, 64
Textiles. *See* Industry
Thompson, Flora, 43, 51, 55, 73, 78–79, 81–83, 151, 155–56, 159
Thompson, Sir Henry, 61
Tomato, 138–39, 148
Toulmin, Camilla, 67
Tourism, 59, 74, 77, 163
Transportation, 10, 19–20, 44; canals, 117, 140; rail, 137, 146, 151; roads, 102, 146; sailing ships, 138; steam ships, 87, 137–38
Treacle, 26, 153
Truffles, 152
Truro, 161
Trusler, John, 104, 106
Turtle, 87
Tusser, Thomas, 75–76
Twentieth century, 58, 76–77, 79, 94, 99, 130, 134, 140, 142, 147, 152, 164
Twinning, Thomas, 61–62

Ude, Louis Eustache, 126; *The French Chef*, 132–33
Ukers, William, 59
United States, 19, 87, 117, 120, 140
Upper classes, 30, 32, 37, 44, 66, 104, 116; definition of, 5; diet and dining styles of, 9–10, 45–46, 61, 63, 65, 72–73, 93, 102, 110, 113, 126–31, 133, 139, 146, 151, 158; income range of, 5, 133; occupations of, 5, 88–89
Urban. *See* Cities
Uruguay, 87

Valentines, gingerbread, 163
Vegetables, 4, 42, 46–47, 49, 78–79, 83, 92. *See also individual types*
Vegetarianism, 146
Victoria, Queen, 11–12, 14, 53, 73, 149
Vinegar, 92, 132–33, 139
Vitamins and minerals, 8, 42, 46, 85, 91, 98

Wales, 81–82, 89
Walnuts, 7, 10
Water, 29, 98, 119–20; for drinking, 21, 72, 107; safety of, 64, 110; sanitation, 21; sources of, 110
Webb, Beatrice Potter, 98
West Sussex, 15
Wheat, 19, 83, 90–91, 93, 159. *See also* Corn Laws; Grain
Whitby, 74
Whiting, 35
Willis Family manuscript cookery book, 97
Wiltshire, 15, 74
Wine and spirits, 7, 9, 49, 53, 72, 76, 104, 106–9, 130–33, 150–51, 153–55, 158
Women: dining-out options, 53–54, 56, 146–47; duties during dinner, 104, 106–9, 115–16, 128–31; as mothers, 47–48, 86; relationship with husbands, 86; roles as housewives, 6–7, 19, 26–40, 50–51, 66–68, 71–73, 131, 142; work outside the home, 76, 96–97, 133–34, 146–47. *See also* Middle classes; Servants; Upper classes; Working classes
Wood. *See* Fuel
Wordsworth, Dorothy and William, 163
Work Houses, 79–80, 92, 150–51. *See also* Poverty
Working classes: definition of, 5; diet of, 16–17, 19, 25–26, 31, 48–49, 51, 54–57, 63, 79, 81–99, 137, 150–51, 159–60; income range, 14, 16, 27, 56, 63, 79–81;

mobility of, 17, 27, 92, 133–34, 147; occupations, 14–16, 54–55, 79–81, 133–34; size of, 5. *See also* Agriculture, laborers; Servants
World War I, 98–99
Yarmouth, 86
Yarrow (Yarb) Beer, 83
Yeast. *See* Leavening agents
York, 85, 98–99, 162
Yorkshire, 60, 82, 74–75, 153, 162, 164

## About the Author

ANDREA BROOMFIELD is associate professor of English at Johnson County Community College. She is coeditor of *Prose by Victorian Women: An Anthology* and has published several book chapters and journal articles.